STEPHEN STRANGE WAS A PRE-EMINENT SURGEON UNTIL A CAR ACCIDENT DAMAGED THE NERVES IN HIS HANDS. HIS EGO DROVE HIM TO SCOUR THE GLOBE FOR A MIRACLE CURE. INST
CALLED THE ANCIENT ONE WHO TAUGHT HIM MAGIC AND THAT THERE A
HIMSELF. THESE LESSONS ENABLED STEPHEN TO BECOME THE SORCE
AGAINST ALL MANNER OF MAGICAL THREATS. HIS PATIENTS

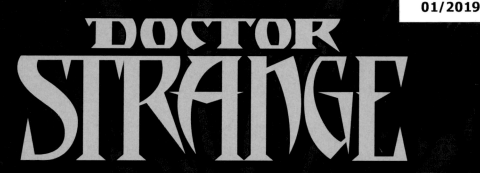

DOCTOR STRANGE

STEPHEN STRANGE REGAINED THE TITLE AND DUTIES OF SORCERER SUPREME, WHICH WERE BRIEFLY USURPED BY LOKI. FORTUNATELY, THE TRICKSTER GOD'S LAST ACTS WERE TO USE ALL THE POWER AT HIS DISPOSAL TO GIVE EARTH'S MAGIC LEVELS A SORELY NEEDED BOOST AND TO RESURRECT STEPHEN'S DOG (ALBEIT AS A GHOST). UNFORTUNATELY, THE LENGTHS TO WHICH STRANGE WAS FORCED TO GO TO RECLAIM HIS POSITION ALIENATED THE LAST OF HIS HUMAN ALLIES. IT'S TIME TO PROVE TO HIMSELF--AND EVERYONE ELSE—THAT STEPHEN STRANGE IS THE RIGHTFUL MYSTICAL DEFENDER OF OUR REALM.

~ City of Sin ~

WRITER
Donny Cates

ARTISTS
Niko Henrichon (#386-389) & *Frazer Irving* (#390)

COLOR ASSISTANT, #386-389
Laurent Grossat

LETTERER
VC's Cory Petit

COVER ART
Niko Henrichon (#386) & *Mike del Mundo* (#387-390)

ASSISTANT EDITOR
Kathleen Wisneski

EDITOR
Nick Lowe

DOCTOR STRANGE CREATED BY STAN LEE & STEVE DITKO

COLLECTION EDITOR: JENNIFER GRÜNWALD
ASSISTANT EDITOR: CAITLIN O'CONNELL
ASSOCIATE MANAGING EDITOR: KATER
EDITOR, SPECIAL PROJECTS: MARK D.

VP PRODUCTION & SPECIAL PROJECTS: JEFF YOUNGQUIST
SVP PRINT, SALES & MARKETING: DAVID GABRIEL

EDITOR IN CHIEF: C.B. CEBULSKI
CHIEF CREATIVE OFFICER: JOE QUESADA
PRESIDENT: DAN BUCKLEY
EXECUTIVE PRODUCER: ALAN FINE

DOCTOR STRANGE BY DONNY CATES VOL. 2: CIT ...). First printing 2018. ISBN 978-1-302-91065-5. Published by MARVEL WORLDWIDE, INC., a subsidiary of MARVEL ENTER ... © 2018 MARVEL No similarity between any of the names, characters, persons, and/or institutions in this magazine with t ... st is purely coincidental. **Printed in Canada.** DAN BUCKLEY, President, Marvel Entertainment; JOHN NEE, Publisher; JOE QU ... s Affairs & Operations, Publishing & Partnership; DAVID GABRIEL, SVP of Sales & Marketing, Publishing; JEFF YOUNGQUIST, V ... MORALES, Director of Publishing Operations; DAN EDINGTON, Managing Editor; SUSAN CRESPI, Production Manager; STAN L ... , please contact Vit DeBellis, Custom Solutions & Integrated Advertising Manager, at vdebellis@marvel.com. For Marvel subscription inquiries, please call 888-511-5480. **Manufactured between 8/10/2018 and 9/11/2018 by SOLISCO PRINTERS, SCOTT, QC, CANADA.**

10 9 8 7 6 5 4 3 2 1

THE EVENTS OF THIS ISSUE TAKE PLACE CONCURRENTLY WITH, BUT MOSTLY AFTER THOSE IN *DOCTOR STRANGE: DAMNATION #1.*

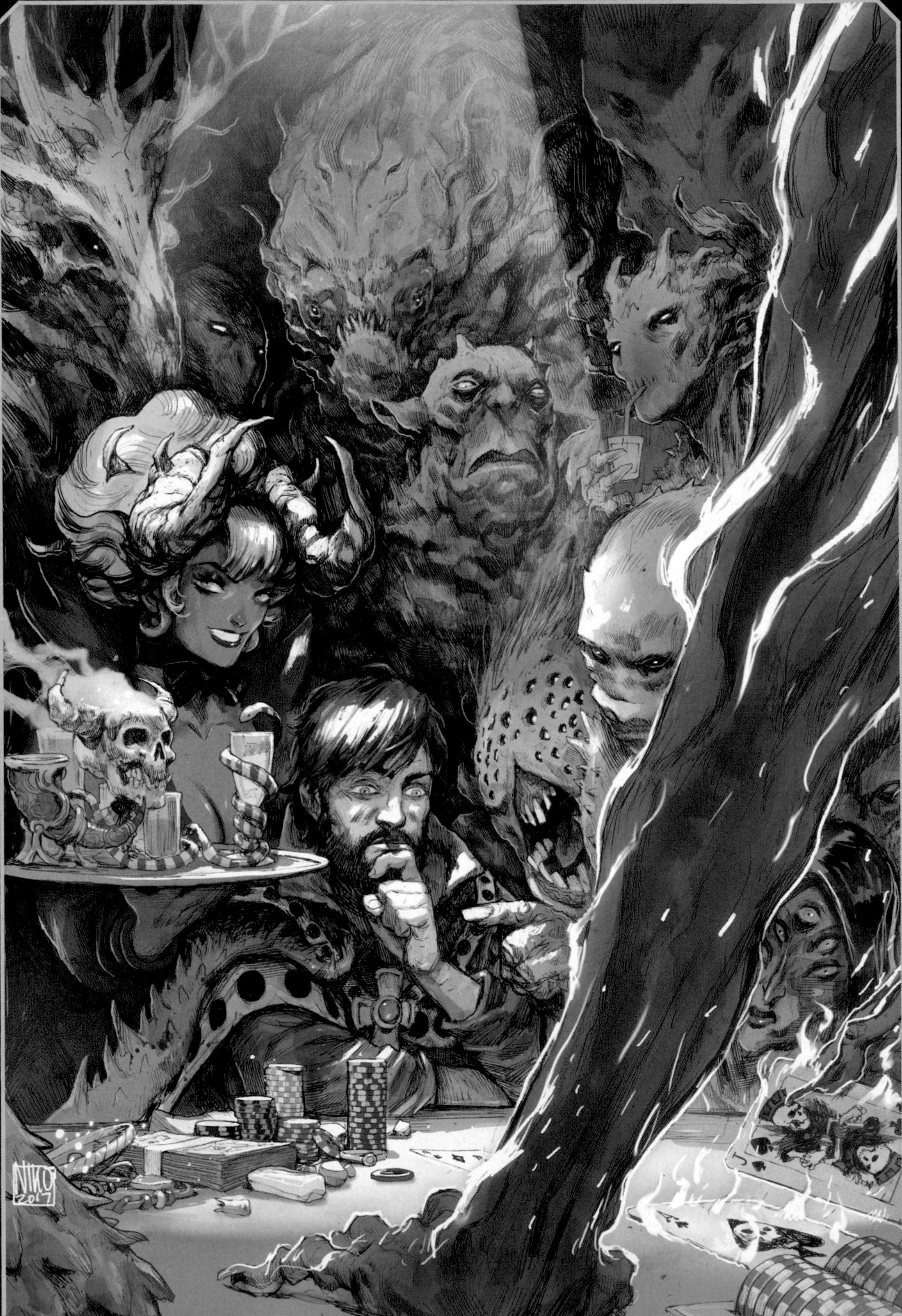

386

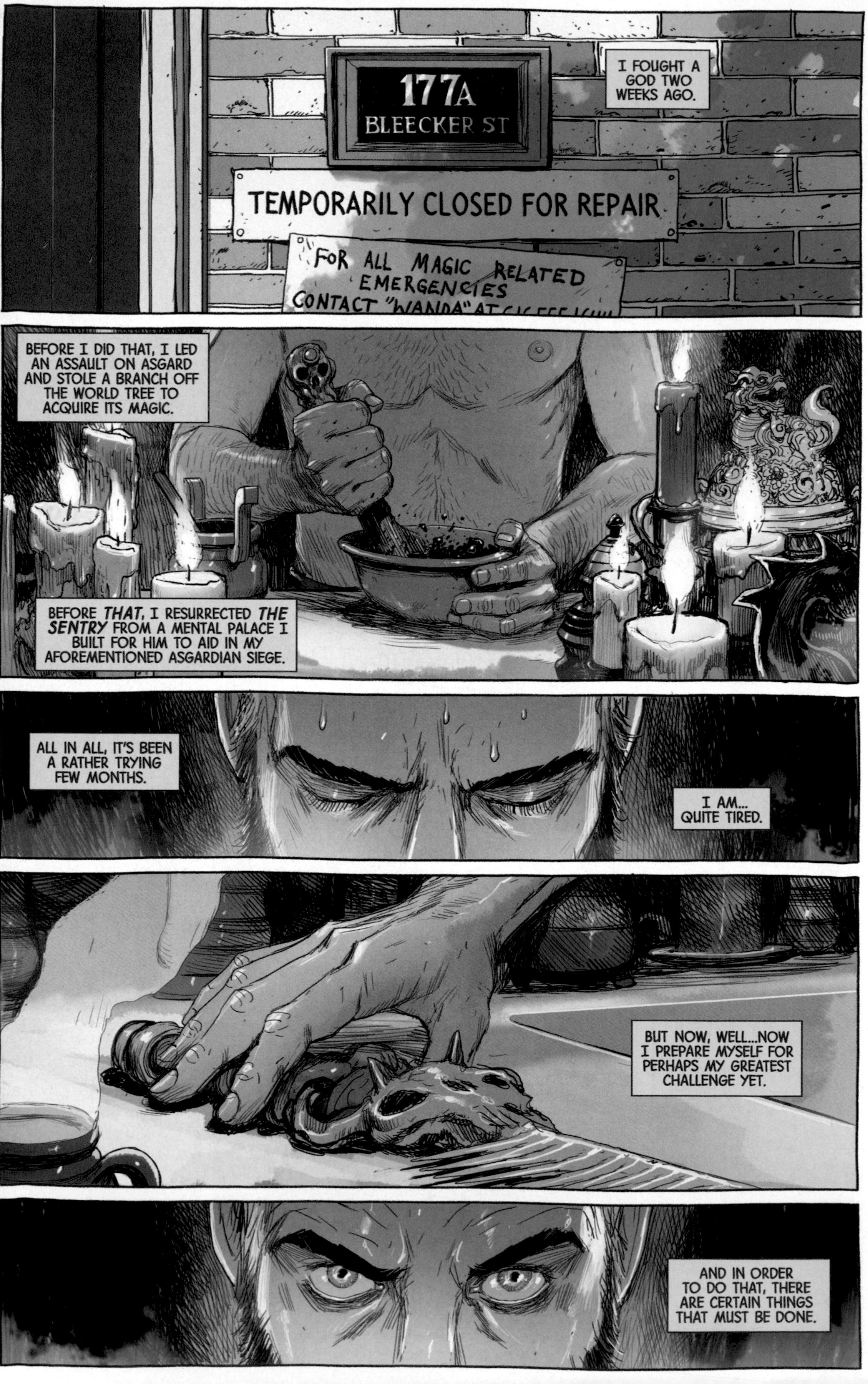

177A
BLEECKER ST
I FOUGHT A GOD TWO WEEKS AGO.
TEMPORARILY CLOSED FOR REPAIR
FOR ALL MAGIC RELATED EMERGENCIES CONTACT "WANDA"
BEFORE I DID THAT, I LED AN ASSAULT ON ASGARD AND STOLE A BRANCH OFF THE WORLD TREE TO ACQUIRE ITS MAGIC.
BEFORE *THAT*, I RESURRECTED *THE SENTRY* FROM A MENTAL PALACE I BUILT FOR HIM TO AID IN MY AFOREMENTIONED ASGARDIAN SIEGE.
ALL IN ALL, IT'S BEEN A RATHER TRYING FEW MONTHS.
I AM... QUITE TIRED.
BUT NOW, WELL...NOW I PREPARE *MYSELF* FOR PERHAPS MY GREATEST CHALLENGE YET.
AND IN ORDER TO DO THAT, THERE ARE CERTAIN THINGS THAT MUST BE DONE.

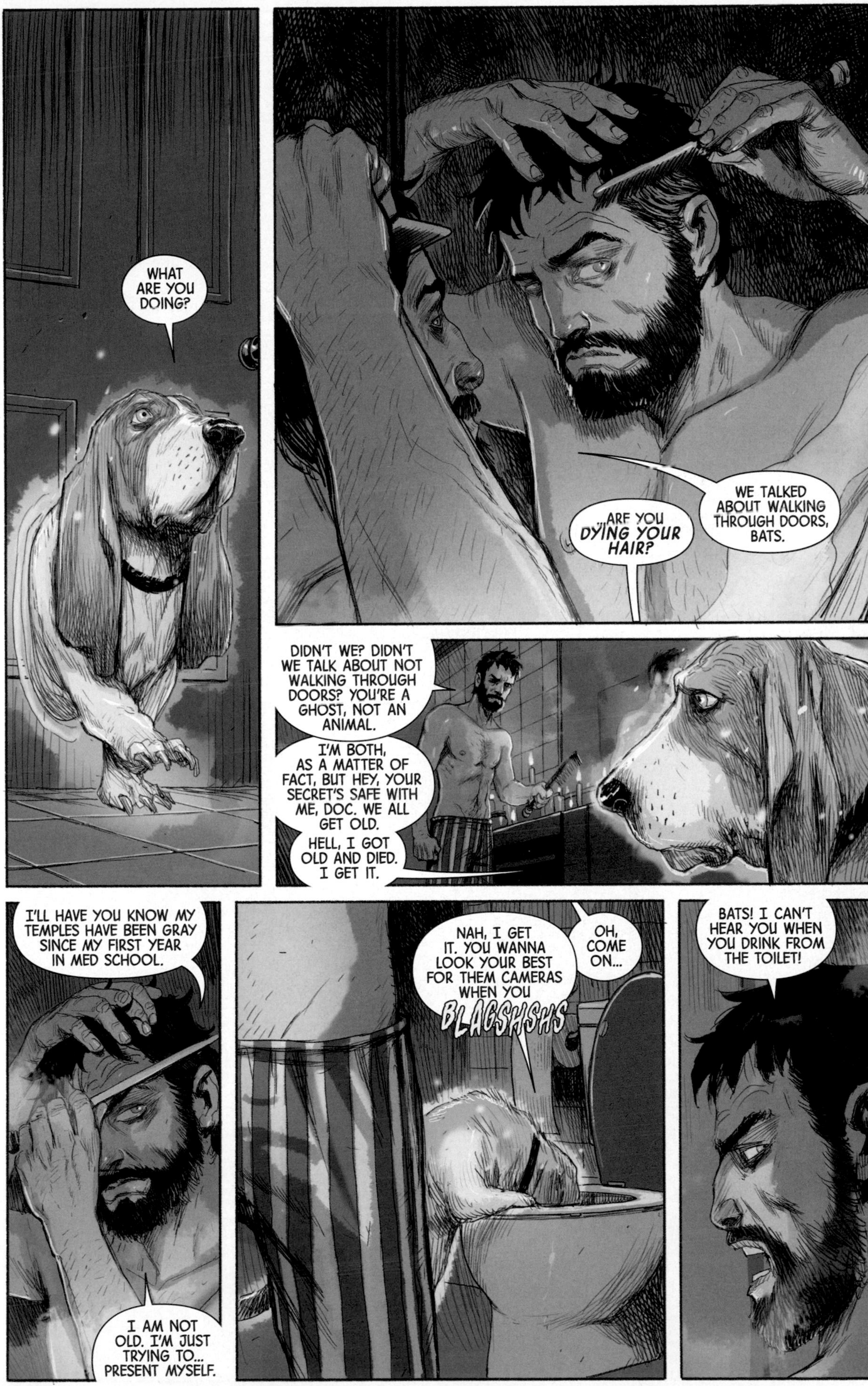
WHAT ARE YOU DOING?
WE TALKED ABOUT WALKING THROUGH DOORS, BATS.
...ARE YOU DYING YOUR HAIR?
DIDN'T WE? DIDN'T WE TALK ABOUT NOT WALKING THROUGH DOORS? YOU'RE A GHOST, NOT AN ANIMAL.
I'M BOTH, AS A MATTER OF FACT, BUT HEY, YOUR SECRET'S SAFE WITH ME, DOC. WE ALL GET OLD.
HELL, I GOT OLD AND DIED. I GET IT.
I'LL HAVE YOU KNOW MY TEMPLES HAVE BEEN GRAY SINCE MY FIRST YEAR IN MED SCHOOL.
I AM NOT OLD. I'M JUST TRYING TO... PRESENT MYSELF.
OH, COME ON...
NAH, I GET IT. YOU WANNA LOOK YOUR BEST FOR THEM CAMERAS WHEN YOU
BLAGSHSHS
BATS! I CAN'T HEAR YOU WHEN YOU DRINK FROM THE TOILET!

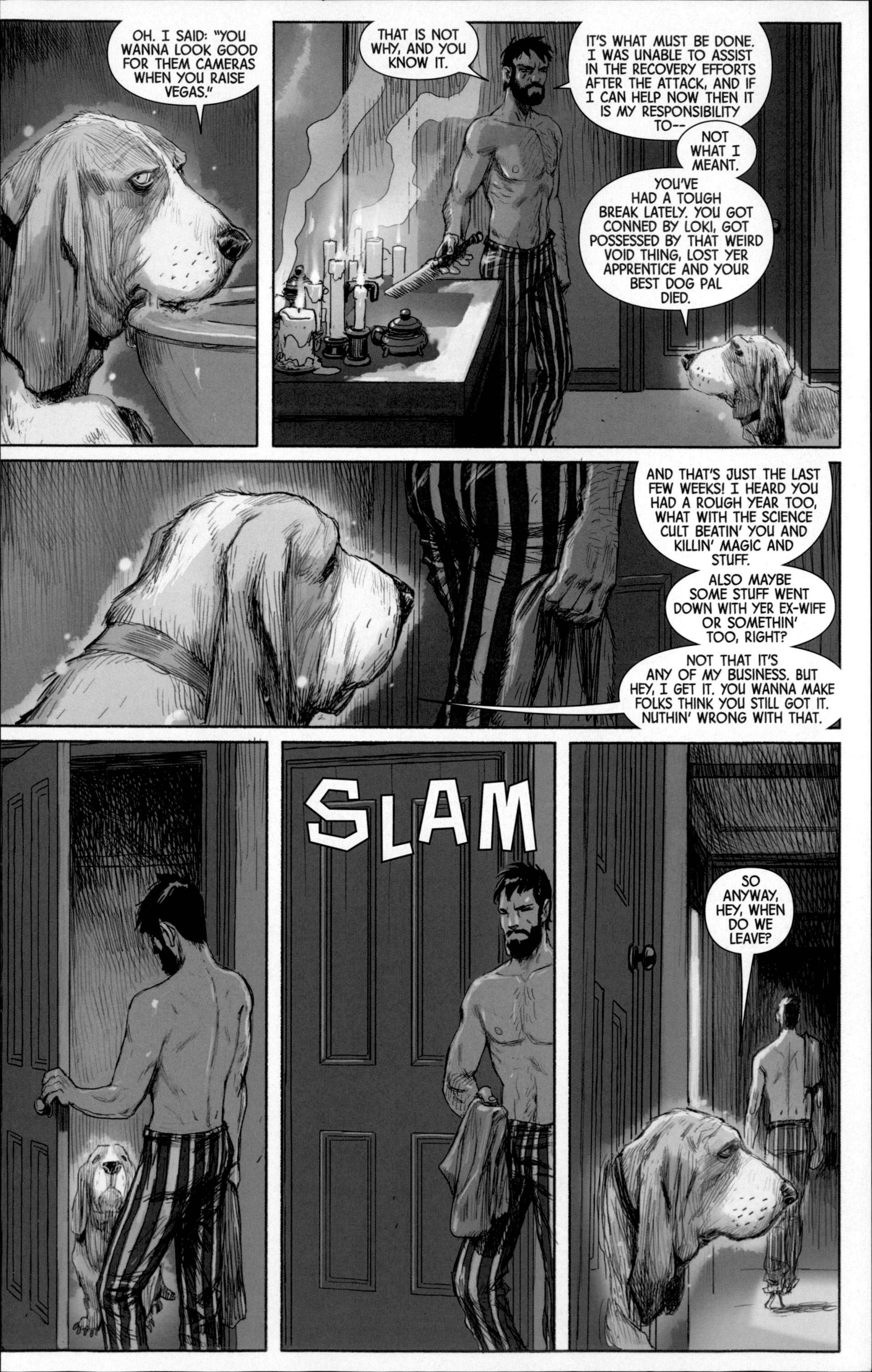
OH. I SAID: "YOU WANNA LOOK GOOD FOR THEM CAMERAS WHEN YOU RAISE VEGAS."
THAT IS NOT WHY, AND YOU KNOW IT.
IT'S WHAT MUST BE DONE. I WAS UNABLE TO ASSIST IN THE RECOVERY EFFORTS AFTER THE ATTACK, AND IF I CAN HELP NOW THEN IT IS MY RESPONSIBILITY TO--
NOT WHAT I MEANT.
YOU'VE HAD A TOUGH BREAK LATELY. YOU GOT CONNED BY LOKI, GOT POSSESSED BY THAT WEIRD VOID THING, LOST YER APPRENTICE AND YOUR BEST DOG PAL DIED.
AND THAT'S JUST THE LAST FEW WEEKS! I HEARD YOU HAD A ROUGH YEAR TOO, WHAT WITH THE SCIENCE CULT BEATIN' YOU AND KILLIN' MAGIC AND STUFF.
ALSO MAYBE SOME STUFF WENT DOWN WITH YER EX-WIFE OR SOMETHIN' TOO, RIGHT?
NOT THAT IT'S ANY OF MY BUSINESS. BUT HEY, I GET IT. YOU WANNA MAKE FOLKS THINK YOU STILL GOT IT. NUTHIN' WRONG WITH THAT.
SLAM
SO ANYWAY, HEY, WHEN DO WE LEAVE?

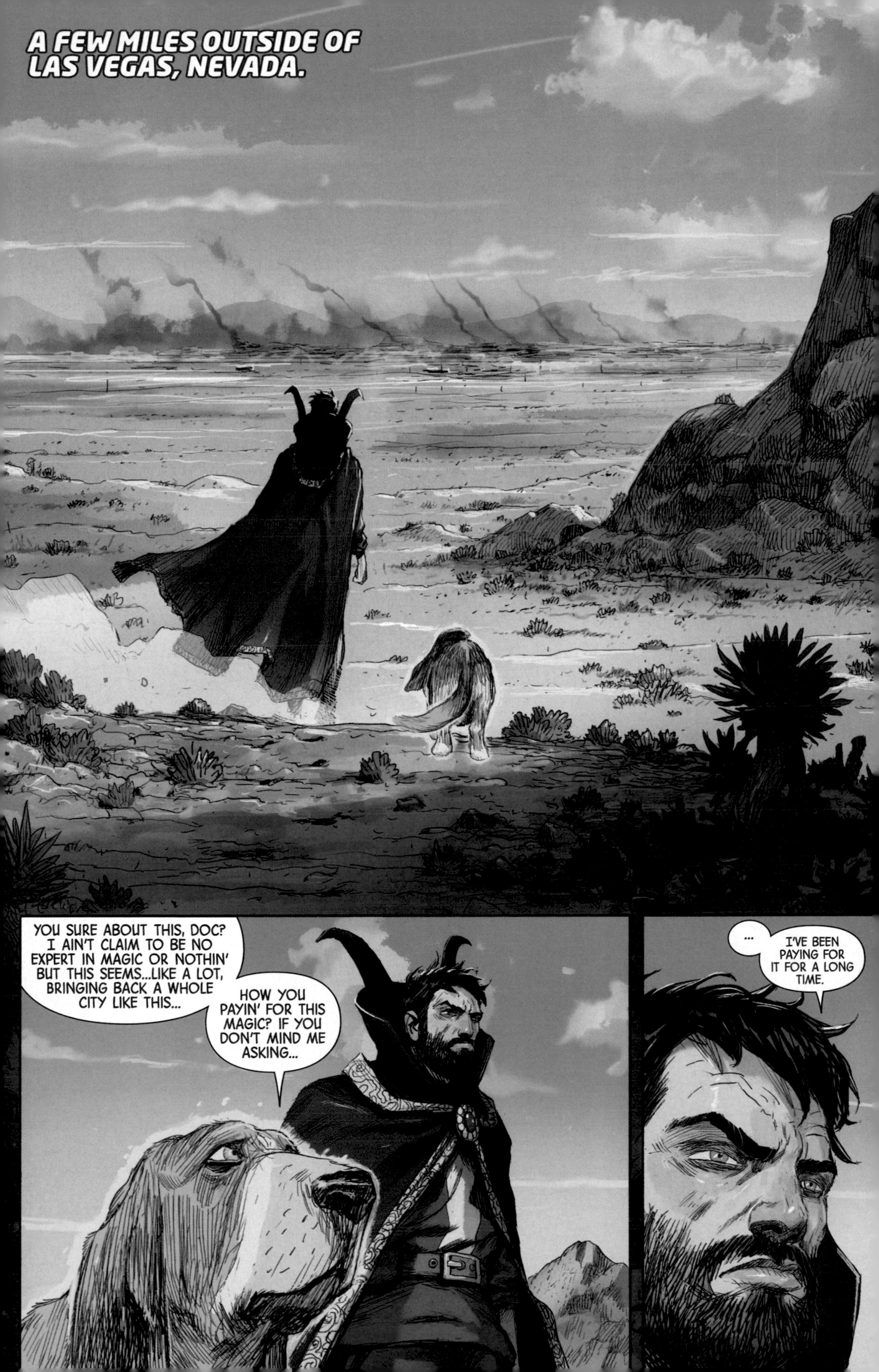
A FEW MILES OUTSIDE OF LAS VEGAS, NEVADA.
YOU SURE ABOUT THIS, DOC? I AIN'T CLAIM TO BE NO EXPERT IN MAGIC OR NOTHIN' BUT THIS SEEMS...LIKE A LOT, BRINGING BACK A WHOLE CITY LIKE THIS...
HOW YOU PAYIN' FOR THIS MAGIC? IF YOU DON'T MIND ME ASKING...
...
I'VE BEEN PAYING FOR IT FOR A LONG TIME.

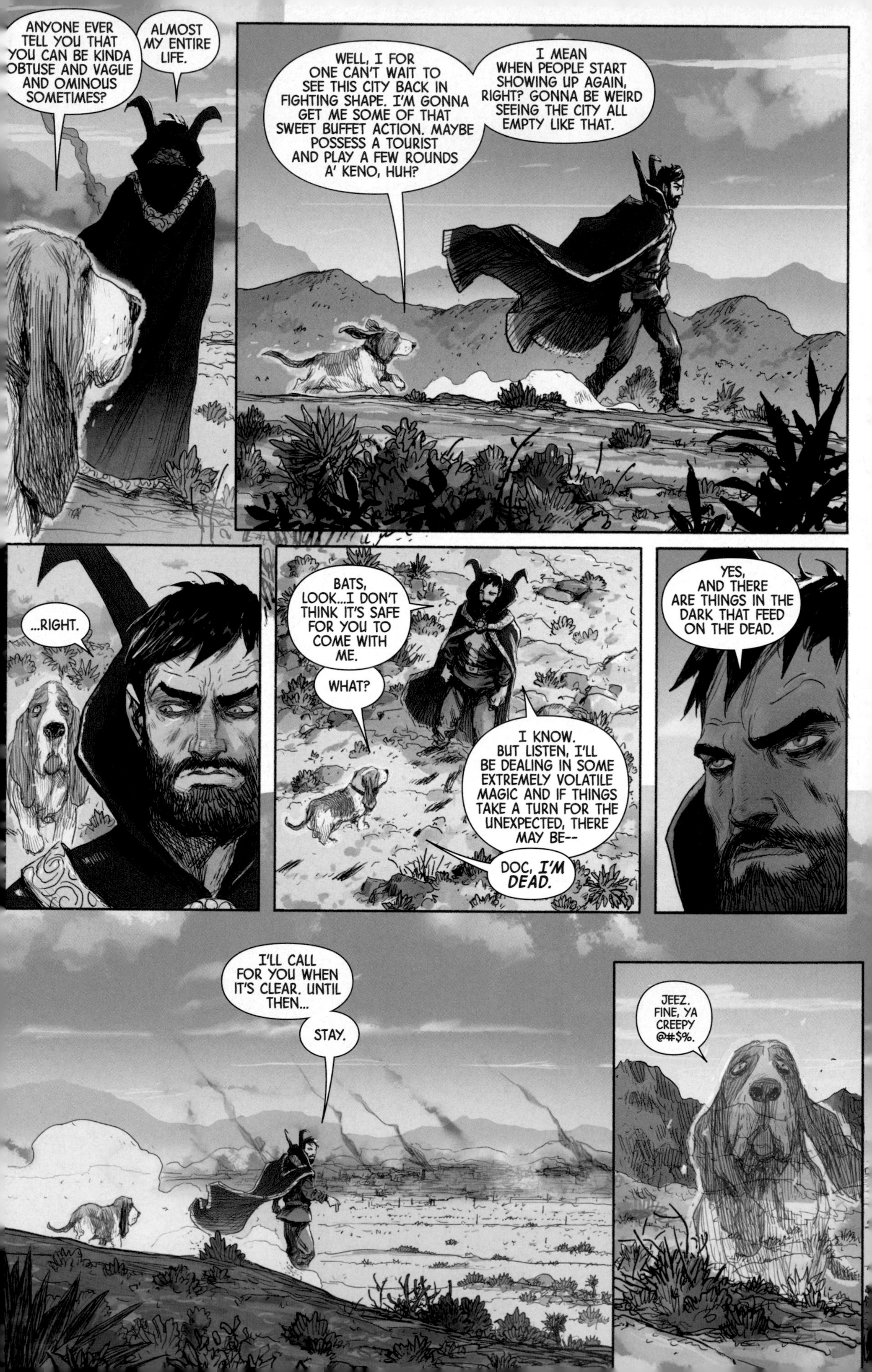
ANYONE EVER TELL YOU THAT YOU CAN BE KINDA OBTUSE AND VAGUE AND OMINOUS SOMETIMES?
ALMOST MY ENTIRE LIFE.
WELL, I FOR ONE CAN'T WAIT TO SEE THIS CITY BACK IN FIGHTING SHAPE. I'M GONNA GET ME SOME OF THAT SWEET BUFFET ACTION. MAYBE POSSESS A TOURIST AND PLAY A FEW ROUNDS A' KENO, HUH?
I MEAN WHEN PEOPLE START SHOWING UP AGAIN, RIGHT? GONNA BE WEIRD SEEING THE CITY ALL EMPTY LIKE THAT.
...RIGHT.
BATS, LOOK...I DON'T THINK IT'S SAFE FOR YOU TO COME WITH ME.
WHAT?
I KNOW. BUT LISTEN, I'LL BE DEALING IN SOME EXTREMELY VOLATILE MAGIC AND IF THINGS TAKE A TURN FOR THE UNEXPECTED, THERE MAY BE--
DOC, ***I'M DEAD.***
YES, AND THERE ARE THINGS IN THE DARK THAT FEED ON THE DEAD.
I'LL CALL FOR YOU WHEN IT'S CLEAR. UNTIL THEN...
STAY.
JEEZ. FINE, YA CREEPY @#$%.

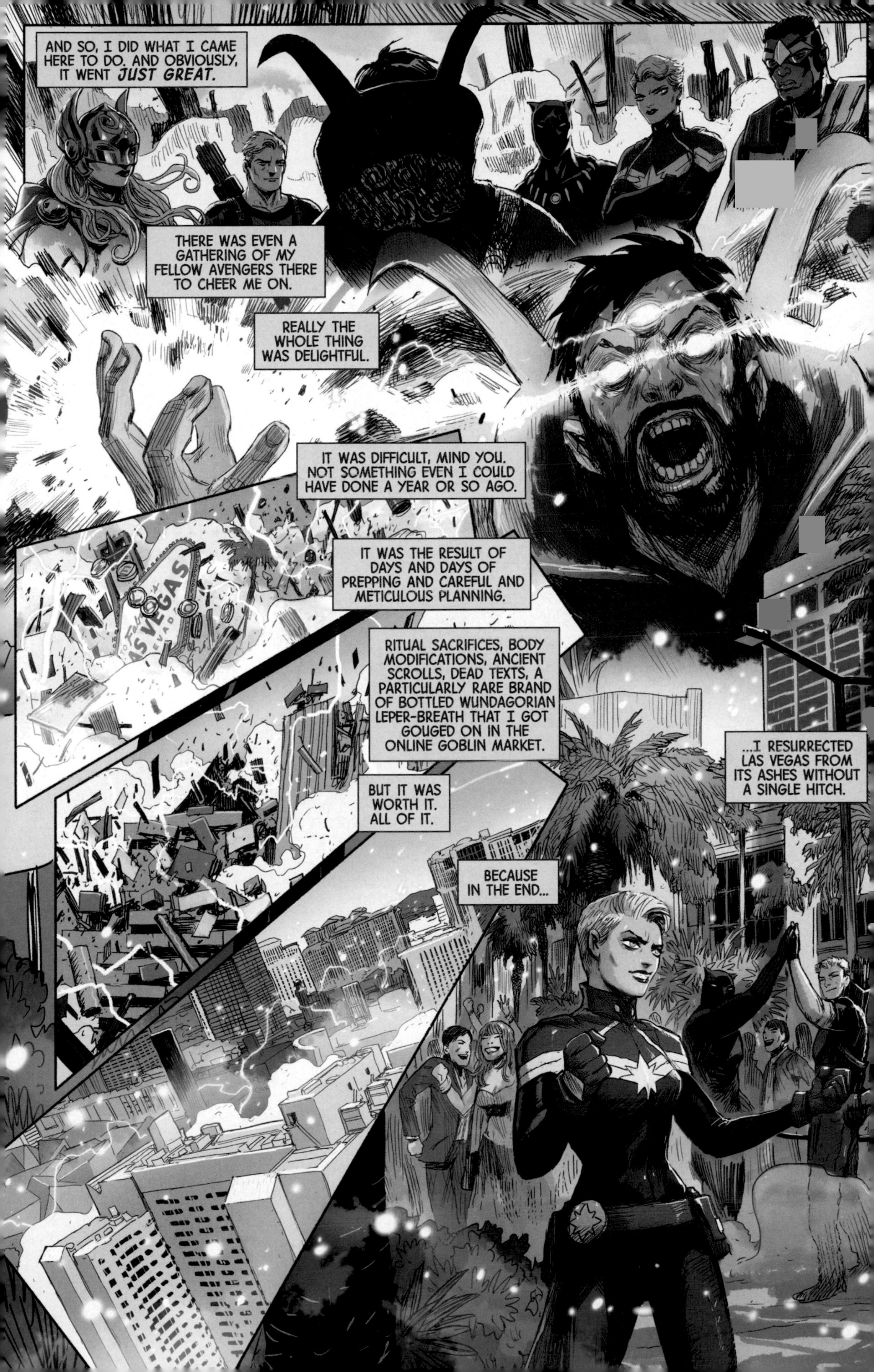
AND SO, I DID WHAT I CAME HERE TO DO. AND OBVIOUSLY, IT WENT JUST GREAT.
THERE WAS EVEN A GATHERING OF MY FELLOW AVENGERS THERE TO CHEER ME ON.
REALLY THE WHOLE THING WAS DELIGHTFUL.
IT WAS DIFFICULT, MIND YOU. NOT SOMETHING EVEN I COULD HAVE DONE A YEAR OR SO AGO.
IT WAS THE RESULT OF DAYS AND DAYS OF PREPPING AND CAREFUL AND METICULOUS PLANNING.
RITUAL SACRIFICES, BODY MODIFICATIONS, ANCIENT SCROLLS, DEAD TEXTS, A PARTICULARLY RARE BRAND OF BOTTLED WUNDAGORIAN LEPER-BREATH THAT I GOT GOUGED ON IN THE ONLINE GOBLIN MARKET.
BUT IT WAS WORTH IT. ALL OF IT.
BECAUSE IN THE END...
...I RESURRECTED LAS VEGAS FROM ITS ASHES WITHOUT A SINGLE HITCH.
LAS VEGAS

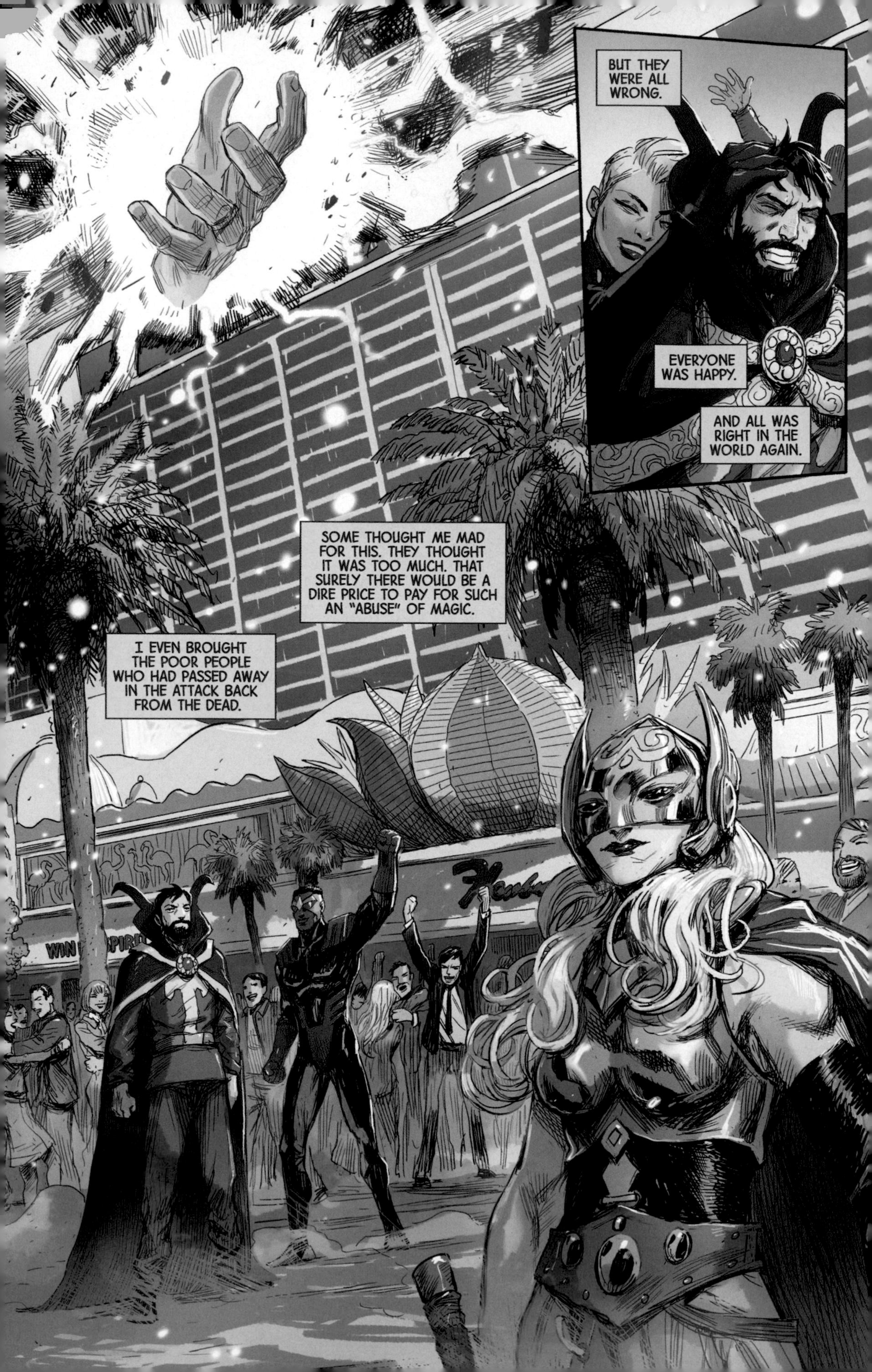
BUT THEY WERE ALL WRONG.
EVERYONE WAS HAPPY.
AND ALL WAS RIGHT IN THE WORLD AGAIN.
SOME THOUGHT ME MAD FOR THIS. THEY THOUGHT IT WAS TOO MUCH. THAT SURELY THERE WOULD BE A DIRE PRICE TO PAY FOR SUCH AN "ABUSE" OF MAGIC.
I EVEN BROUGHT THE POOR PEOPLE WHO HAD PASSED AWAY IN THE ATTACK BACK FROM THE DEAD.

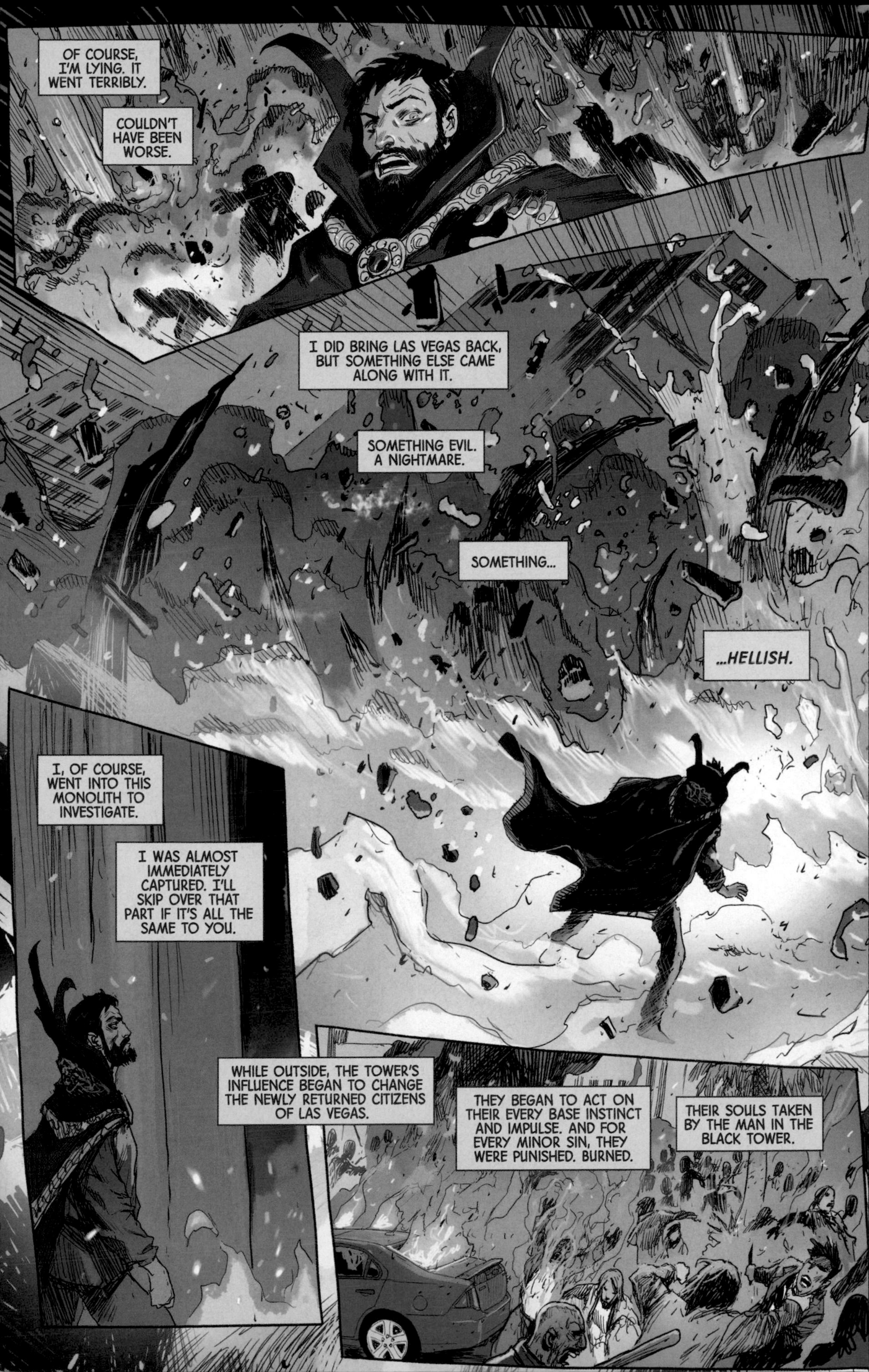
OF COURSE, I'M LYING. IT WENT TERRIBLY.
COULDN'T HAVE BEEN WORSE.
I DID BRING LAS VEGAS BACK, BUT SOMETHING ELSE CAME ALONG WITH IT.
SOMETHING EVIL. A NIGHTMARE.
SOMETHING...
...HELLISH.
I, OF COURSE, WENT INTO THIS MONOLITH TO INVESTIGATE.
I WAS ALMOST IMMEDIATELY CAPTURED. I'LL SKIP OVER THAT PART IF IT'S ALL THE SAME TO YOU.
WHILE OUTSIDE, THE TOWER'S INFLUENCE BEGAN TO CHANGE THE NEWLY RETURNED CITIZENS OF LAS VEGAS.
THEY BEGAN TO ACT ON THEIR EVERY BASE INSTINCT AND IMPULSE. AND FOR EVERY MINOR SIN, THEY WERE PUNISHED. BURNED.
THEIR SOULS TAKEN BY THE MAN IN THE BLACK TOWER.

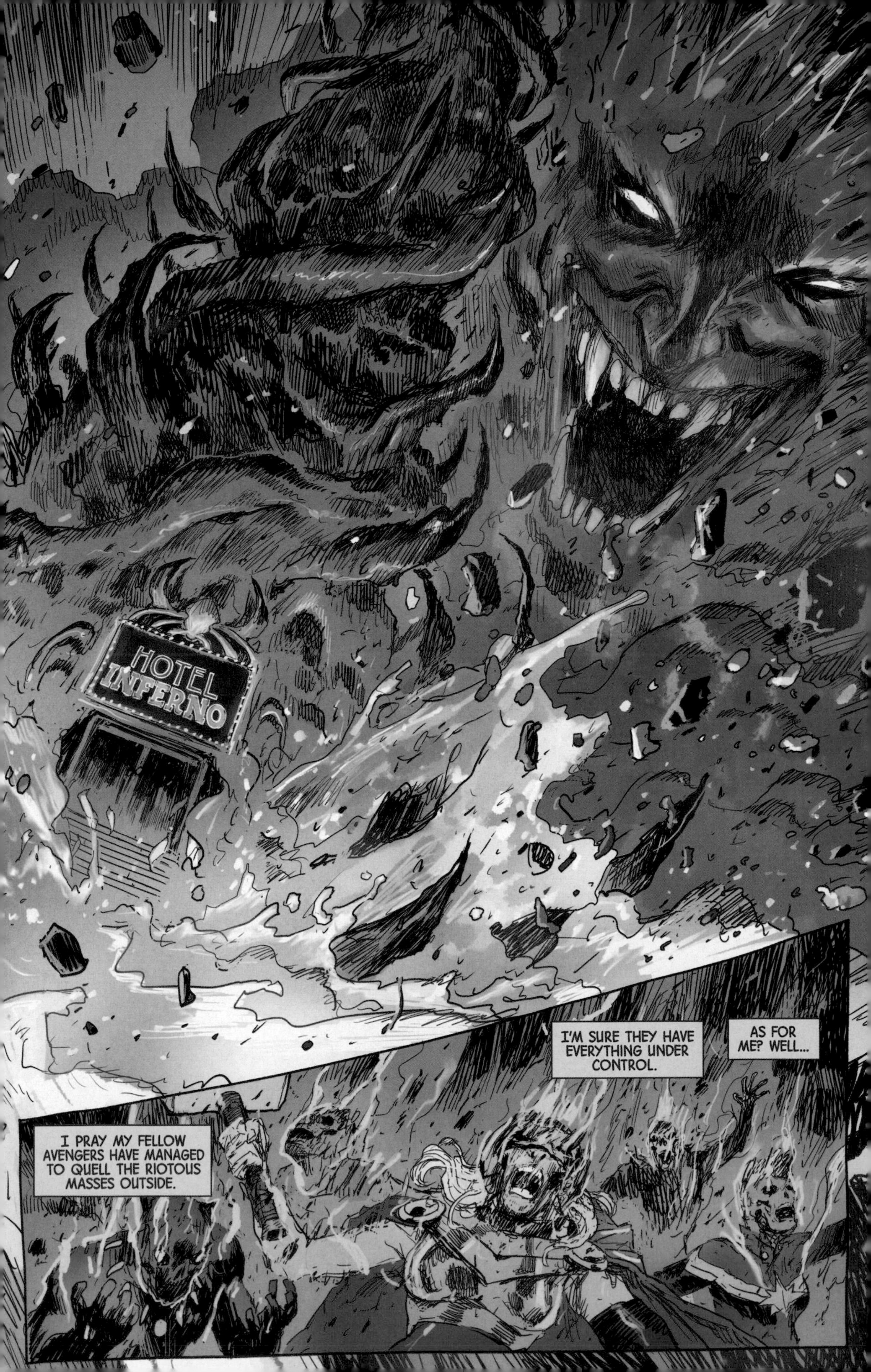
HOTEL INFERNO
I'M SURE THEY HAVE EVERYTHING UNDER CONTROL.
AS FOR ME? WELL...
I PRAY MY FELLOW AVENGERS HAVE MANAGED TO QUELL THE RIOTOUS MASSES OUTSIDE.

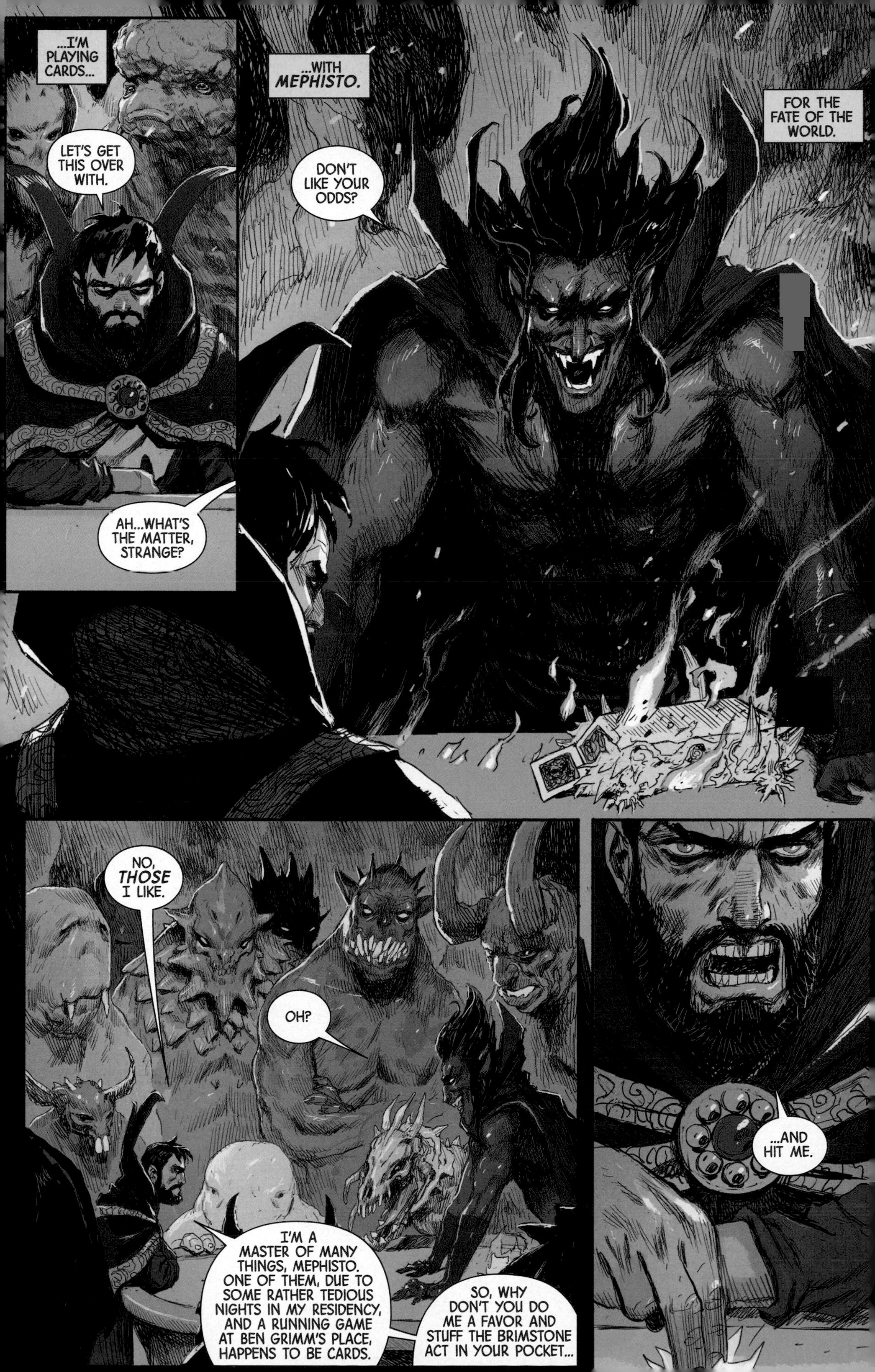
...I'M PLAYING CARDS...
...WITH *MEPHISTO.*
FOR THE FATE OF THE WORLD.
LET'S GET THIS OVER WITH.
AH...WHAT'S THE MATTER, STRANGE?
DON'T LIKE YOUR ODDS?
NO, *THOSE* I LIKE.
OH?
I'M A MASTER OF MANY THINGS, MEPHISTO. ONE OF THEM, DUE TO SOME RATHER TEDIOUS NIGHTS IN MY RESIDENCY, AND A RUNNING GAME AT BEN GRIMM'S PLACE, HAPPENS TO BE CARDS.
SO, WHY DON'T YOU DO ME A FAVOR AND STUFF THE BRIMSTONE ACT IN YOUR POCKET...
...AND HIT ME.

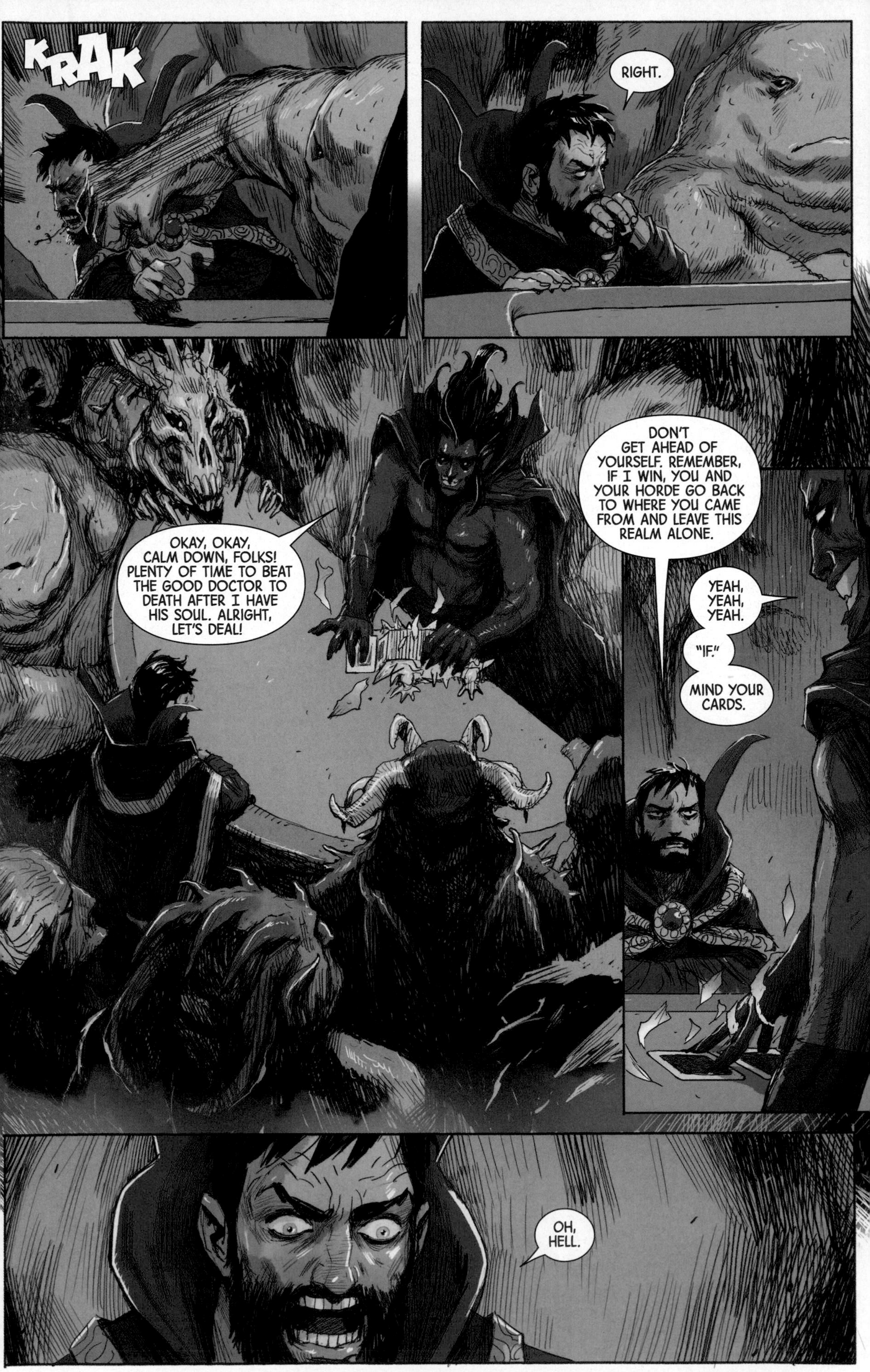
KRAK
RIGHT.
OKAY, OKAY, CALM DOWN, FOLKS! PLENTY OF TIME TO BEAT THE GOOD DOCTOR TO DEATH AFTER I HAVE HIS SOUL. ALRIGHT, LET'S DEAL!
DON'T GET AHEAD OF YOURSELF. REMEMBER, IF I WIN, YOU AND YOUR HORDE GO BACK TO WHERE YOU CAME FROM AND LEAVE THIS REALM ALONE.
YEAH, YEAH, YEAH.
"IF."
MIND YOUR CARDS.
OH, HELL.

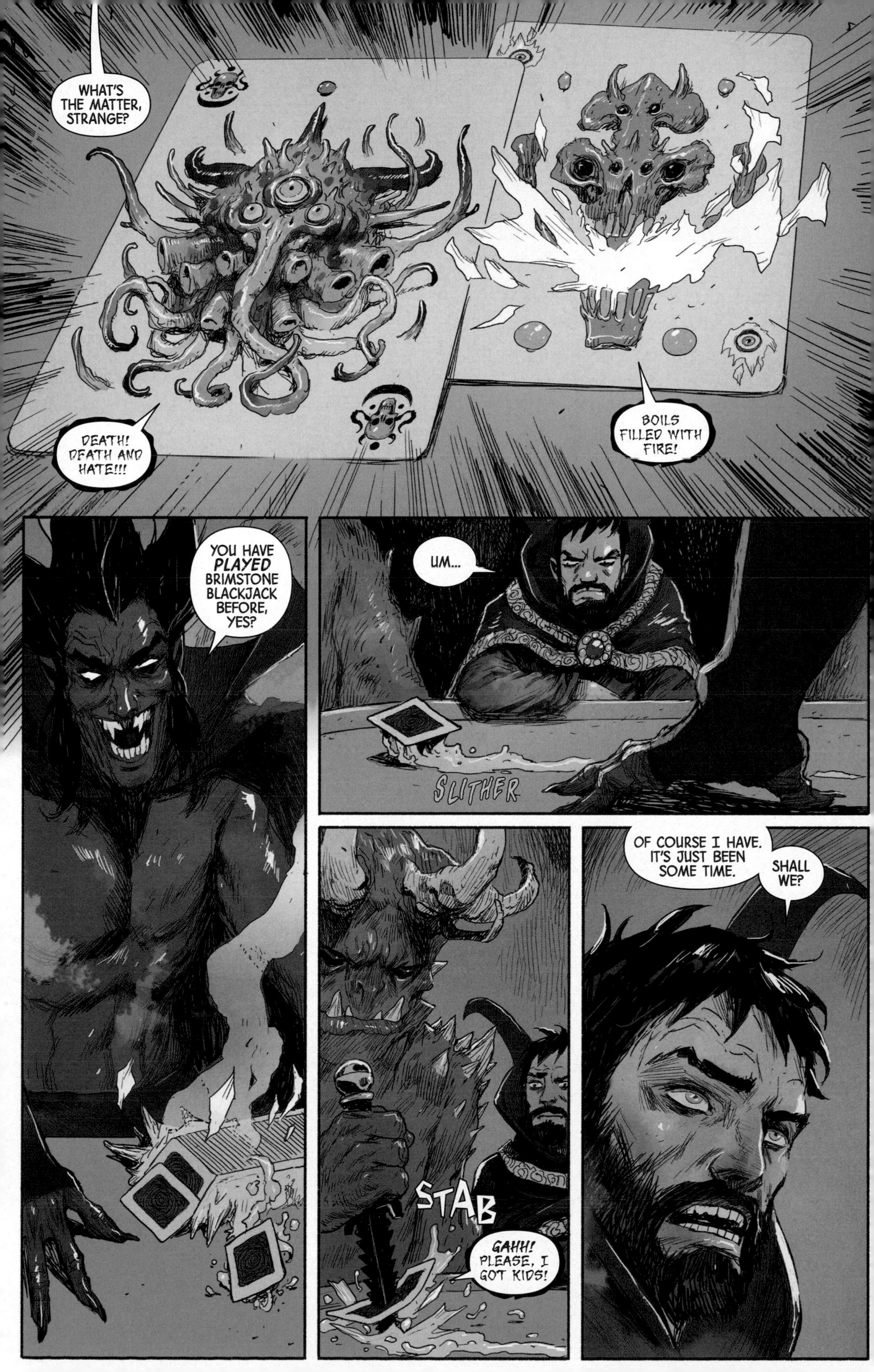

WHAT'S THE MATTER, STRANGE?
DEATH! DEATH AND HATE!!!
BOILS FILLED WITH FIRE!
YOU HAVE *PLAYED* BRIMSTONE BLACKJACK BEFORE, YES?
UM...
SLITHER
STAB
GAHH! PLEASE, I GOT KIDS!
OF COURSE I HAVE. IT'S JUST BEEN SOME TIME.
SHALL WE?

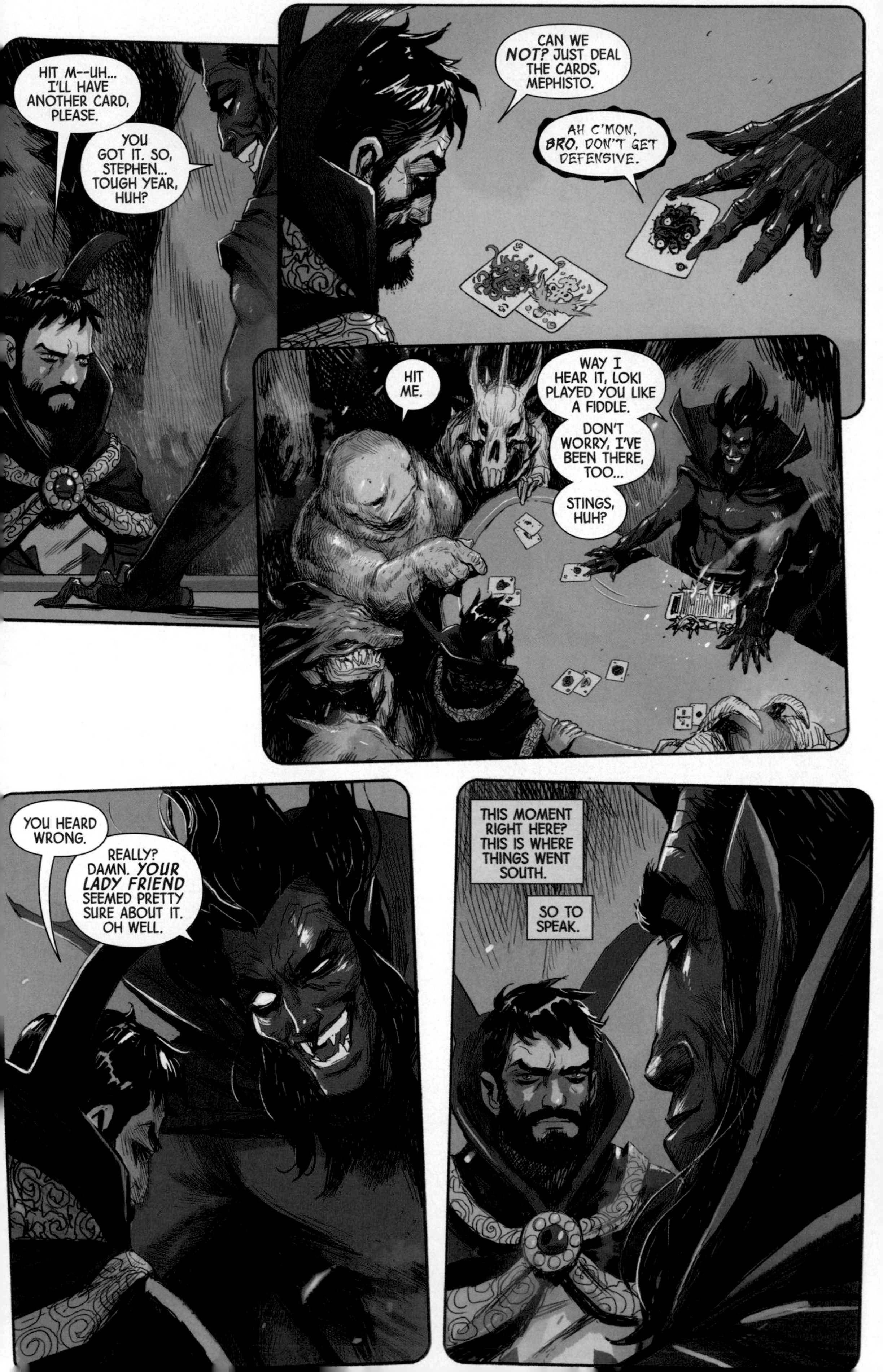
HIT M--UH... I'LL HAVE ANOTHER CARD, PLEASE.
YOU GOT IT. SO, STEPHEN... TOUGH YEAR, HUH?
CAN WE NOT? JUST DEAL THE CARDS, MEPHISTO.
AH C'MON, BRO, DON'T GET DEFENSIVE.
HIT ME.
WAY I HEAR IT, LOKI PLAYED YOU LIKE A FIDDLE.
DON'T WORRY, I'VE BEEN THERE, TOO...
STINGS, HUH?
YOU HEARD WRONG.
REALLY? DAMN. YOUR LADY FRIEND SEEMED PRETTY SURE ABOUT IT. OH WELL.
THIS MOMENT RIGHT HERE? THIS IS WHERE THINGS WENT SOUTH.
SO TO SPEAK.

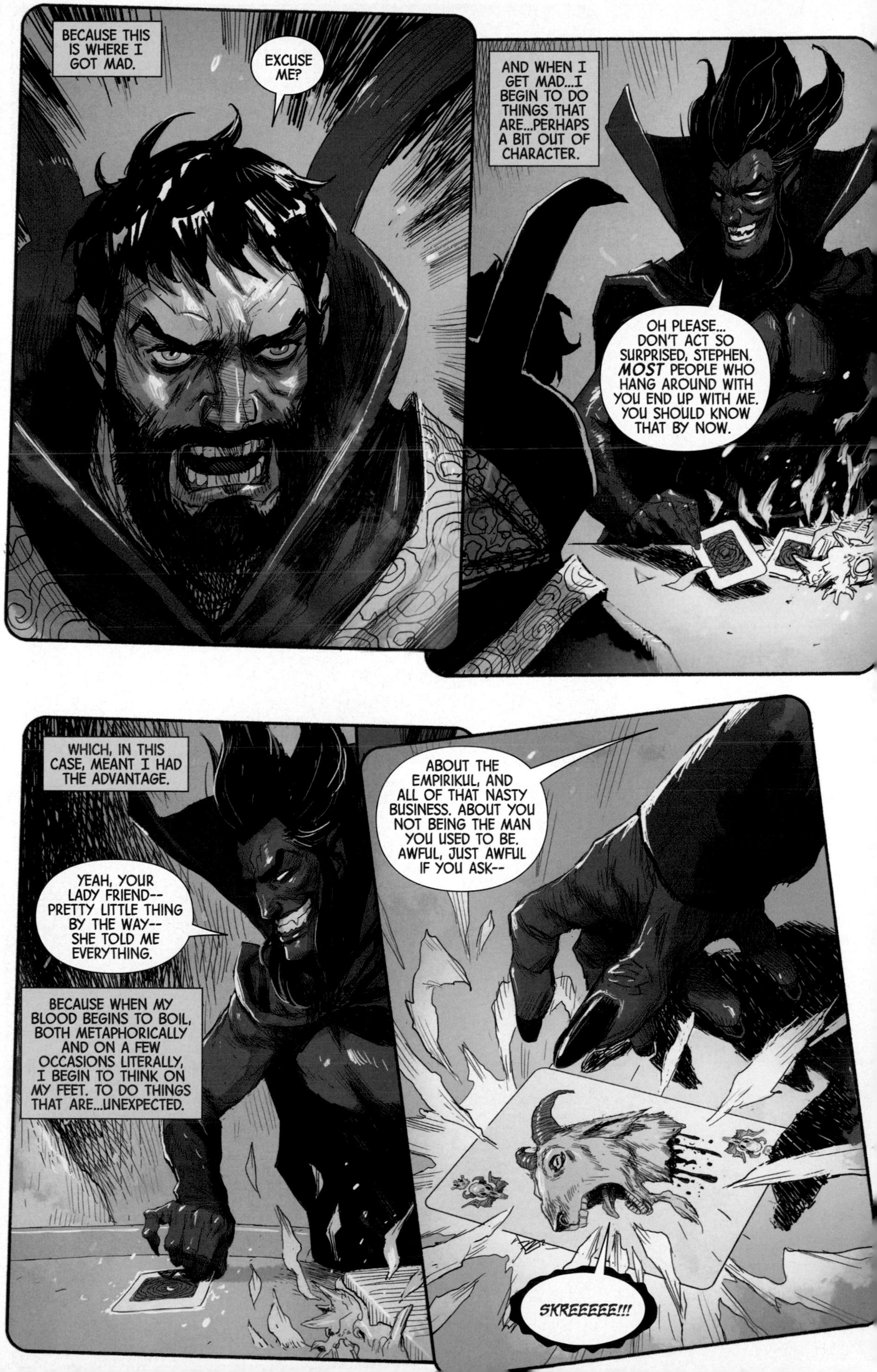
BECAUSE THIS IS WHERE I GOT MAD.
EXCUSE ME?
AND WHEN I GET MAD...I BEGIN TO DO THINGS THAT ARE...PERHAPS A BIT OUT OF CHARACTER.
OH PLEASE... DON'T ACT SO SURPRISED, STEPHEN. *MOST* PEOPLE WHO HANG AROUND WITH YOU END UP WITH ME. YOU SHOULD KNOW THAT BY NOW.
WHICH, IN THIS CASE, MEANT I HAD THE ADVANTAGE.
YEAH, YOUR LADY FRIEND-- PRETTY LITTLE THING BY THE WAY-- SHE TOLD ME EVERYTHING.
BECAUSE WHEN MY BLOOD BEGINS TO BOIL, BOTH METAPHORICALLY AND ON A FEW OCCASIONS LITERALLY, I BEGIN TO THINK ON MY FEET. TO DO THINGS THAT ARE...UNEXPECTED.
ABOUT THE EMPIRIKUL, AND ALL OF THAT NASTY BUSINESS. ABOUT YOU NOT BEING THE MAN YOU USED TO BE. AWFUL, JUST AWFUL IF YOU ASK--
SKREEEEEE!!!

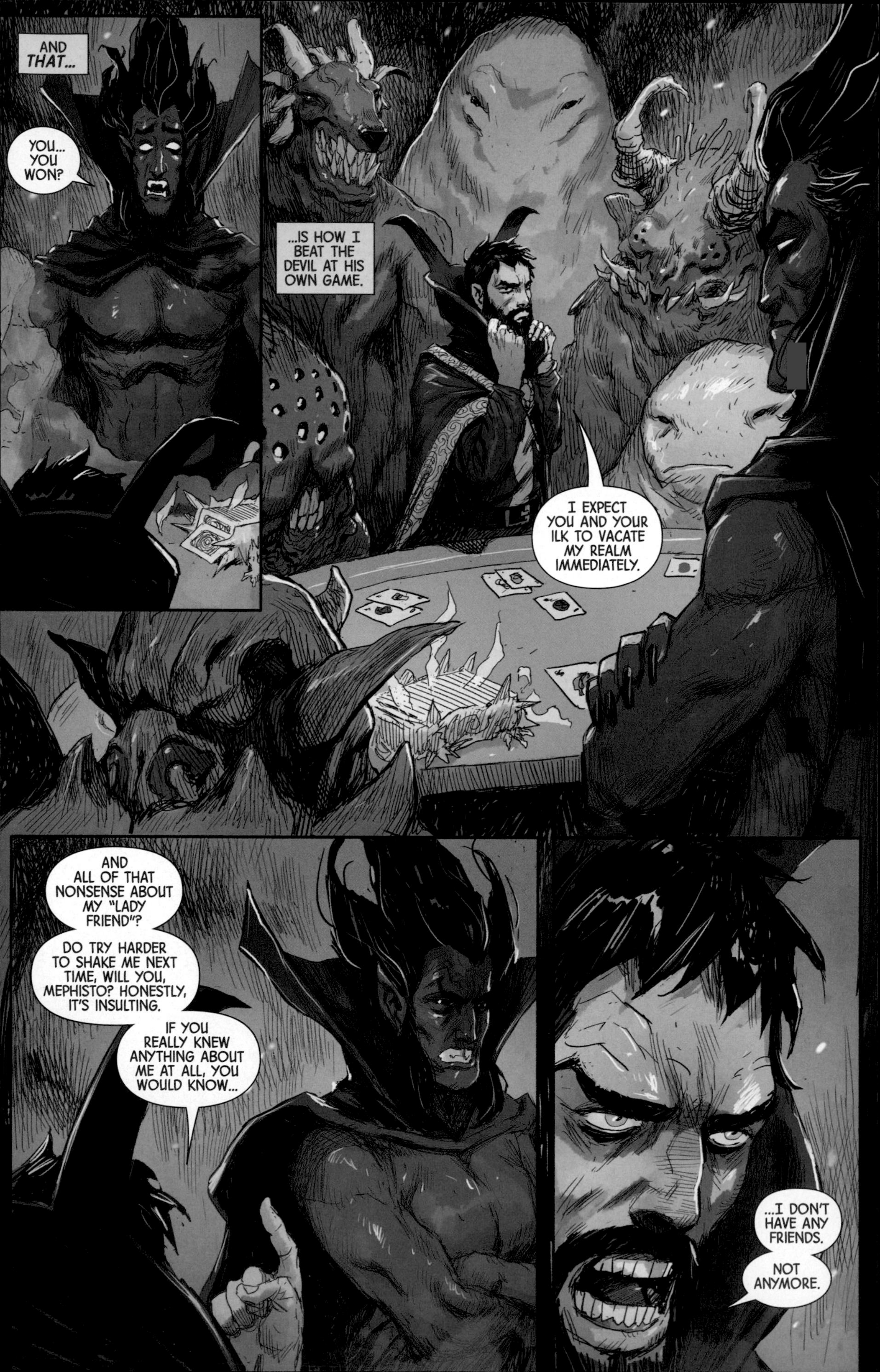
AND THAT...
YOU... YOU WON?
...IS HOW I BEAT THE DEVIL AT HIS OWN GAME.
I EXPECT YOU AND YOUR ILK TO VACATE MY REALM IMMEDIATELY.
AND ALL OF THAT NONSENSE ABOUT MY "LADY FRIEND"?
DO TRY HARDER TO SHAKE ME NEXT TIME, WILL YOU, MEPHISTO? HONESTLY, IT'S INSULTING.
IF YOU REALLY KNEW ANYTHING ABOUT ME AT ALL, YOU WOULD KNOW...
...I DON'T HAVE ANY FRIENDS.
NOT ANYMORE.

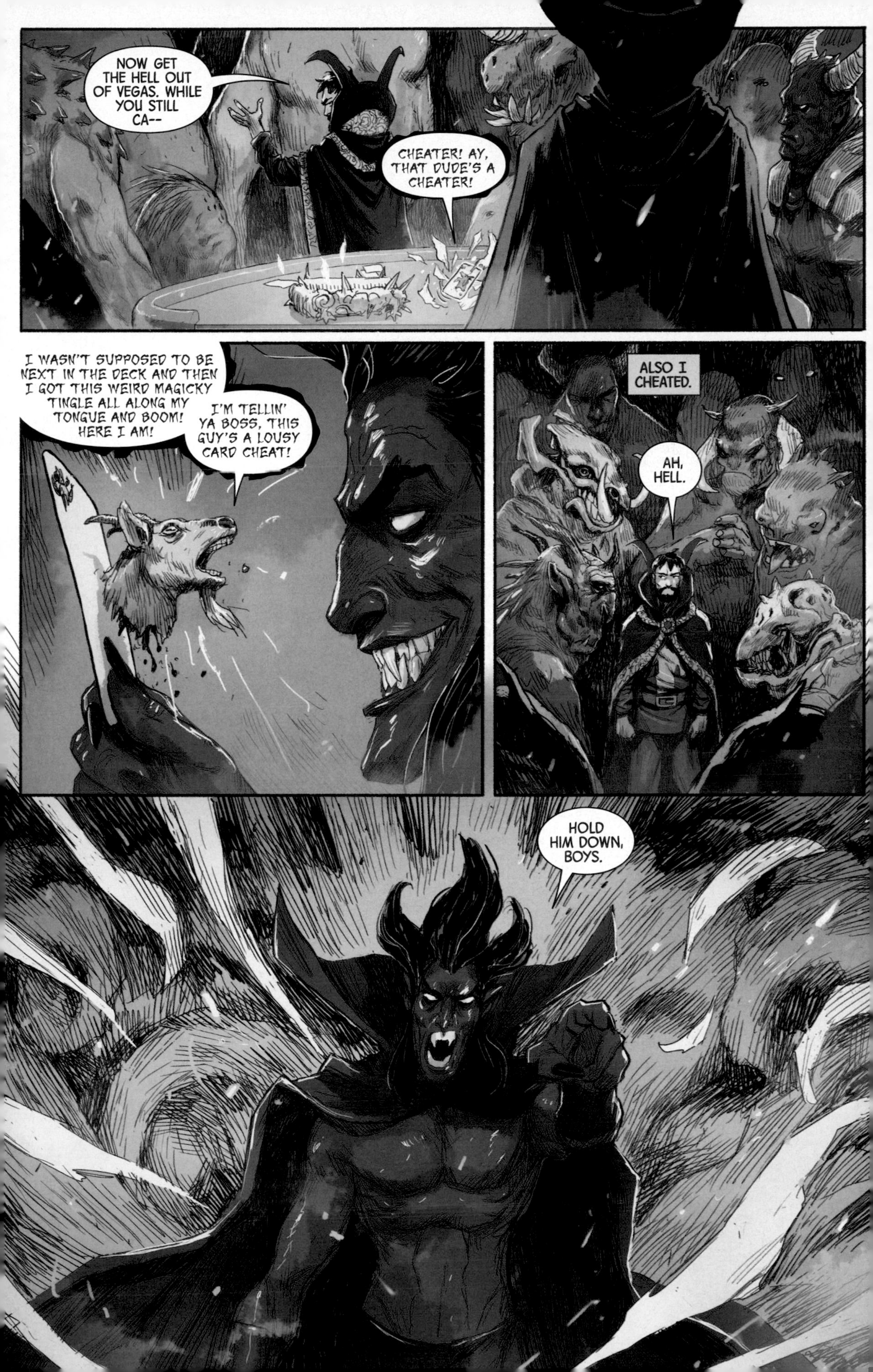
NOW GET THE HELL OUT OF VEGAS. WHILE YOU STILL CA--
CHEATER! AY, THAT DUDE'S A CHEATER!
I WASN'T SUPPOSED TO BE NEXT IN THE DECK AND THEN I GOT THIS WEIRD MAGICKY TINGLE ALL ALONG MY TONGUE AND BOOM! HERE I AM!
I'M TELLIN' YA BOSS, THIS GUY'S A LOUSY CARD CHEAT!
ALSO I CHEATED.
AH, HELL.
HOLD HIM DOWN, BOYS.

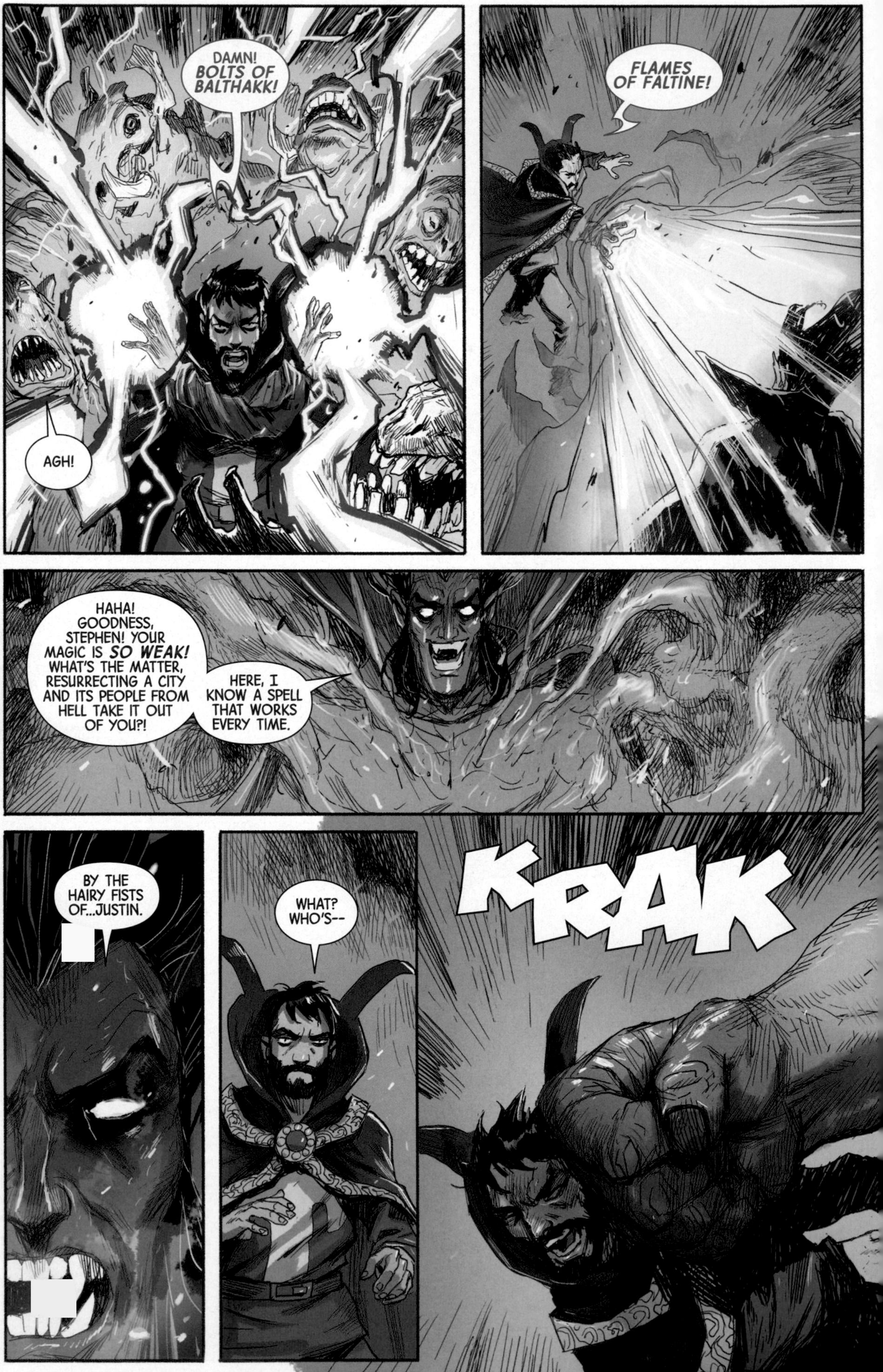
DAMN! BOLTS OF BALTHAKK!
AGH!
FLAMES OF FALTINE!
HAHA! GOODNESS, STEPHEN! YOUR MAGIC IS SO WEAK! WHAT'S THE MATTER, RESURRECTING A CITY AND ITS PEOPLE FROM HELL TAKE IT OUT OF YOU?!
HERE, I KNOW A SPELL THAT WORKS EVERY TIME.
BY THE HAIRY FISTS OF...JUSTIN.
WHAT? WHO'S--
KRAK

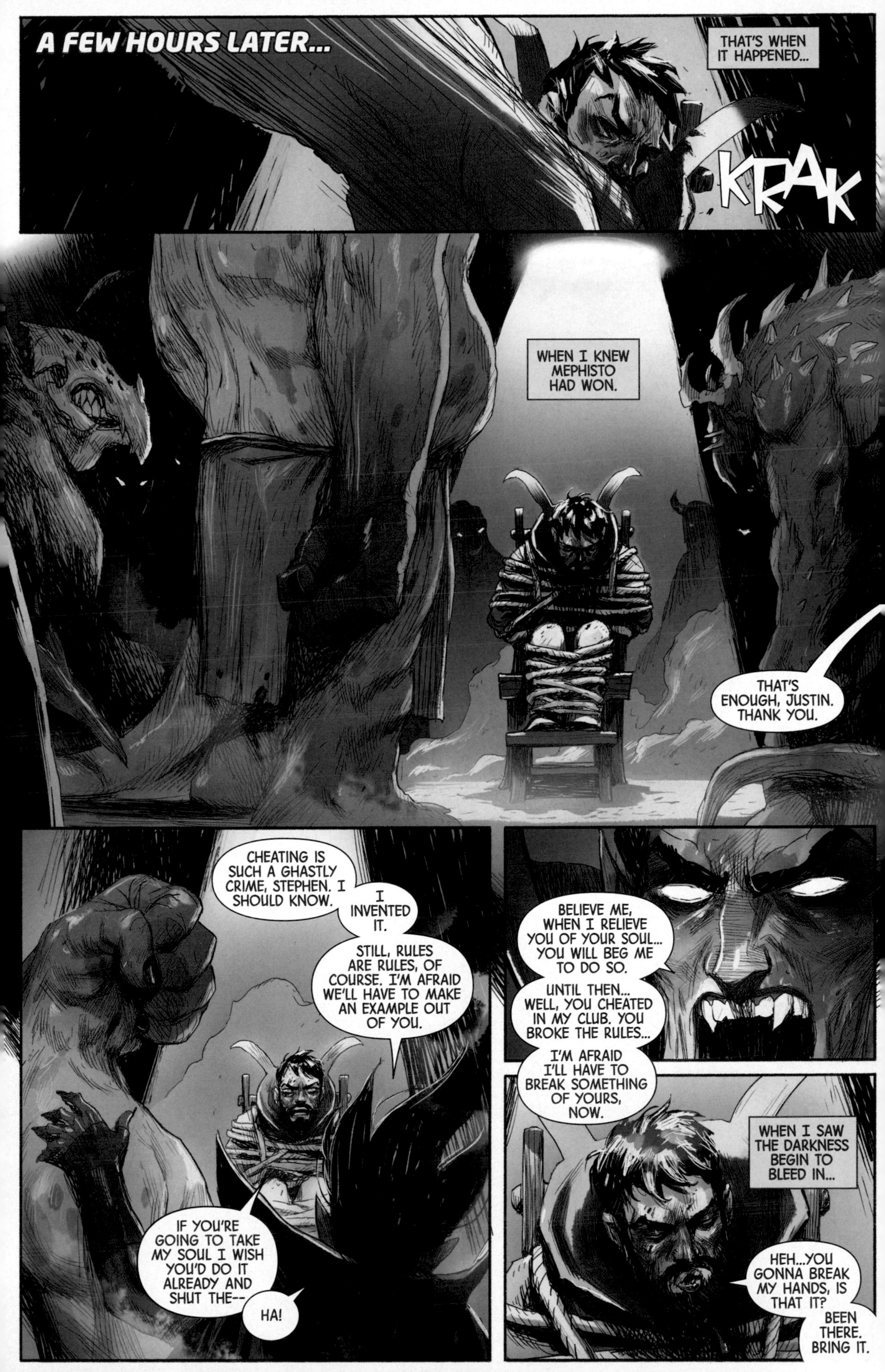
A FEW HOURS LATER...
THAT'S WHEN IT HAPPENED...
KRAK
WHEN I KNEW MEPHISTO HAD WON.
THAT'S ENOUGH, JUSTIN. THANK YOU.
CHEATING IS SUCH A GHASTLY CRIME, STEPHEN. I SHOULD KNOW.
I INVENTED IT.
STILL, RULES ARE RULES, OF COURSE. I'M AFRAID WE'LL HAVE TO MAKE AN EXAMPLE OUT OF YOU.
IF YOU'RE GOING TO TAKE MY SOUL I WISH YOU'D DO IT ALREADY AND SHUT THE--
HA!
BELIEVE ME, WHEN I RELIEVE YOU OF YOUR SOUL... YOU WILL BEG ME TO DO SO.
UNTIL THEN... WELL, YOU CHEATED IN MY CLUB. YOU BROKE THE RULES...
I'M AFRAID I'LL HAVE TO BREAK SOMETHING OF YOURS, NOW.
WHEN I SAW THE DARKNESS BEGIN TO BLEED IN...
HEH...YOU GONNA BREAK MY HANDS, IS THAT IT?
BEEN THERE. BRING IT.

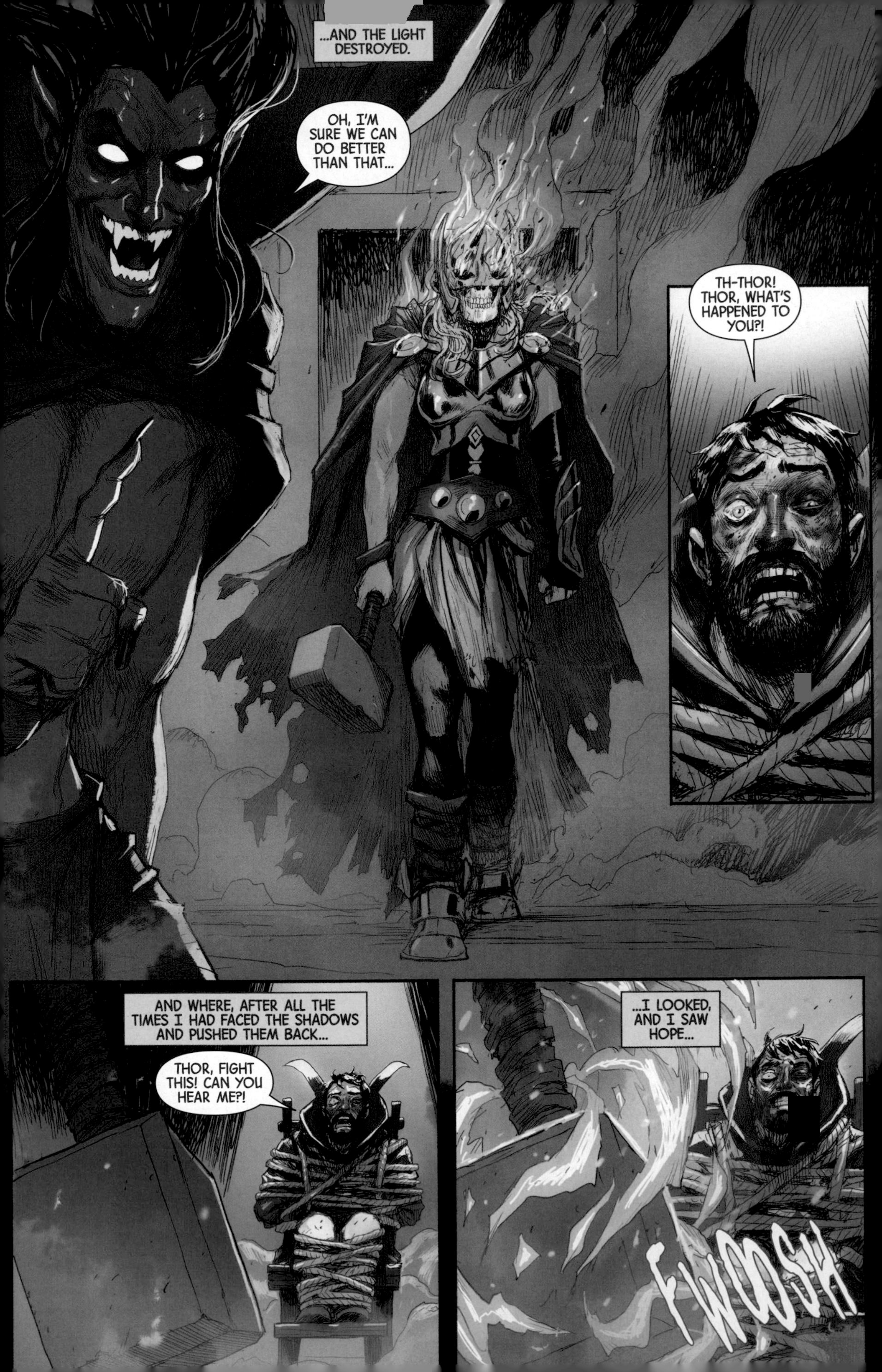

...AND THE LIGHT DESTROYED.
OH, I'M SURE WE CAN DO BETTER THAN THAT...
TH-THOR! THOR, WHAT'S HAPPENED TO YOU?!
AND WHERE, AFTER ALL THE TIMES I HAD FACED THE SHADOWS AND PUSHED THEM BACK...
THOR, FIGHT THIS! CAN YOU HEAR ME?!
...I LOOKED, AND I SAW HOPE...
FWOOSH

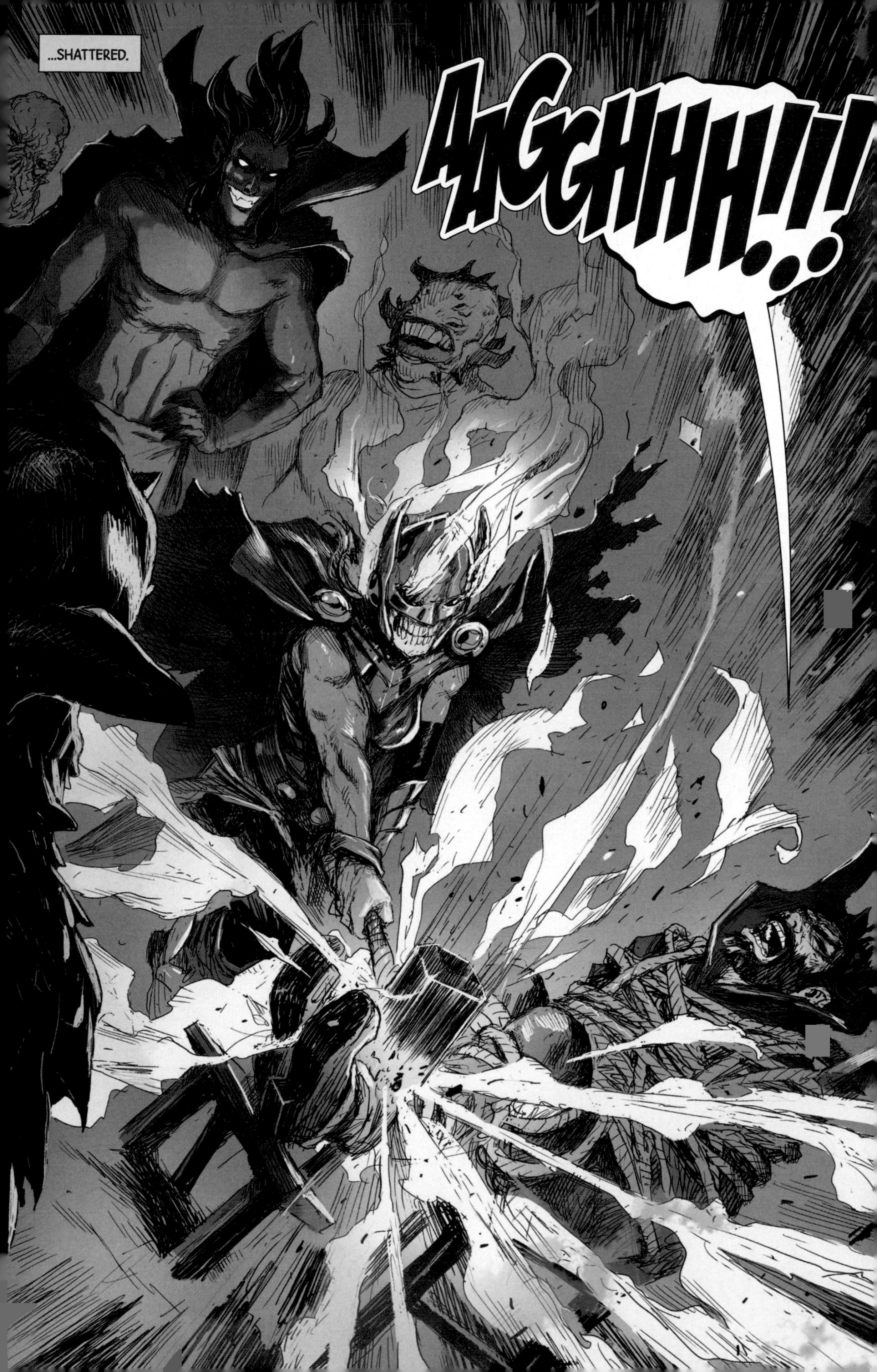
...SHATTERED.
AAGGHHHH!!...

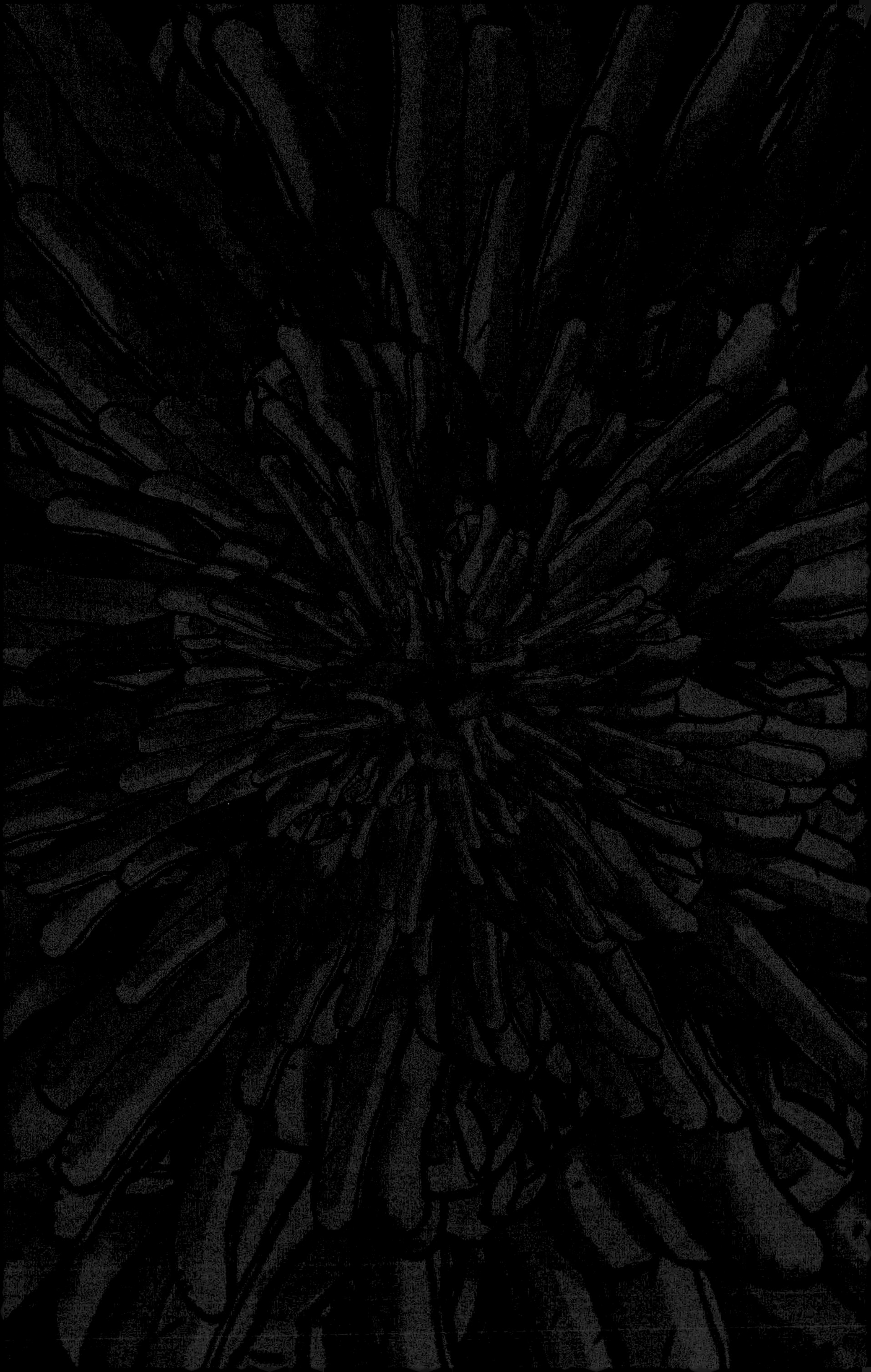

THE EVENTS OF THIS ISSUE TAKE PLACE CONCURRENTLY WITH THOSE IN *DOCTOR STRANGE: DAMNATION* #2.

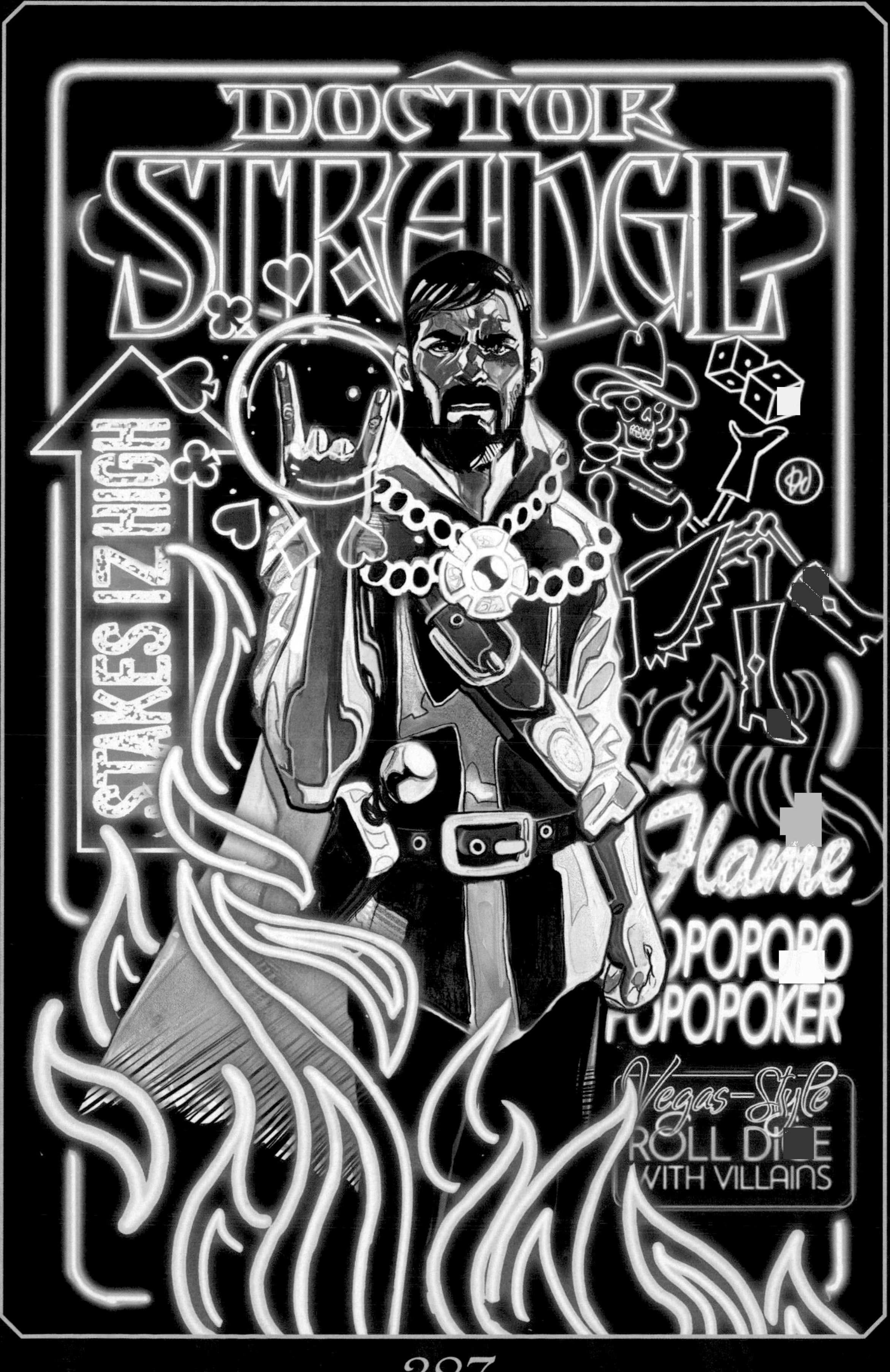
DOCTOR
STRANGE
STAKES IZ HIGH
la Flame
Vegas-Style
WITH VILLAINS

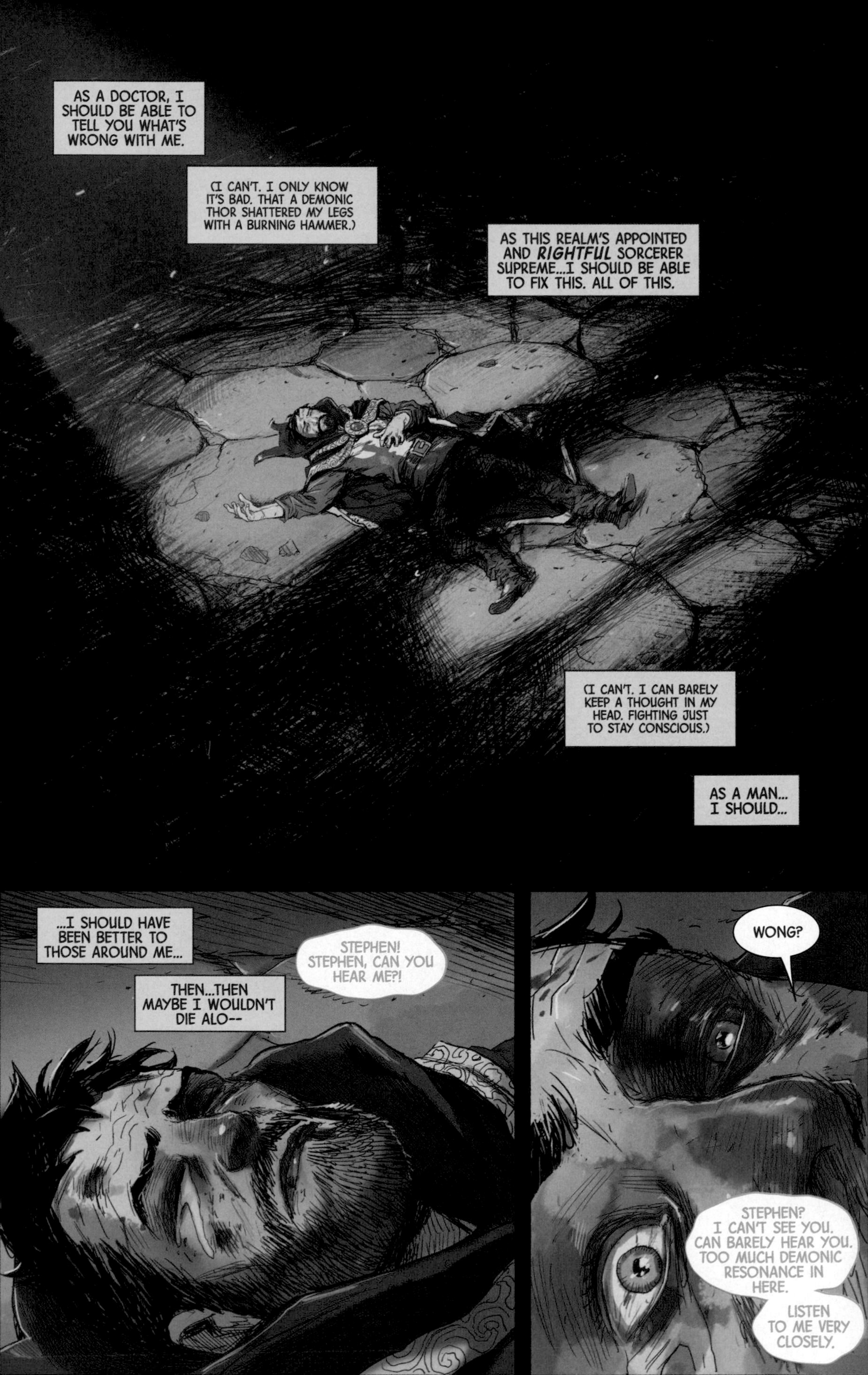
AS A DOCTOR, I SHOULD BE ABLE TO TELL YOU WHAT'S WRONG WITH ME.
(I CAN'T. I ONLY KNOW IT'S BAD. THAT A DEMONIC THOR SHATTERED MY LEGS WITH A BURNING HAMMER.)
AS THIS REALM'S APPOINTED AND *RIGHTFUL* SORCERER SUPREME...I SHOULD BE ABLE TO FIX THIS. ALL OF THIS.
(I CAN'T. I CAN BARELY KEEP A THOUGHT IN MY HEAD. FIGHTING JUST TO STAY CONSCIOUS.)
AS A MAN... I SHOULD...
...I SHOULD HAVE BEEN BETTER TO THOSE AROUND ME...
THEN...THEN MAYBE I WOULDN'T DIE ALO--
STEPHEN! STEPHEN, CAN YOU HEAR ME?!
WONG?
STEPHEN? I CAN'T SEE YOU. CAN BARELY HEAR YOU. TOO MUCH DEMONIC RESONANCE IN HERE.
LISTEN TO ME VERY CLOSELY.

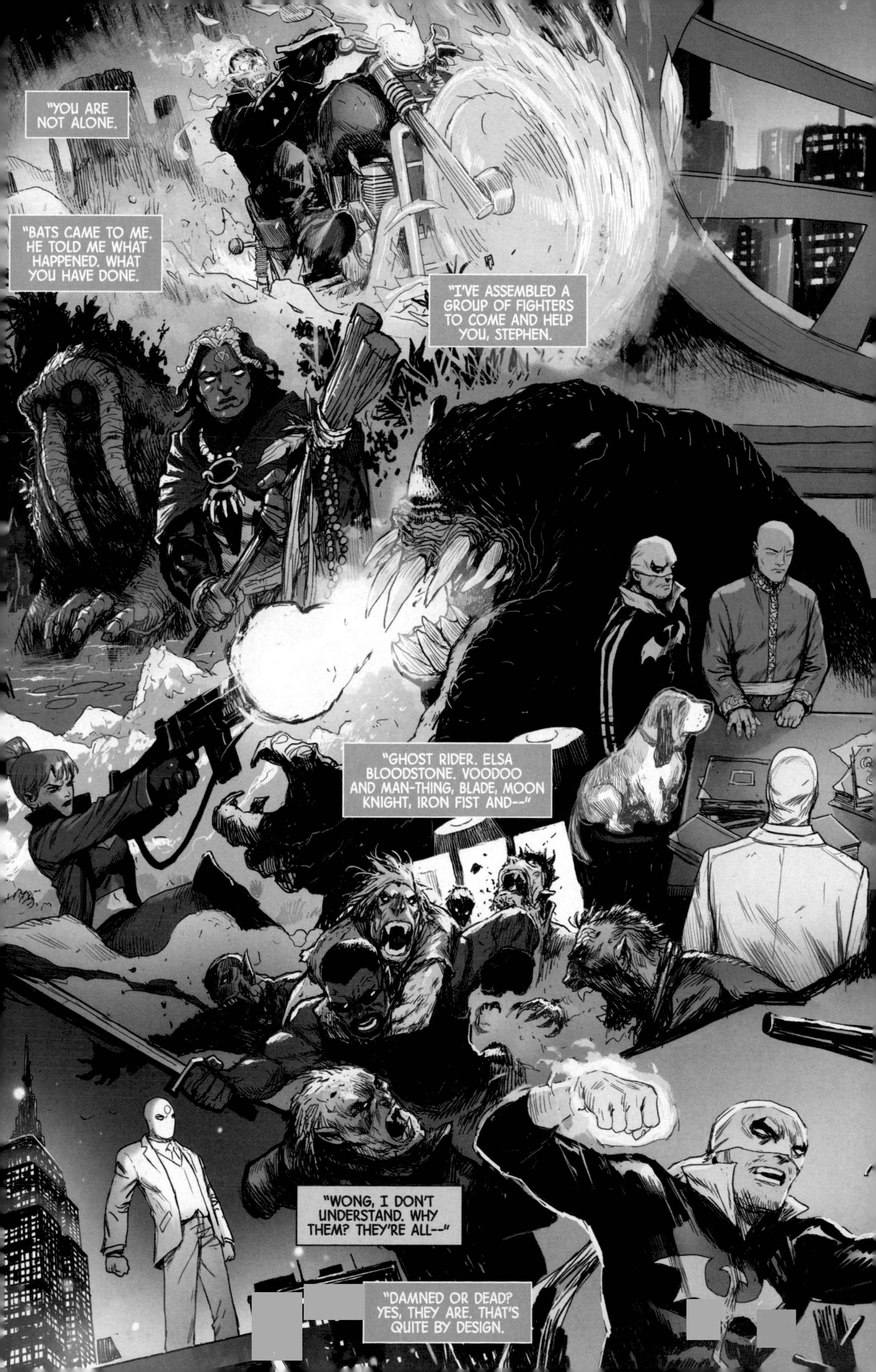
"YOU ARE NOT ALONE.
"BATS CAME TO ME. HE TOLD ME WHAT HAPPENED. WHAT YOU HAVE DONE.
"I'VE ASSEMBLED A GROUP OF FIGHTERS TO COME AND HELP YOU, STEPHEN.
"GHOST RIDER. ELSA BLOODSTONE. VOODOO AND MAN-THING, BLADE, MOON KNIGHT, IRON FIST AND--"
"WONG, I DON'T UNDERSTAND. WHY THEM? THEY'RE ALL--"
"DAMNED OR DEAD? YES, THEY ARE. THAT'S QUITE BY DESIGN.

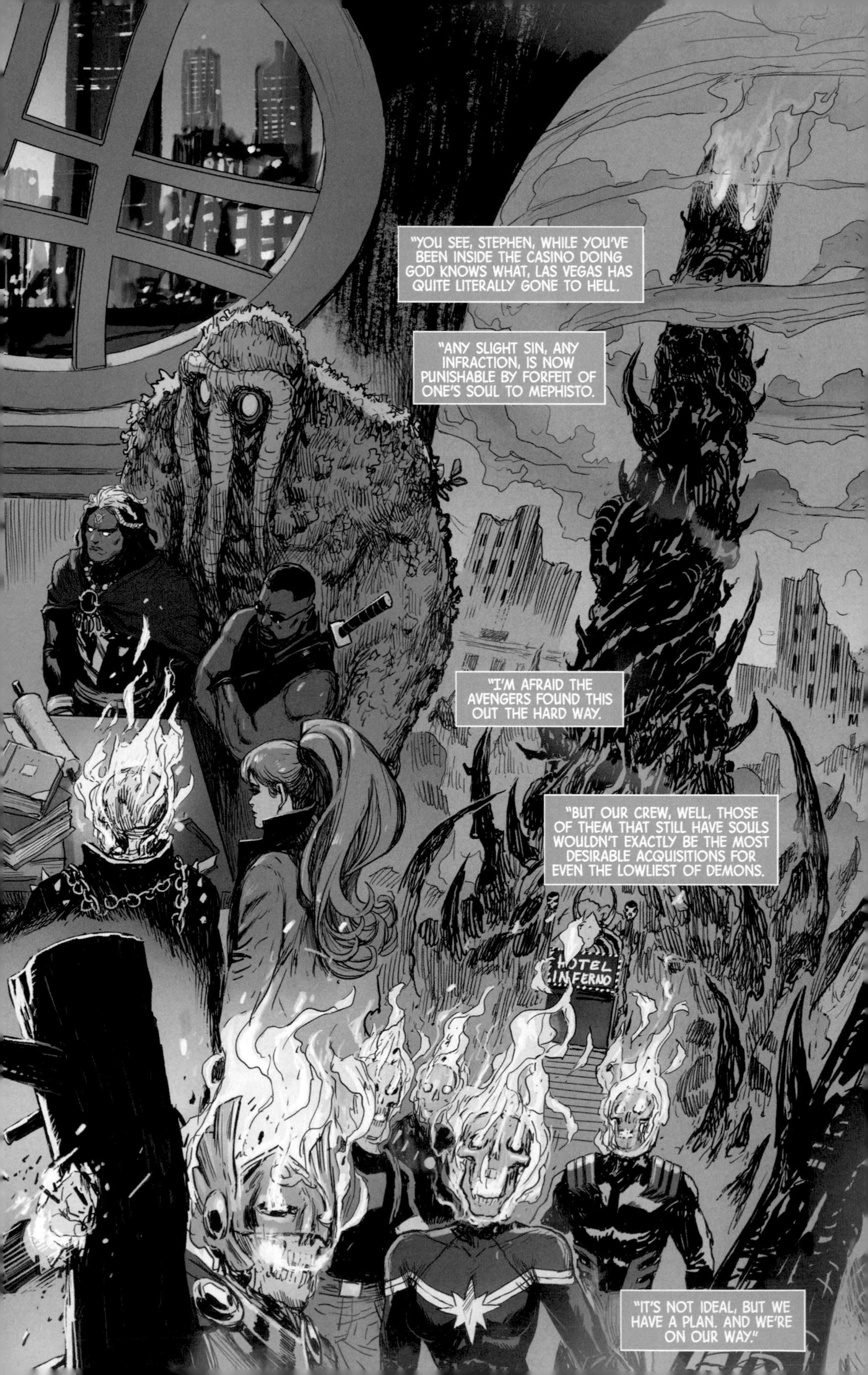
"YOU SEE, STEPHEN, WHILE YOU'VE BEEN INSIDE THE CASINO DOING GOD KNOWS WHAT, LAS VEGAS HAS QUITE LITERALLY GONE TO HELL.
"ANY SLIGHT SIN, ANY INFRACTION, IS NOW PUNISHABLE BY FORFEIT OF ONE'S SOUL TO MEPHISTO.
"I'M AFRAID THE AVENGERS FOUND THIS OUT THE HARD WAY.
"BUT OUR CREW, WELL, THOSE OF THEM THAT STILL HAVE SOULS WOULDN'T EXACTLY BE THE MOST DESIRABLE ACQUISITIONS FOR EVEN THE LOWLIEST OF DEMONS.
HOTEL INFERNO
"IT'S NOT IDEAL, BUT WE HAVE A PLAN. AND WE'RE ON OUR WAY."

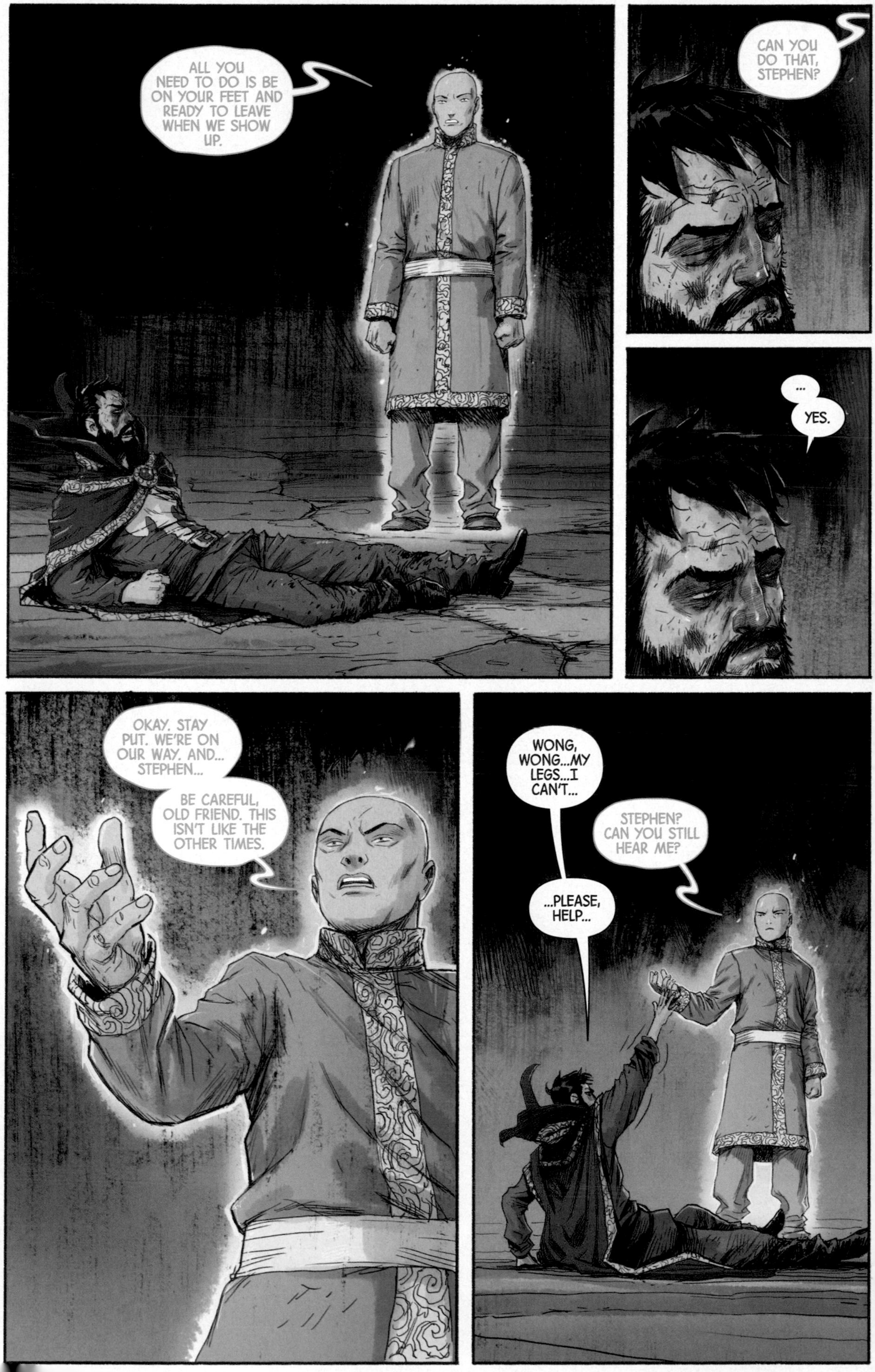
ALL YOU NEED TO DO IS BE ON YOUR FEET AND READY TO LEAVE WHEN WE SHOW UP.
CAN YOU DO THAT, STEPHEN?
...
YES.
OKAY. STAY PUT. WE'RE ON OUR WAY. AND... STEPHEN...
BE CAREFUL, OLD FRIEND. THIS ISN'T LIKE THE OTHER TIMES.
WONG, WONG...MY LEGS...I CAN'T...
STEPHEN? CAN YOU STILL HEAR ME?
...PLEASE, HELP...

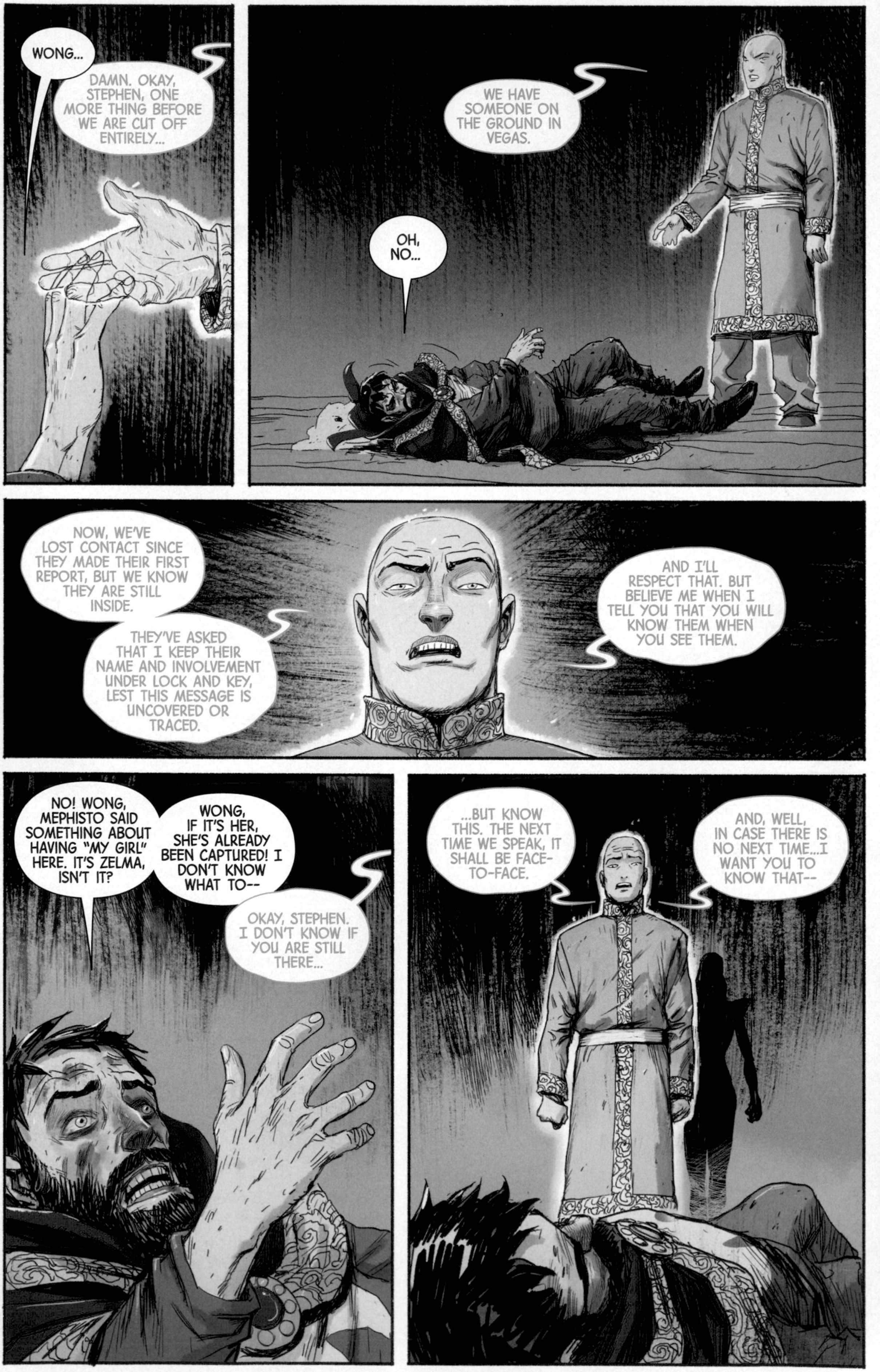
WONG...
DAMN. OKAY, STEPHEN, ONE MORE THING BEFORE WE ARE CUT OFF ENTIRELY...
WE HAVE SOMEONE ON THE GROUND IN VEGAS.
OH, NO...
NOW, WE'VE LOST CONTACT SINCE THEY MADE THEIR FIRST REPORT, BUT WE KNOW THEY ARE STILL INSIDE.
THEY'VE ASKED THAT I KEEP THEIR NAME AND INVOLVEMENT UNDER LOCK AND KEY, LEST THIS MESSAGE IS UNCOVERED OR TRACED.
AND I'LL RESPECT THAT. BUT BELIEVE ME WHEN I TELL YOU THAT YOU WILL KNOW THEM WHEN YOU SEE THEM.
NO! WONG, MEPHISTO SAID SOMETHING ABOUT HAVING "MY GIRL" HERE. IT'S ZELMA, ISN'T IT?
WONG, IF IT'S HER, SHE'S ALREADY BEEN CAPTURED! I DON'T KNOW WHAT TO--
OKAY, STEPHEN. I DON'T KNOW IF YOU ARE STILL THERE...
...BUT KNOW THIS. THE NEXT TIME WE SPEAK, IT SHALL BE FACE-TO-FACE.
AND, WELL, IN CASE THERE IS NO NEXT TIME...I WANT YOU TO KNOW THAT--

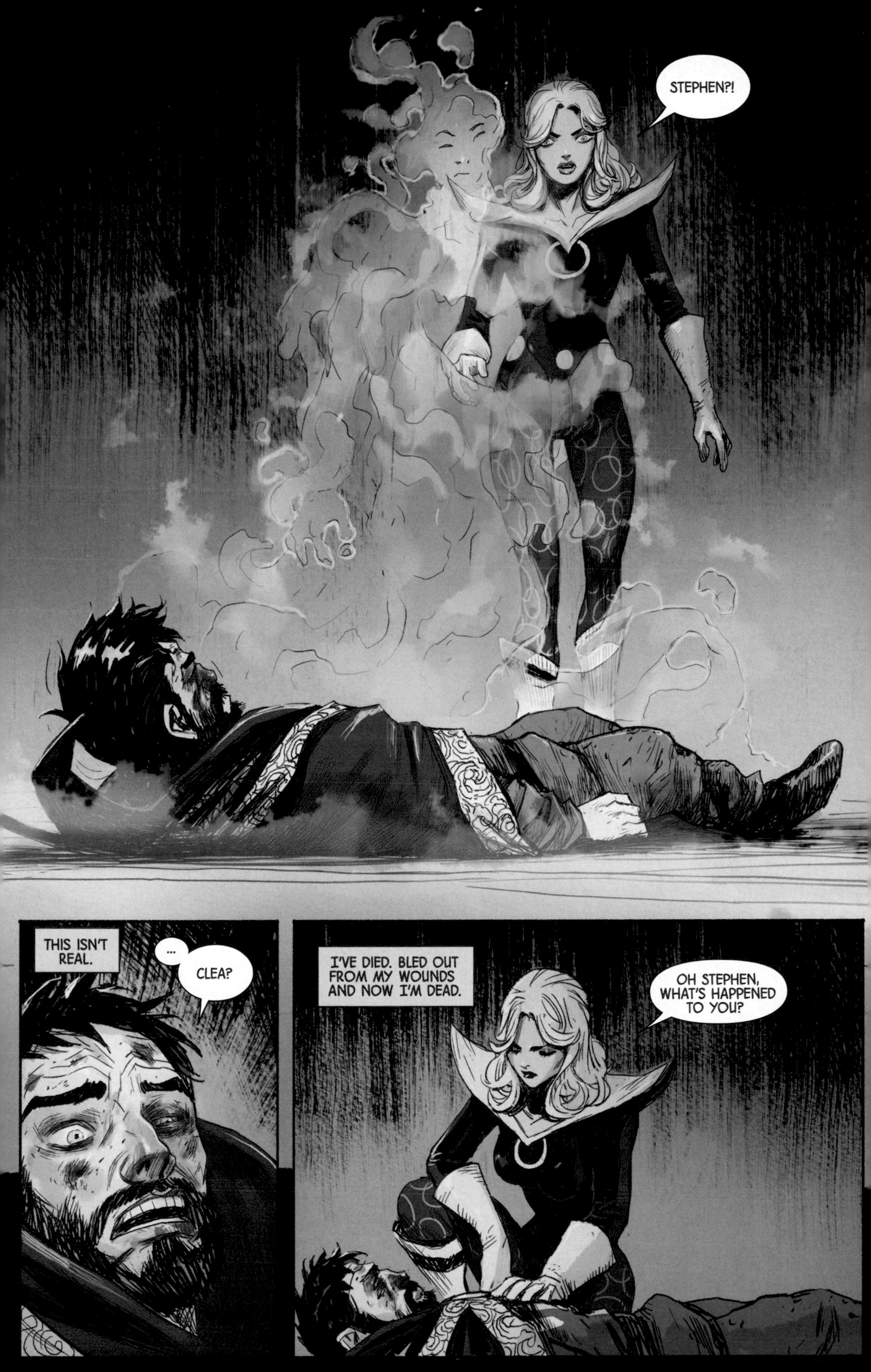
STEPHEN?!
THIS ISN'T REAL.
...
CLEA?
I'VE DIED. BLED OUT FROM MY WOUNDS AND NOW I'M DEAD.
OH STEPHEN, WHAT'S HAPPENED TO YOU?

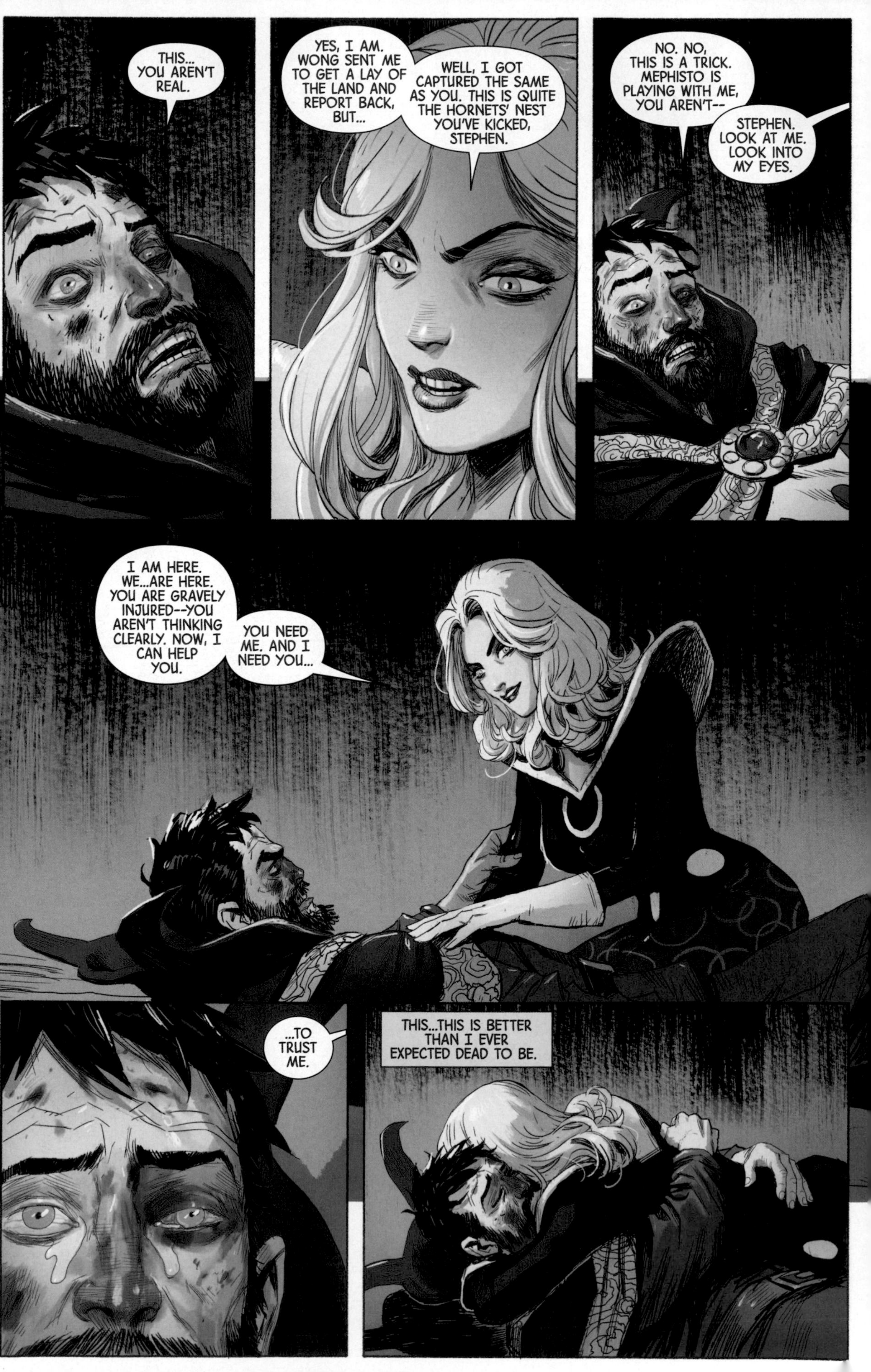
THIS... YOU AREN'T REAL.
YES, I AM. WONG SENT ME TO GET A LAY OF THE LAND AND REPORT BACK, BUT...
WELL, I GOT CAPTURED THE SAME AS YOU. THIS IS QUITE THE HORNETS' NEST YOU'VE KICKED, STEPHEN.
NO. NO, THIS IS A TRICK. MEPHISTO IS PLAYING WITH ME, YOU AREN'T--
STEPHEN. LOOK AT ME. LOOK INTO MY EYES.
I AM HERE. WE...ARE HERE. YOU ARE GRAVELY INJURED--YOU AREN'T THINKING CLEARLY. NOW, I CAN HELP YOU.
YOU NEED ME. AND I NEED YOU...
...TO TRUST ME.
THIS...THIS IS BETTER THAN I EVER EXPECTED DEAD TO BE.

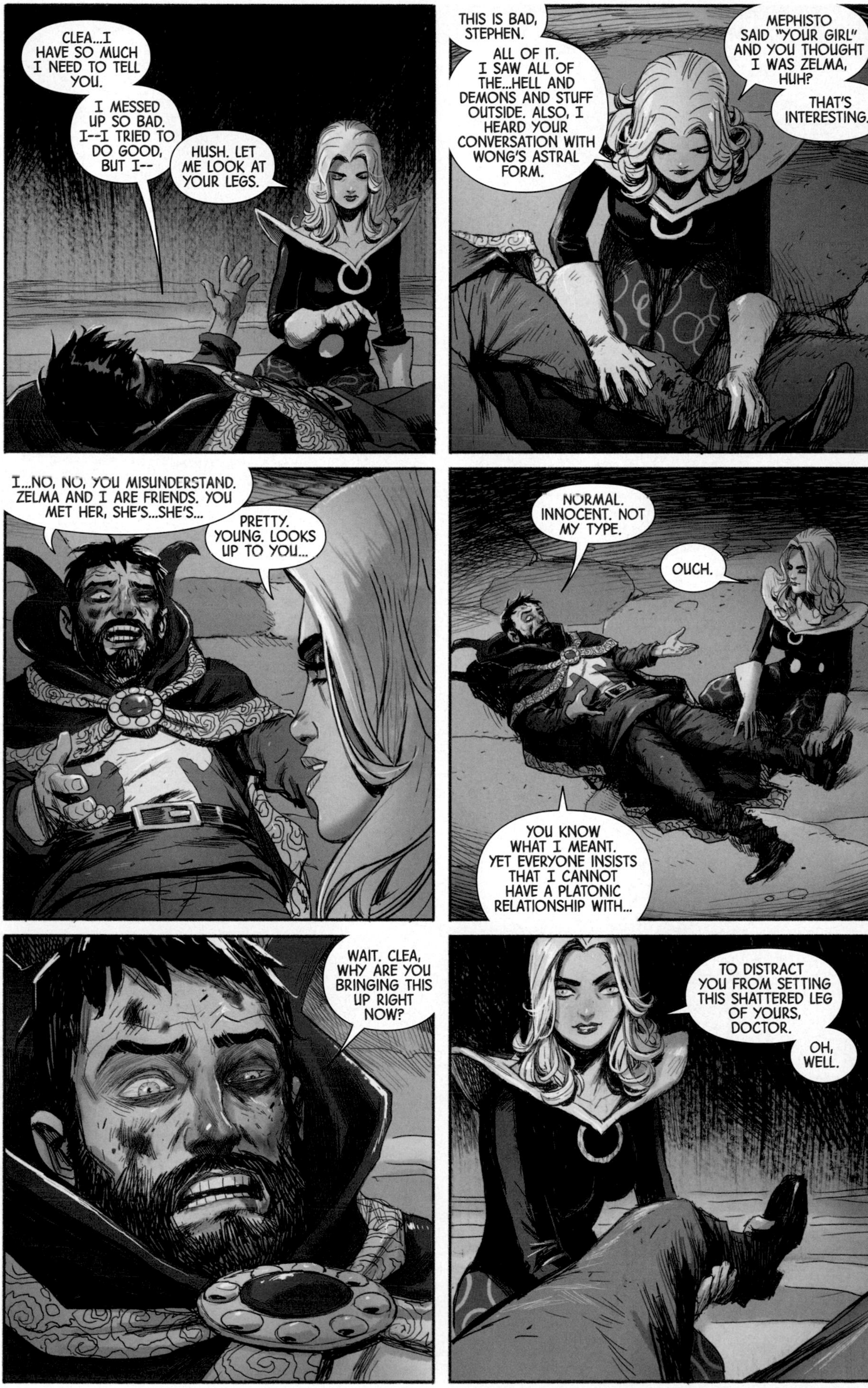
CLEA...I HAVE SO MUCH I NEED TO TELL YOU.
I MESSED UP SO BAD. I--I TRIED TO DO GOOD, BUT I--
HUSH. LET ME LOOK AT YOUR LEGS.
THIS IS BAD, STEPHEN.
ALL OF IT. I SAW ALL OF THE...HELL AND DEMONS AND STUFF OUTSIDE. ALSO, I HEARD YOUR CONVERSATION WITH WONG'S ASTRAL FORM.
MEPHISTO SAID "YOUR GIRL" AND YOU THOUGHT I WAS ZELMA, HUH?
THAT'S INTERESTING.
I...NO, NO, YOU MISUNDERSTAND. ZELMA AND I ARE FRIENDS. YOU MET HER, SHE'S...SHE'S...
PRETTY. YOUNG. LOOKS UP TO YOU...
NORMAL. INNOCENT. NOT MY TYPE.
OUCH.
YOU KNOW WHAT I MEANT. YET EVERYONE INSISTS THAT I CANNOT HAVE A PLATONIC RELATIONSHIP WITH...
WAIT. CLEA, WHY ARE YOU BRINGING THIS UP RIGHT NOW?
TO DISTRACT YOU FROM SETTING THIS SHATTERED LEG OF YOURS, DOCTOR.
OH, WELL.

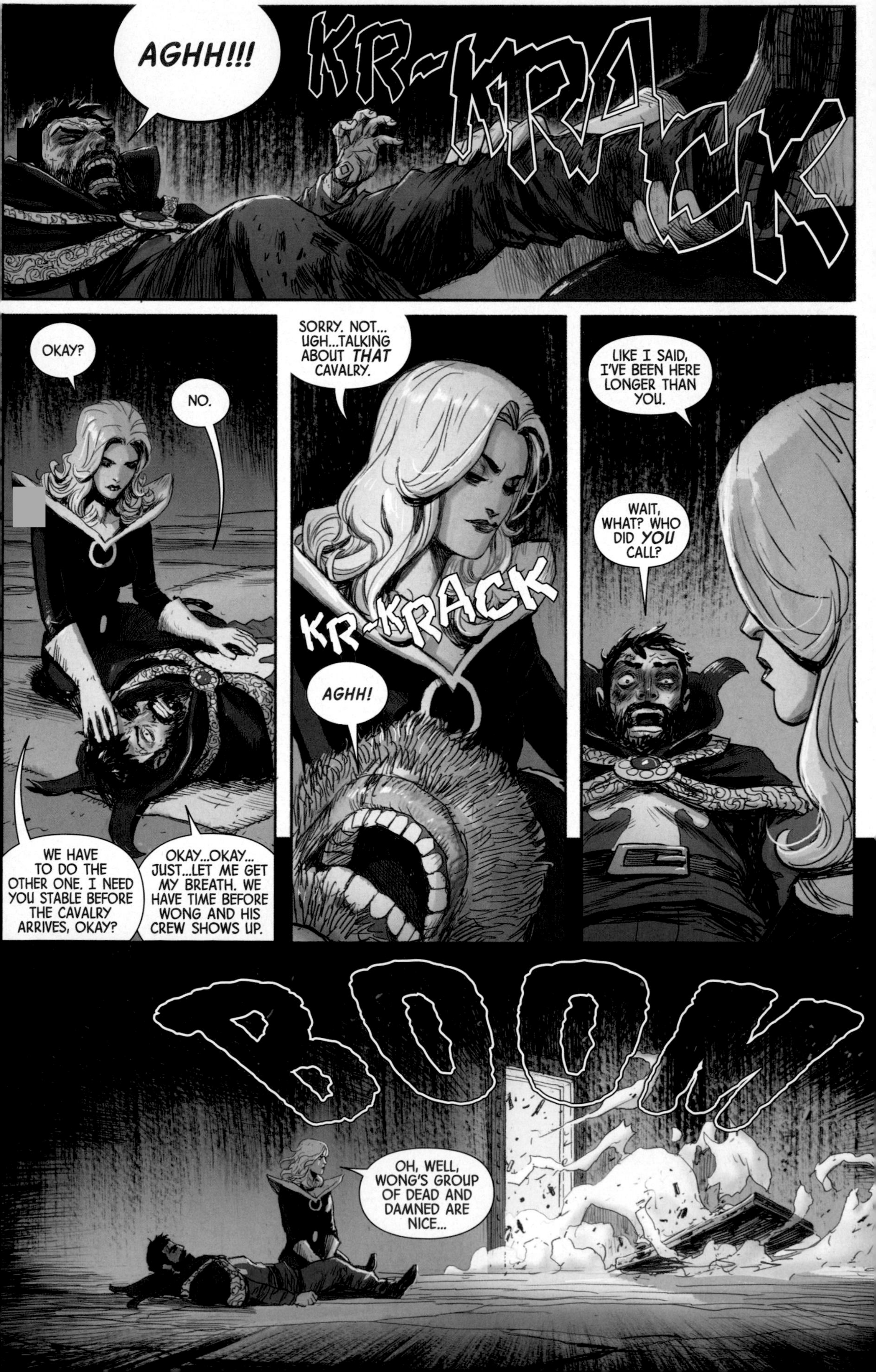
AGHH!!!
KR-KRACK
OKAY?
NO.
WE HAVE TO DO THE OTHER ONE. I NEED YOU STABLE BEFORE THE CAVALRY ARRIVES, OKAY?
OKAY...OKAY... JUST...LET ME GET MY BREATH. WE HAVE TIME BEFORE WONG AND HIS CREW SHOWS UP.
SORRY. NOT... UGH...TALKING ABOUT THAT CAVALRY.
KR-KRACK
AGHH!
LIKE I SAID, I'VE BEEN HERE LONGER THAN YOU.
WAIT, WHAT? WHO DID YOU CALL?
BOOM
OH, WELL, WONG'S GROUP OF DEAD AND DAMNED ARE NICE...

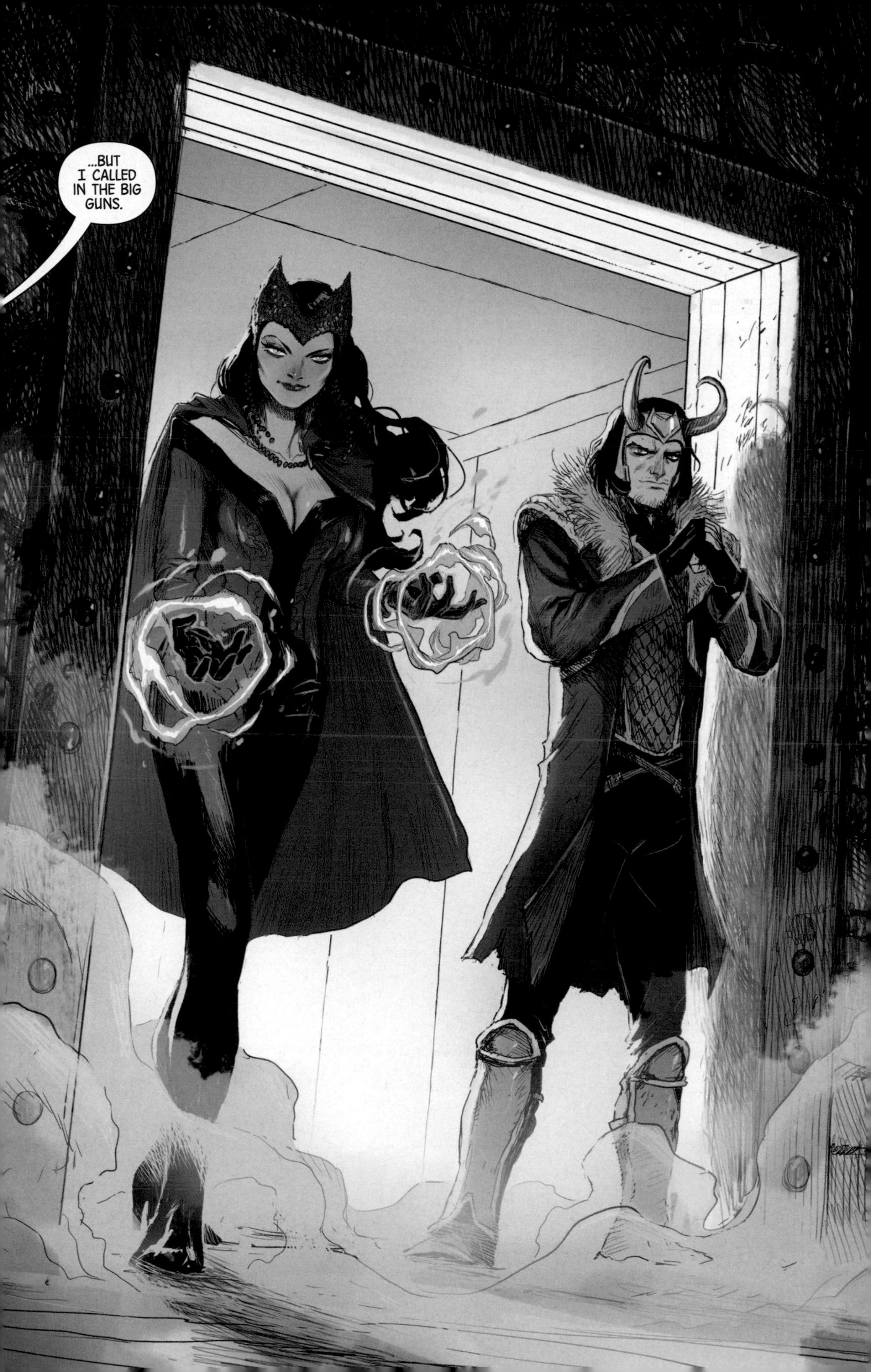
...BUT I CALLED IN THE BIG GUNS.

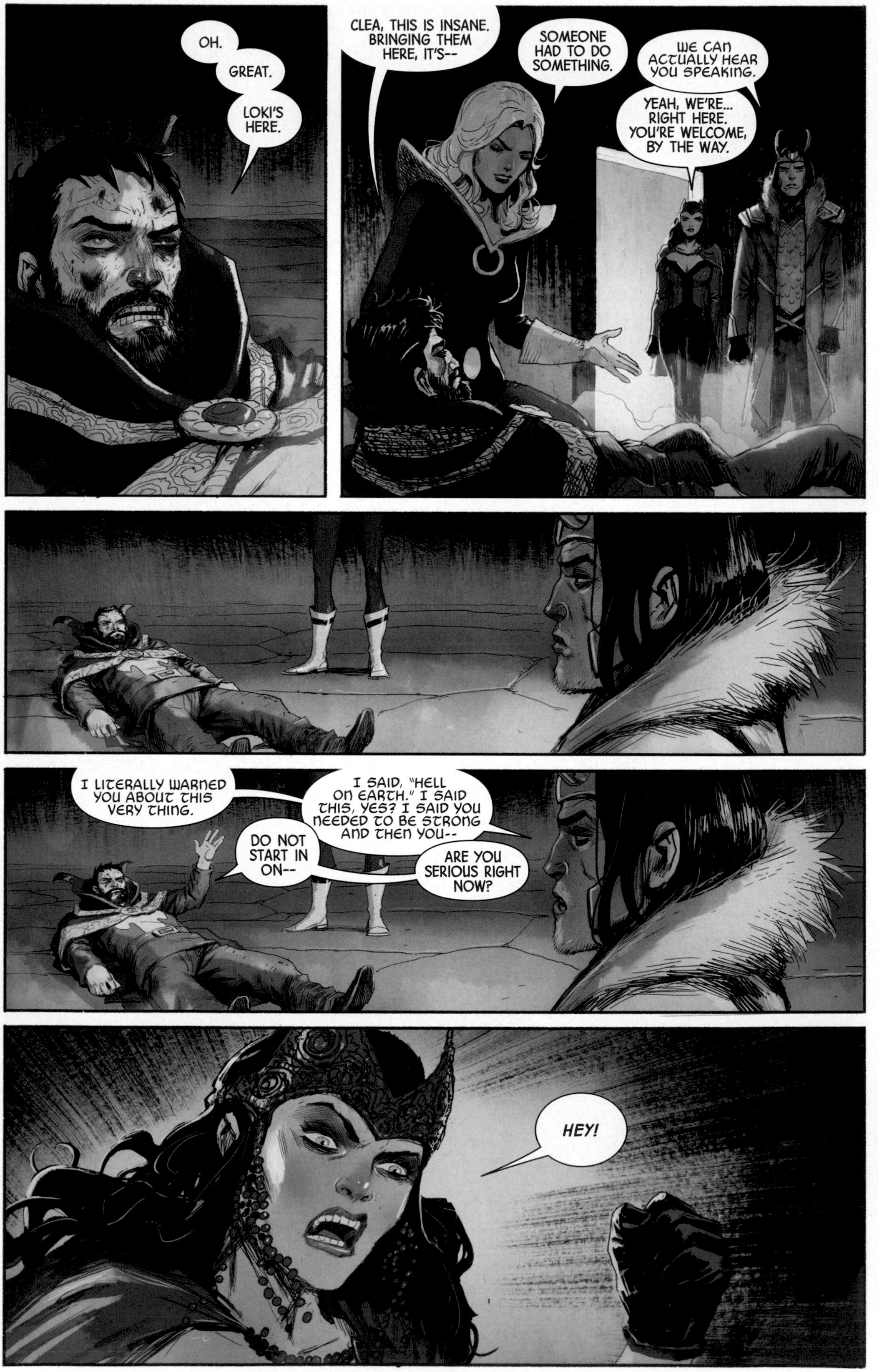
OH.
GREAT.
LOKI'S HERE.
CLEA, THIS IS INSANE. BRINGING THEM HERE, IT'S--
SOMEONE HAD TO DO SOMETHING.
WE CAN ACTUALLY HEAR YOU SPEAKING.
YEAH, WE'RE... RIGHT HERE. YOU'RE WELCOME, BY THE WAY.
I LITERALLY WARNED YOU ABOUT THIS VERY THING.
I SAID, "HELL ON EARTH." I SAID THIS, YES? I SAID YOU NEEDED TO BE STRONG AND THEN YOU--
DO NOT START IN ON--
ARE YOU SERIOUS RIGHT NOW?
HEY!

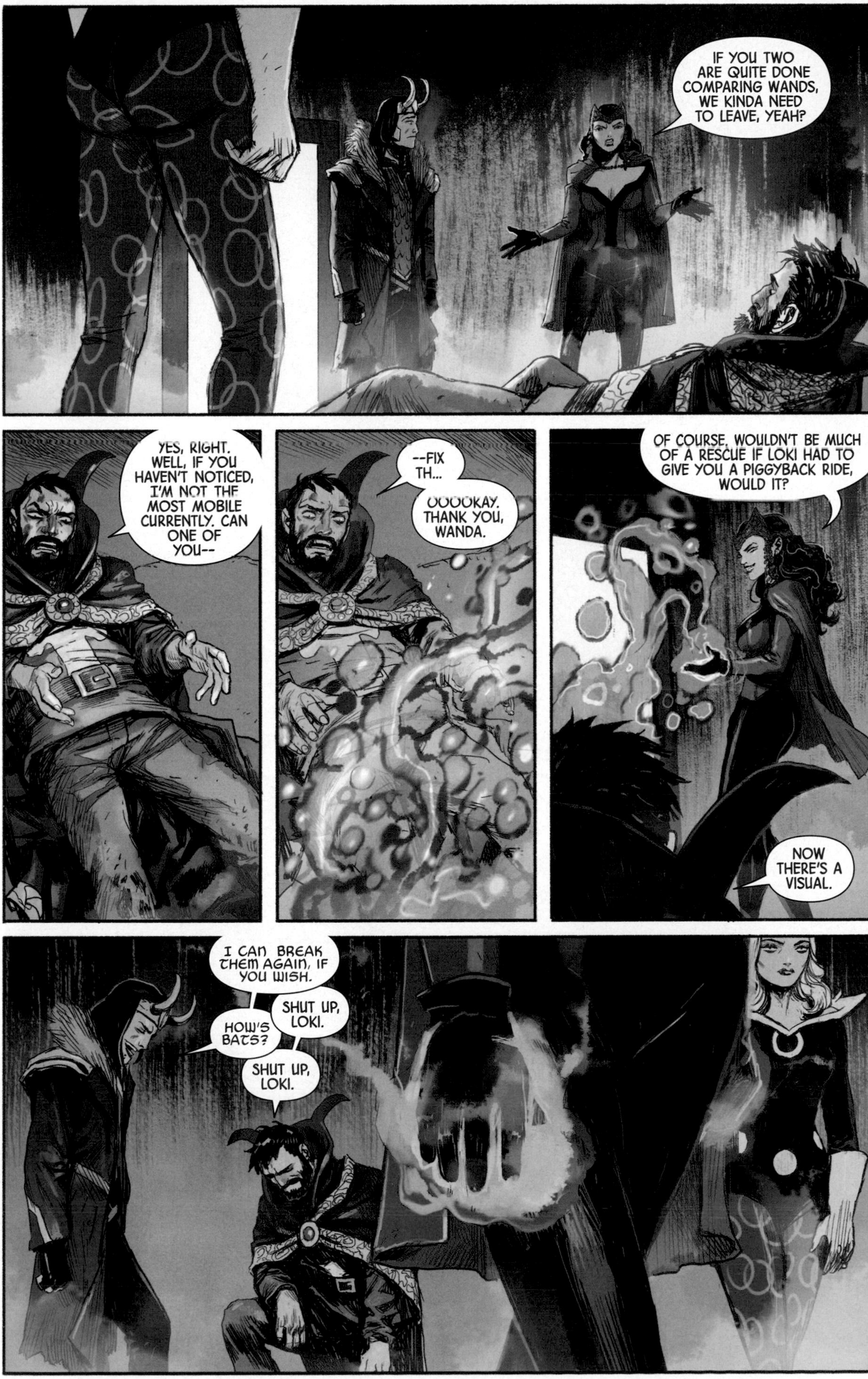
IF YOU TWO ARE QUITE DONE COMPARING WANDS, WE KINDA NEED TO LEAVE, YEAH?
YES, RIGHT. WELL, IF YOU HAVEN'T NOTICED, I'M NOT THE MOST MOBILE CURRENTLY. CAN ONE OF YOU--
--FIX TH...
OOOOKAY. THANK YOU, WANDA.
OF COURSE. WOULDN'T BE MUCH OF A RESCUE IF LOKI HAD TO GIVE YOU A PIGGYBACK RIDE, WOULD IT?
NOW THERE'S A VISUAL.
I CAN BREAK THEM AGAIN, IF YOU WISH.
HOW'S BATS?
SHUT UP, LOKI.
SHUT UP, LOKI.

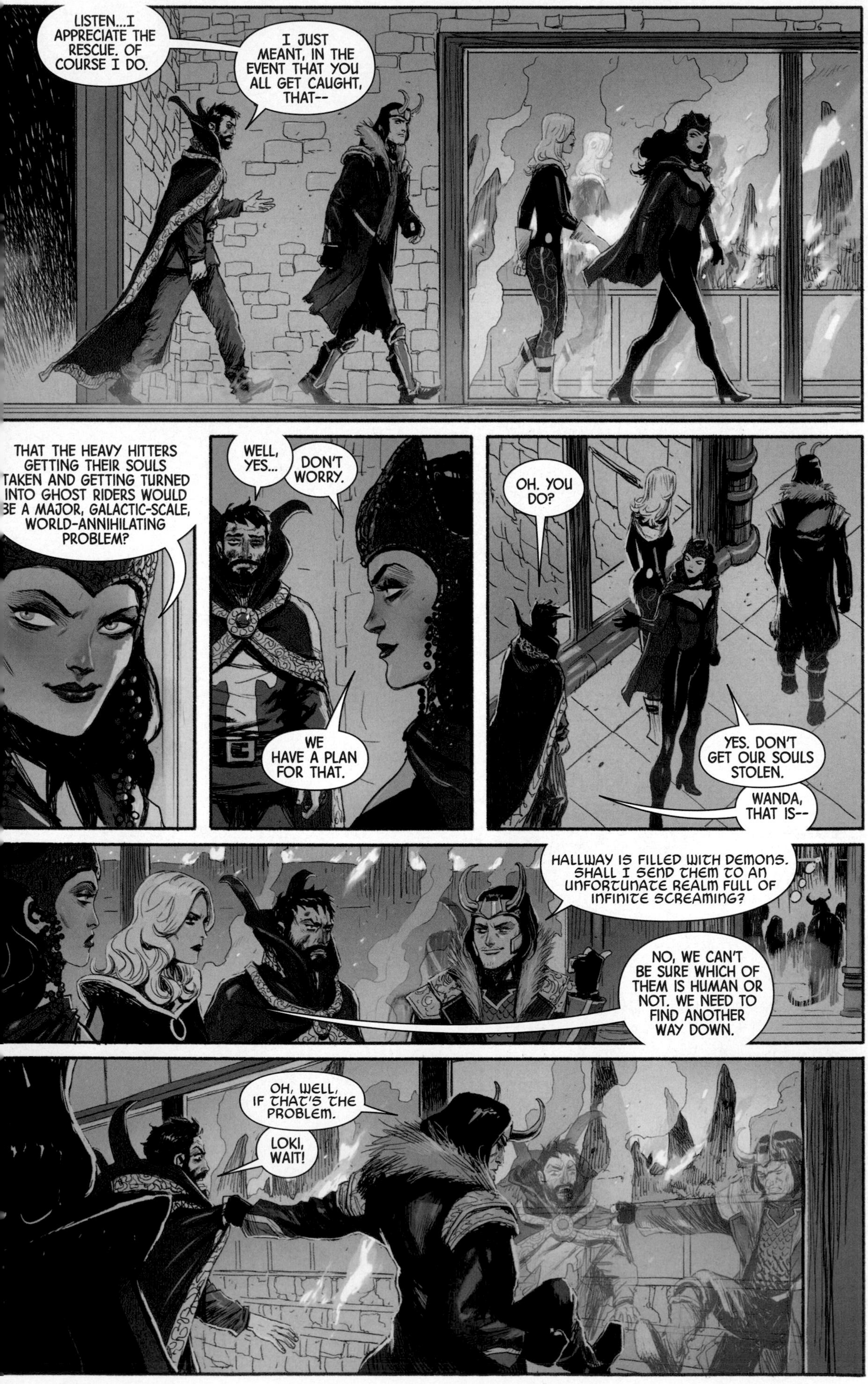
LISTEN...I APPRECIATE THE RESCUE. OF COURSE I DO.
I JUST MEANT, IN THE EVENT THAT YOU ALL GET CAUGHT, THAT--
THAT THE HEAVY HITTERS GETTING THEIR SOULS TAKEN AND GETTING TURNED INTO GHOST RIDERS WOULD BE A MAJOR, GALACTIC-SCALE, WORLD-ANNIHILATING PROBLEM?
WELL, YES...
DON'T WORRY.
WE HAVE A PLAN FOR THAT.
OH. YOU DO?
YES. DON'T GET OUR SOULS STOLEN.
WANDA, THAT IS--
HALLWAY IS FILLED WITH DEMONS. SHALL I SEND THEM TO AN UNFORTUNATE REALM FULL OF INFINITE SCREAMING?
NO, WE CAN'T BE SURE WHICH OF THEM IS HUMAN OR NOT. WE NEED TO FIND ANOTHER WAY DOWN.
OH, WELL, IF THAT'S THE PROBLEM.
LOKI, WAIT!

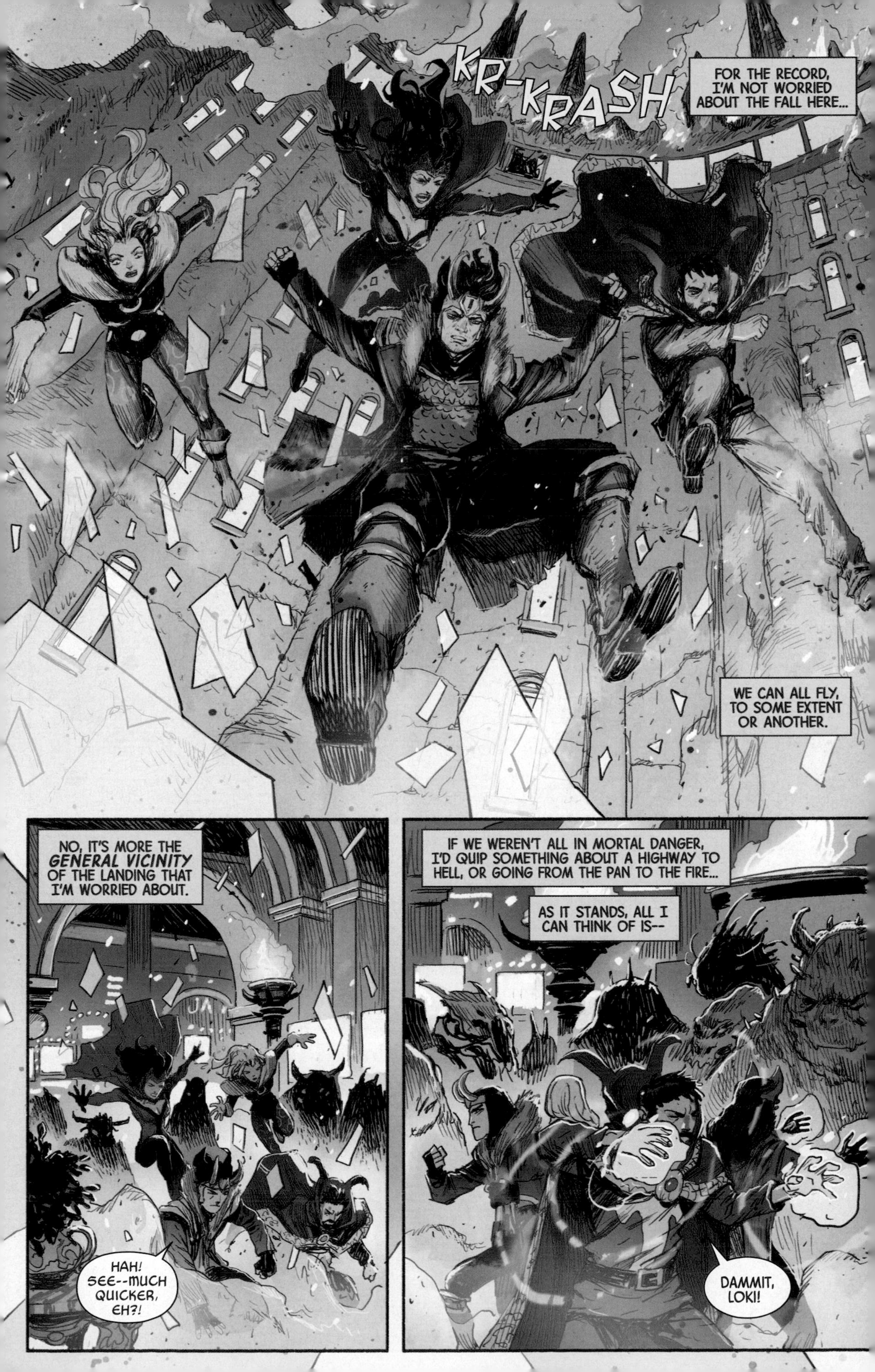
KR-KRASH
FOR THE RECORD, I'M NOT WORRIED ABOUT THE FALL HERE...
WE CAN ALL FLY, TO SOME EXTENT OR ANOTHER.
NO, IT'S MORE THE GENERAL VICINITY OF THE LANDING THAT I'M WORRIED ABOUT.
HAH! SEE--MUCH QUICKER, EH?!
IF WE WEREN'T ALL IN MORTAL DANGER, I'D QUIP SOMETHING ABOUT A HIGHWAY TO HELL, OR GOING FROM THE PAN TO THE FIRE...
AS IT STANDS, ALL I CAN THINK OF IS--
DAMMIT, LOKI!

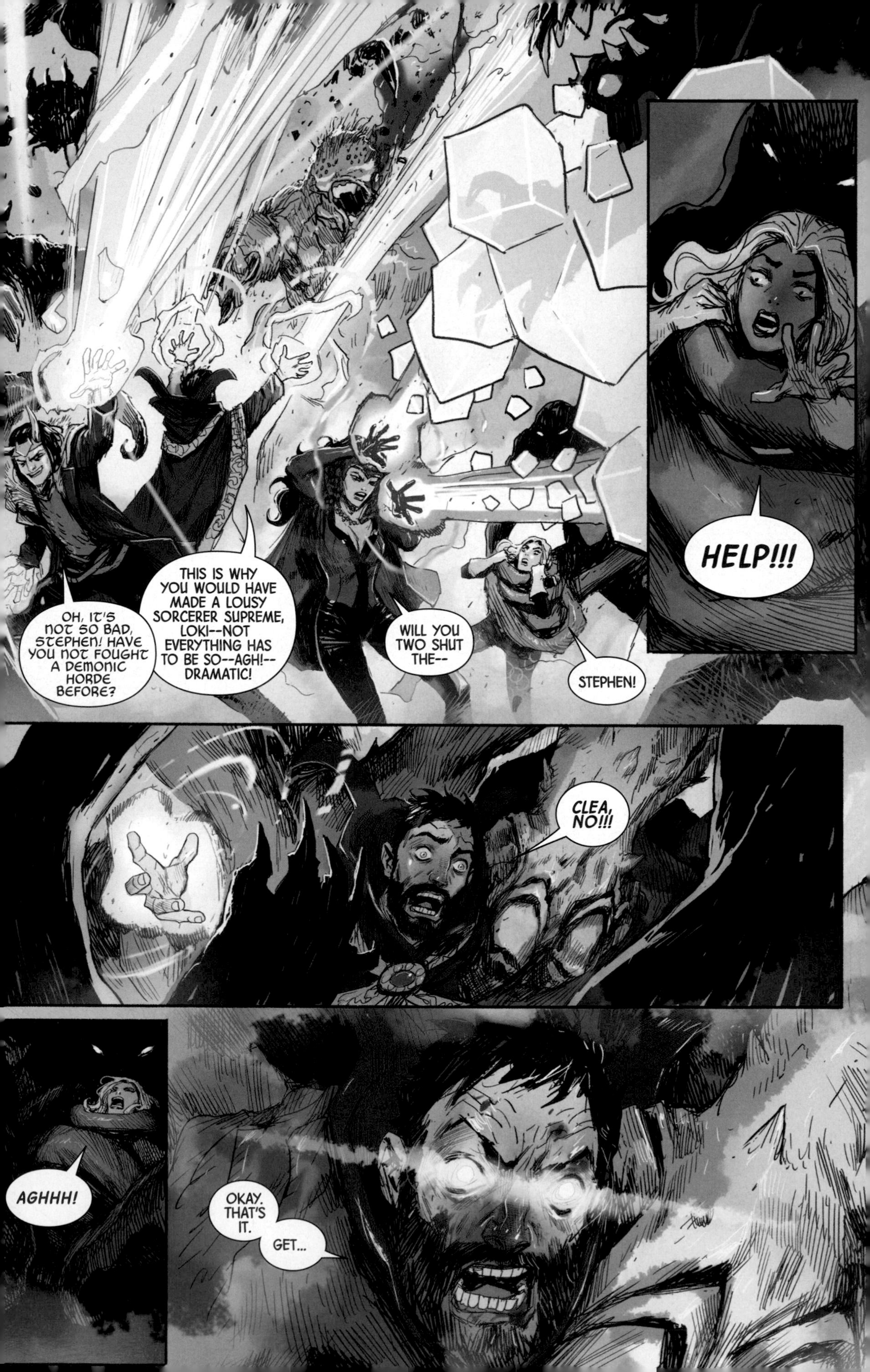
OH, IT'S NOT SO BAD, STEPHEN! HAVE YOU NOT FOUGHT A DEMONIC HORDE BEFORE?
THIS IS WHY YOU WOULD HAVE MADE A LOUSY SORCERER SUPREME, LOKI--NOT EVERYTHING HAS TO BE SO--AGH!--DRAMATIC!
WILL YOU TWO SHUT THE--
STEPHEN!
HELP!!!
CLEA, NO!!!
AGHHH!
OKAY. THAT'S IT.
GET...

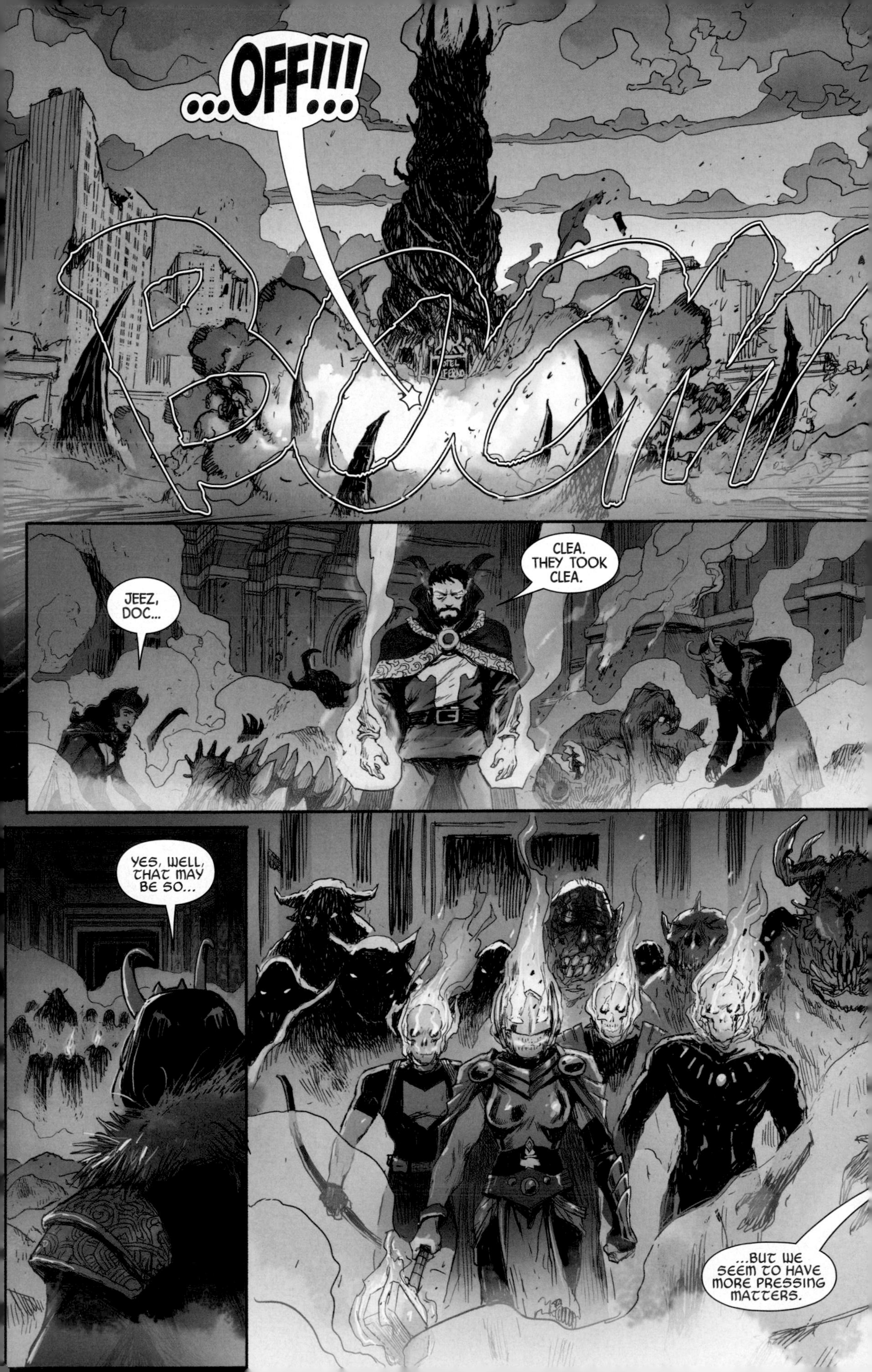
...OFF!!!...
BOOM
JEEZ, DOC...
CLEA. THEY TOOK CLEA.
YES, WELL, THAT MAY BE SO...
...BUT WE SEEM TO HAVE MORE PRESSING MATTERS.

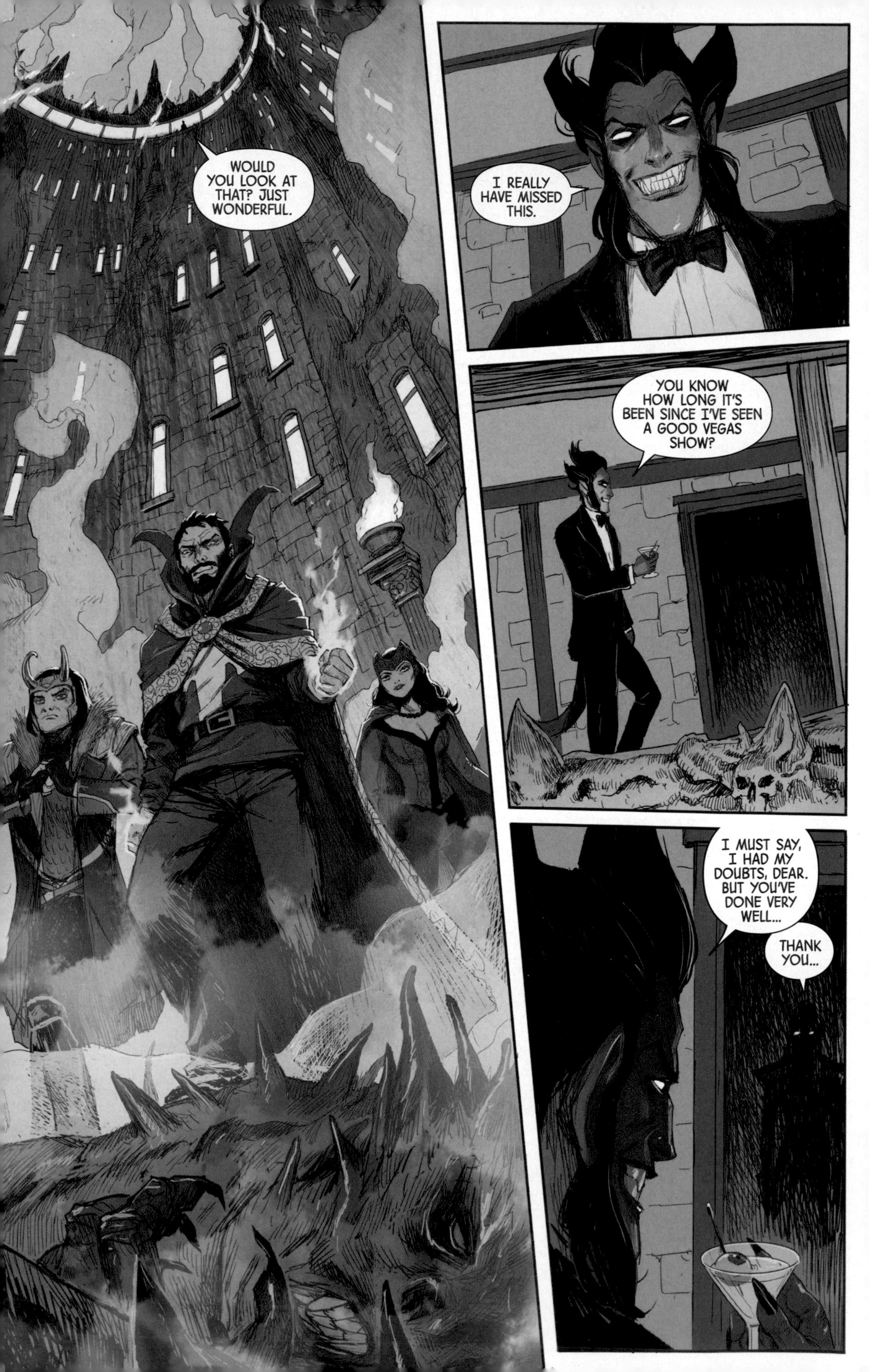
WOULD YOU LOOK AT THAT? JUST WONDERFUL.
I REALLY HAVE MISSED THIS.
YOU KNOW HOW LONG IT'S BEEN SINCE I'VE SEEN A GOOD VEGAS SHOW?
I MUST SAY, I HAD MY DOUBTS, DEAR. BUT YOU'VE DONE VERY WELL...
THANK YOU...

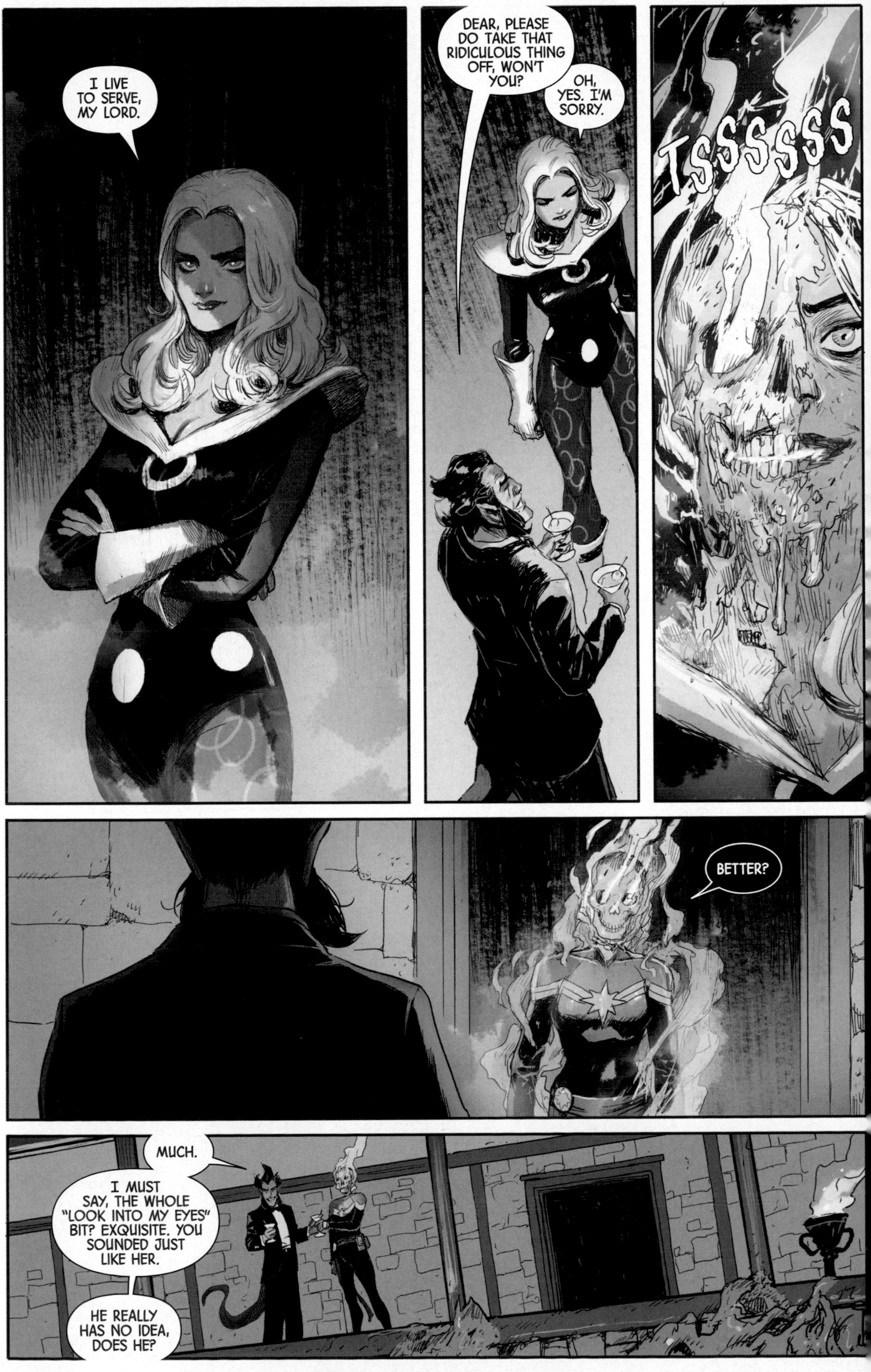
I LIVE TO SERVE, MY LORD.
DEAR, PLEASE DO TAKE THAT RIDICULOUS THING OFF, WON'T YOU?
OH, YES. I'M SORRY.
TSSSSSS
BETTER?
MUCH.
I MUST SAY, THE WHOLE "LOOK INTO MY EYES" BIT? EXQUISITE. YOU SOUNDED JUST LIKE HER.
HE REALLY HAS NO IDEA, DOES HE?

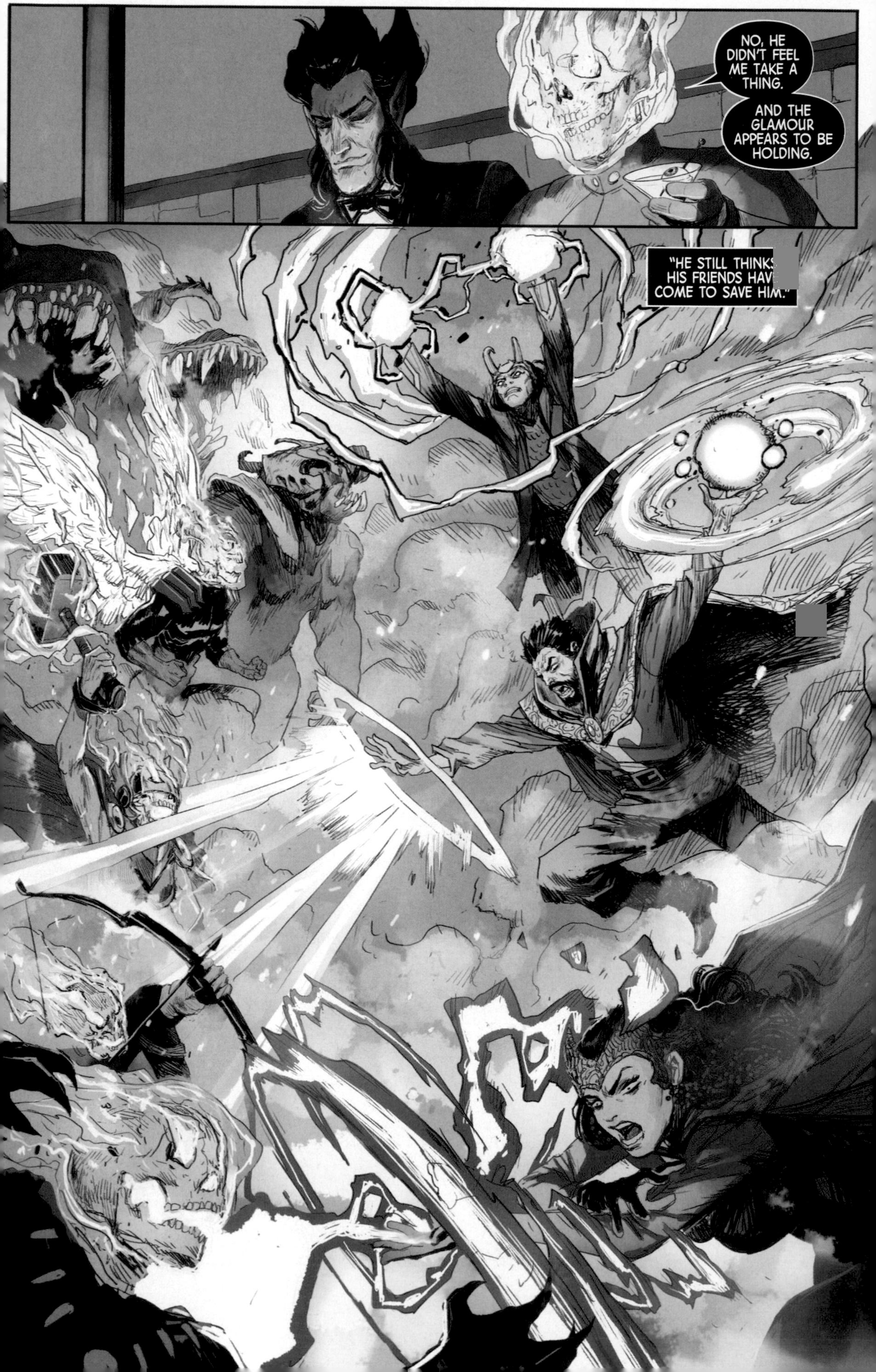
NO, HE DIDN'T FEEL ME TAKE A THING.
AND THE GLAMOUR APPEARS TO BE HOLDING.
"HE STILL THINKS HIS FRIENDS HAVE COME TO SAVE HIM."

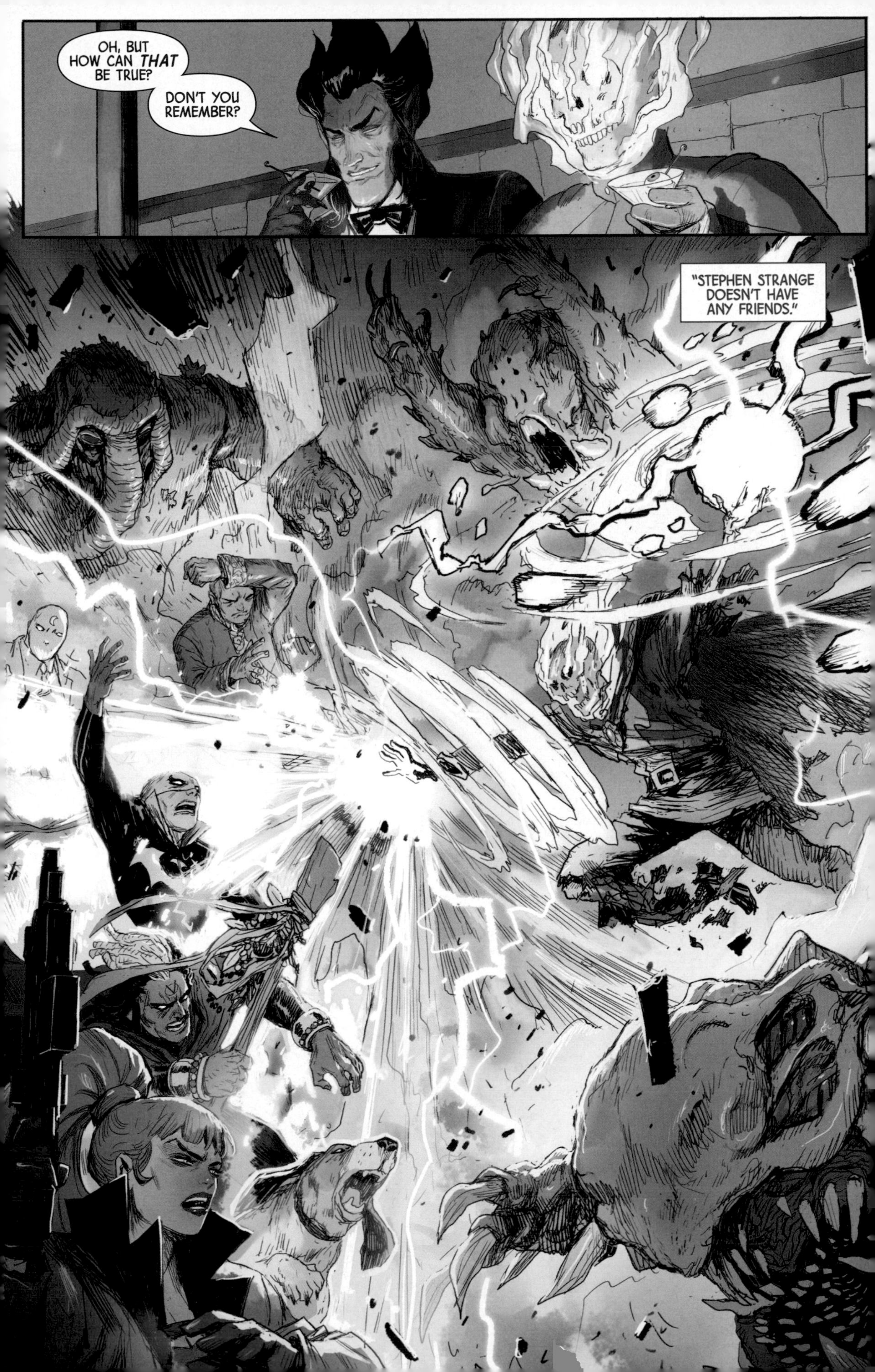
OH, BUT HOW CAN *THAT* BE TRUE?
DON'T YOU REMEMBER?
"STEPHEN STRANGE DOESN'T HAVE ANY FRIENDS."

THE EVENTS OF THIS ISSUE TAKE PLACE AFTER THOSE IN *DOCTOR STRANGE: DAMNATION* #3.

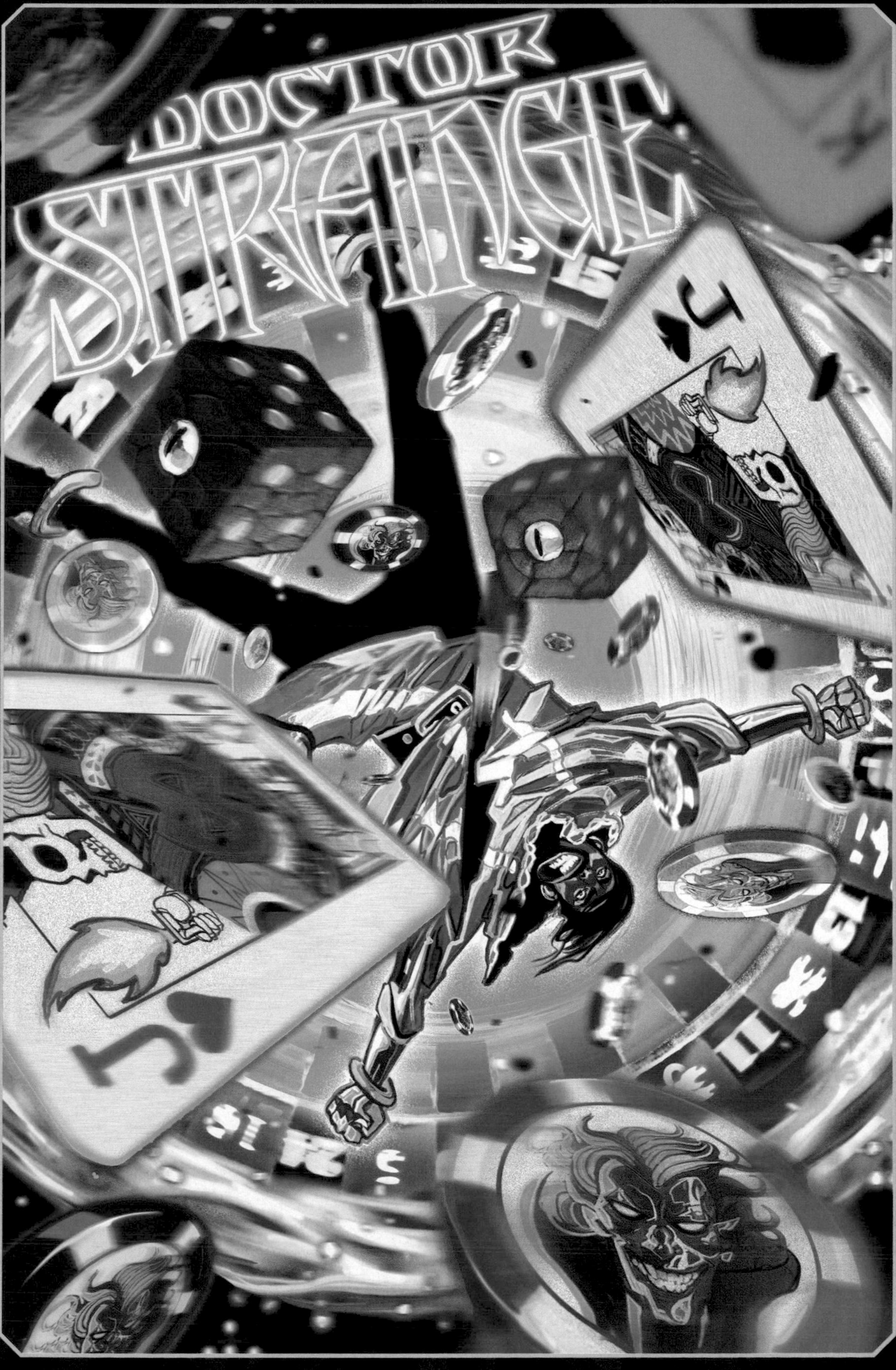
DOCTOR
STRANGE

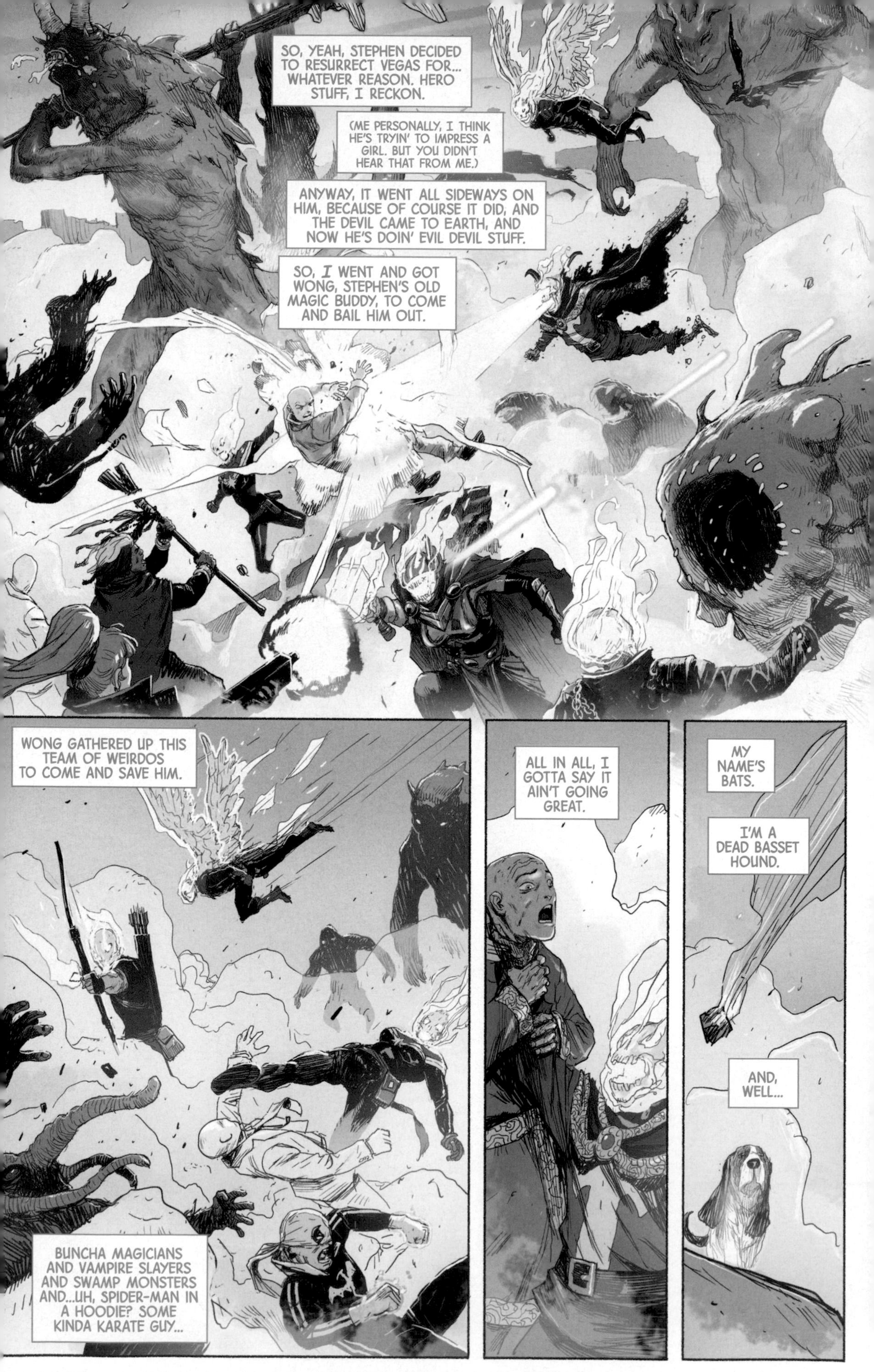
SO, YEAH, STEPHEN DECIDED TO RESURRECT VEGAS FOR... WHATEVER REASON. HERO STUFF, I RECKON.
(ME PERSONALLY, I THINK HE'S TRYIN' TO IMPRESS A GIRL. BUT YOU DIDN'T HEAR THAT FROM ME.)
ANYWAY, IT WENT ALL SIDEWAYS ON HIM, BECAUSE OF COURSE IT DID, AND THE DEVIL CAME TO EARTH, AND NOW HE'S DOIN' EVIL DEVIL STUFF.
SO, *I* WENT AND GOT WONG, STEPHEN'S OLD MAGIC BUDDY, TO COME AND BAIL HIM OUT.
WONG GATHERED UP THIS TEAM OF WEIRDOS TO COME AND SAVE HIM.
BUNCHA MAGICIANS AND VAMPIRE SLAYERS AND SWAMP MONSTERS AND...UH, SPIDER-MAN IN A HOODIE? SOME KINDA KARATE GUY...
ALL IN ALL, I GOTTA SAY IT AIN'T GOING GREAT.
MY NAME'S BATS.
I'M A DEAD BASSET HOUND.
AND, WELL...

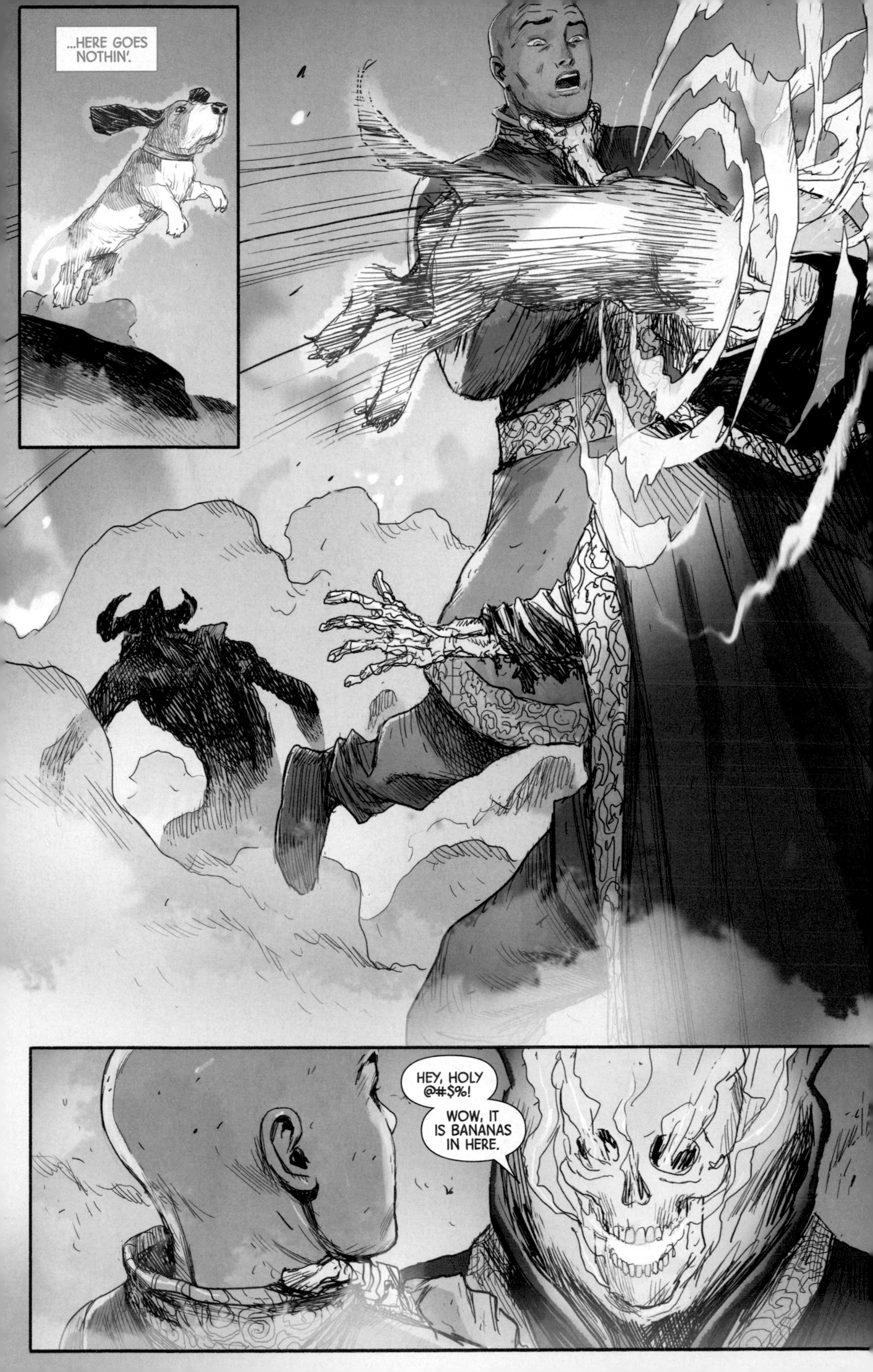
...HERE GOES NOTHIN'.
HEY, HOLY @#$%!
WOW, IT IS BANANAS IN HERE.

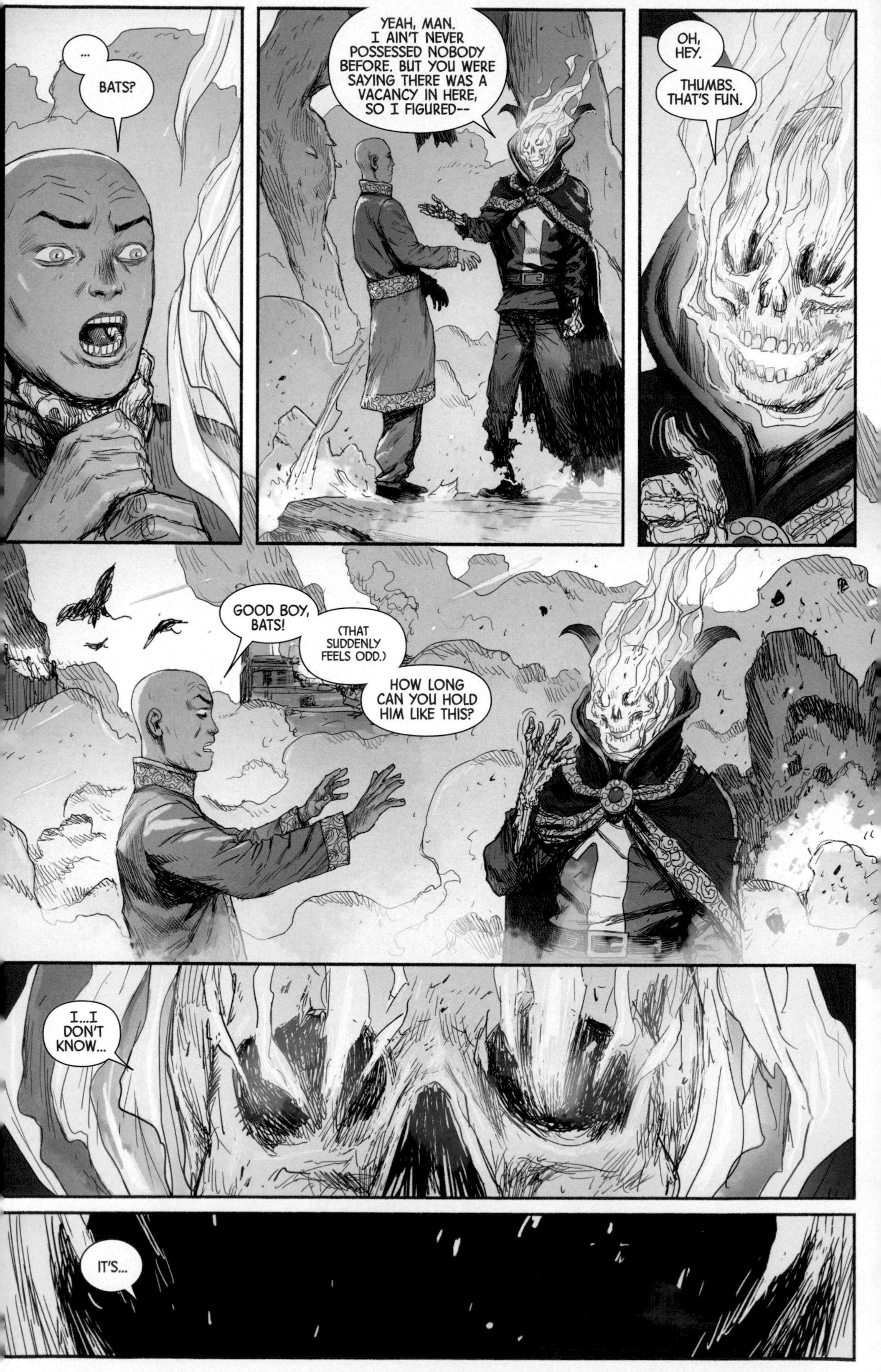
...
BATS?
YEAH, MAN. I AIN'T NEVER POSSESSED NOBODY BEFORE. BUT YOU WERE SAYING THERE WAS A VACANCY IN HERE, SO I FIGURED--
OH, HEY.
THUMBS. THAT'S FUN.
GOOD BOY, BATS!
(THAT SUDDENLY FEELS ODD.)
HOW LONG CAN YOU HOLD HIM LIKE THIS?
I...I DON'T KNOW...
IT'S...

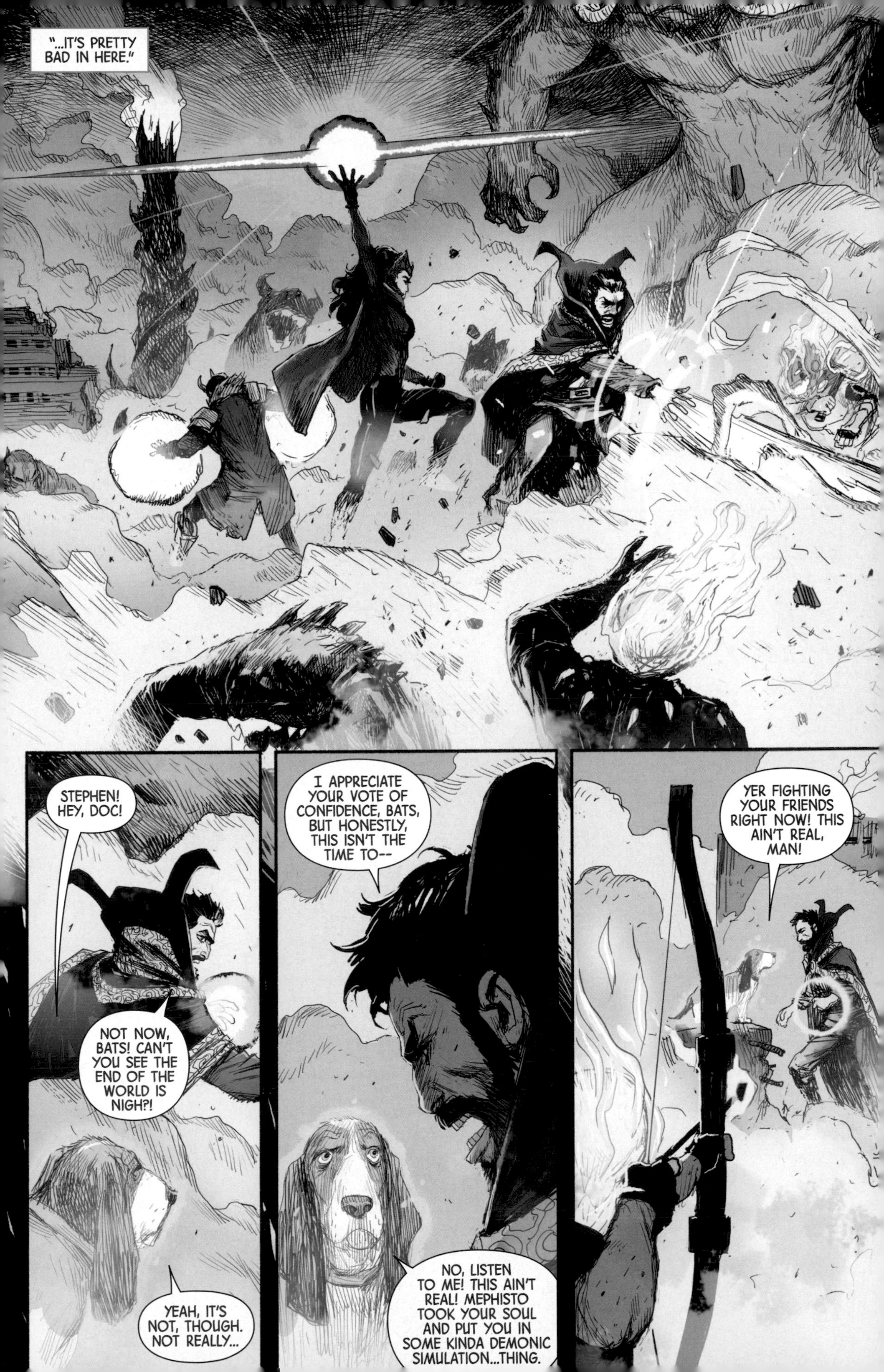
"...IT'S PRETTY BAD IN HERE."
STEPHEN! HEY, DOC!
NOT NOW, BATS! CAN'T YOU SEE THE END OF THE WORLD IS NIGH?!
YEAH, IT'S NOT, THOUGH. NOT REALLY...
I APPRECIATE YOUR VOTE OF CONFIDENCE, BATS, BUT HONESTLY, THIS ISN'T THE TIME TO--
NO, LISTEN TO ME! THIS AIN'T REAL! MEPHISTO TOOK YOUR SOUL AND PUT YOU IN SOME KINDA DEMONIC SIMULATION...THING.
YER FIGHTING YOUR FRIENDS RIGHT NOW! THIS AIN'T REAL, MAN!

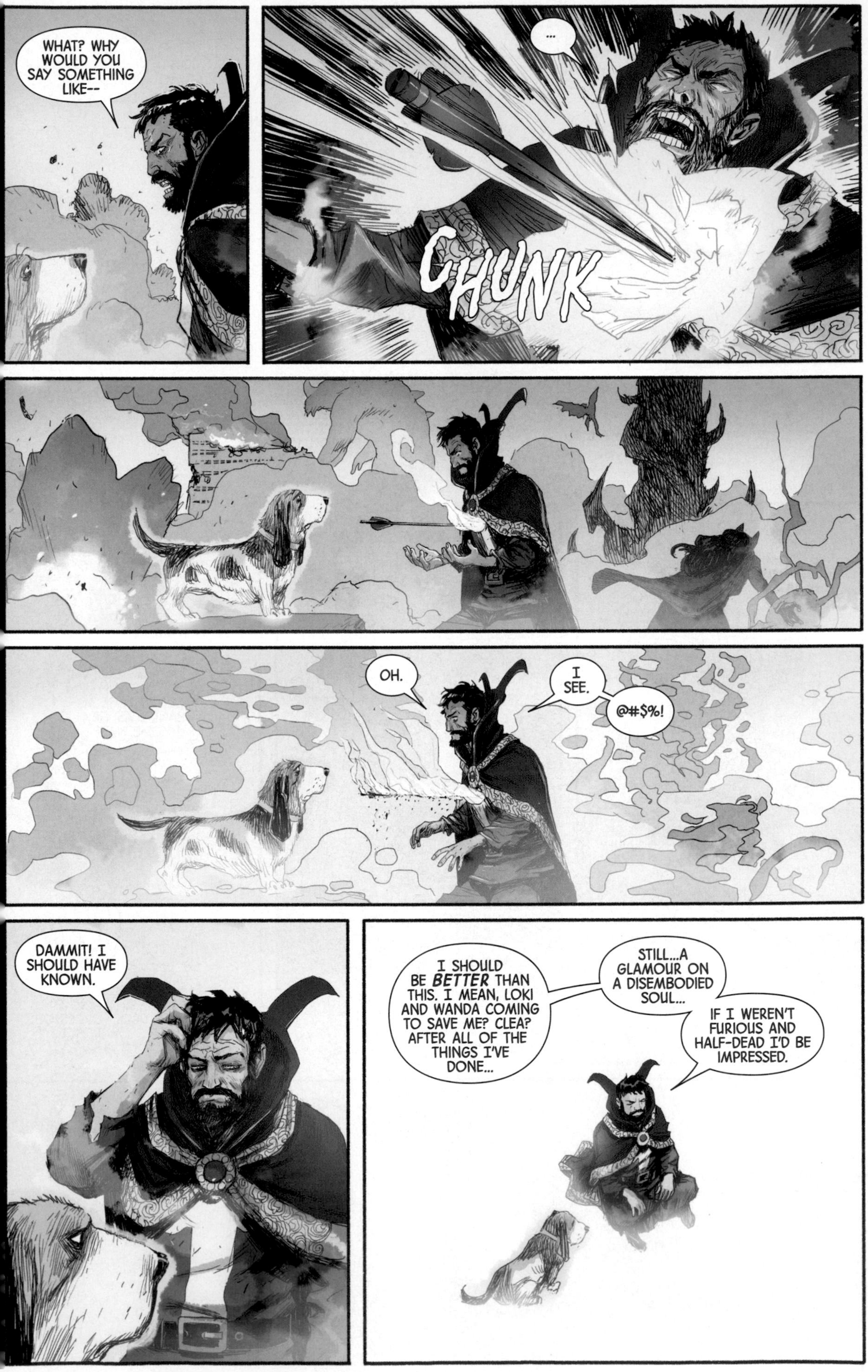
WHAT? WHY WOULD YOU SAY SOMETHING LIKE--
...
CHUNK
OH.
I SEE.
@#$%!
DAMMIT! I SHOULD HAVE KNOWN.
I SHOULD BE BETTER THAN THIS. I MEAN, LOKI AND WANDA COMING TO SAVE ME? CLEA? AFTER ALL OF THE THINGS I'VE DONE...
STILL...A GLAMOUR ON A DISEMBODIED SOUL...
IF I WEREN'T FURIOUS AND HALF-DEAD I'D BE IMPRESSED.

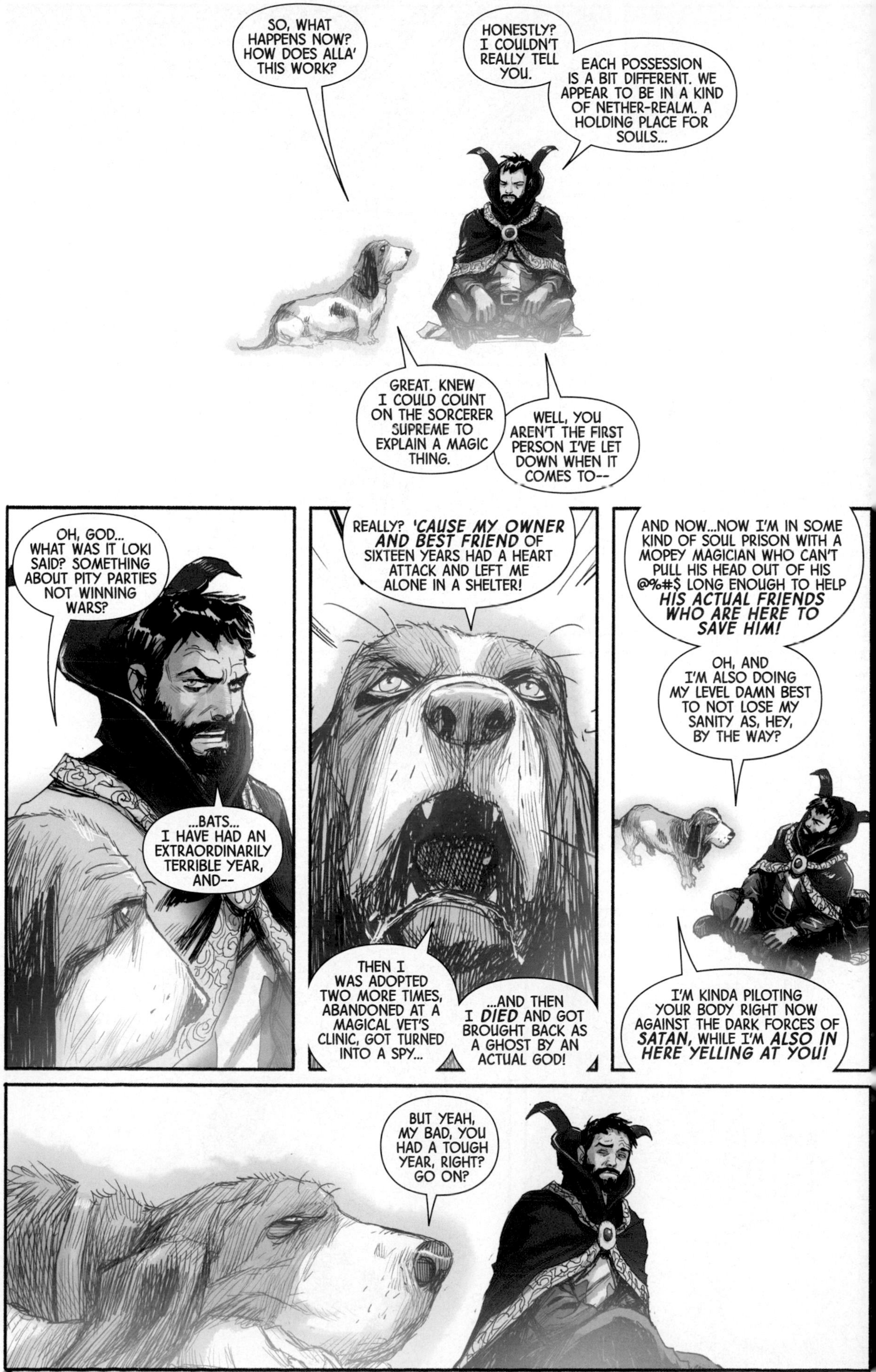
SO, WHAT HAPPENS NOW? HOW DOES ALLA' THIS WORK?
HONESTLY? I COULDN'T REALLY TELL YOU.
EACH POSSESSION IS A BIT DIFFERENT. WE APPEAR TO BE IN A KIND OF NETHER-REALM. A HOLDING PLACE FOR SOULS...
GREAT. KNEW I COULD COUNT ON THE SORCERER SUPREME TO EXPLAIN A MAGIC THING.
WELL, YOU AREN'T THE FIRST PERSON I'VE LET DOWN WHEN IT COMES TO--
OH, GOD... WHAT WAS IT LOKI SAID? SOMETHING ABOUT PITY PARTIES NOT WINNING WARS?
...BATS... I HAVE HAD AN EXTRAORDINARILY TERRIBLE YEAR, AND--
REALLY? *'CAUSE MY OWNER AND BEST FRIEND* OF SIXTEEN YEARS HAD A HEART ATTACK AND LEFT ME ALONE IN A SHELTER!
THEN I WAS ADOPTED TWO MORE TIMES, ABANDONED AT A MAGICAL VET'S CLINIC, GOT TURNED INTO A SPY...
...AND THEN I *DIED* AND GOT BROUGHT BACK AS A GHOST BY AN ACTUAL GOD!
AND NOW...NOW I'M IN SOME KIND OF SOUL PRISON WITH A MOPEY MAGICIAN WHO CAN'T PULL HIS HEAD OUT OF HIS @%#$ LONG ENOUGH TO HELP *HIS ACTUAL FRIENDS WHO ARE HERE TO SAVE HIM!*
OH, AND I'M ALSO DOING MY LEVEL DAMN BEST TO NOT LOSE MY SANITY AS, HEY, BY THE WAY?
I'M KINDA PILOTING YOUR BODY RIGHT NOW AGAINST THE DARK FORCES OF *SATAN*, WHILE I'M *ALSO IN HERE YELLING AT YOU!*
BUT YEAH, MY BAD, YOU HAD A TOUGH YEAR, RIGHT? GO ON?

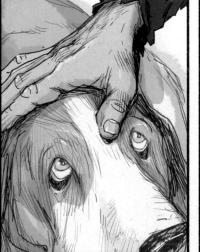

I'M SORRY.

... OKAY.

YOU WANNA GET OUT OF HERE?

YOU GOT A PLAN?

NO, BUT WHILE YOU WERE YELLING AT ME A GIANT DOOR APPEARED ON THE HORIZON WITH THE WORD "EXIT" WRITTEN IN HUGE BLINKING NEON LIGHTS.

HUH. WELL, YEAH, I GUESS THERE'S THAT...

REAL QUICK, JUST SO WE'RE BOTH ON THE SAME PAGE...

OH, IT'S ABSOLUTELY A TRAP.

JUST MAKING SURE.

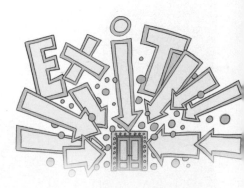

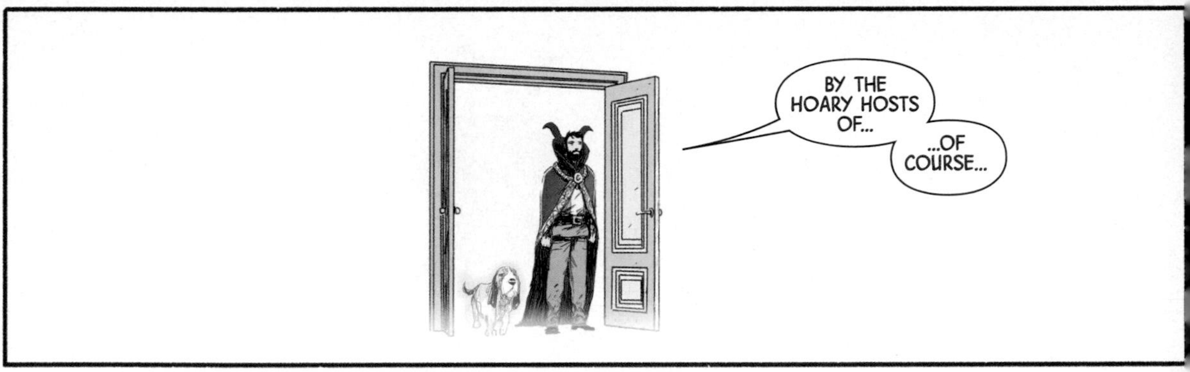
BY THE HOARY HOSTS OF...
...OF COURSE...

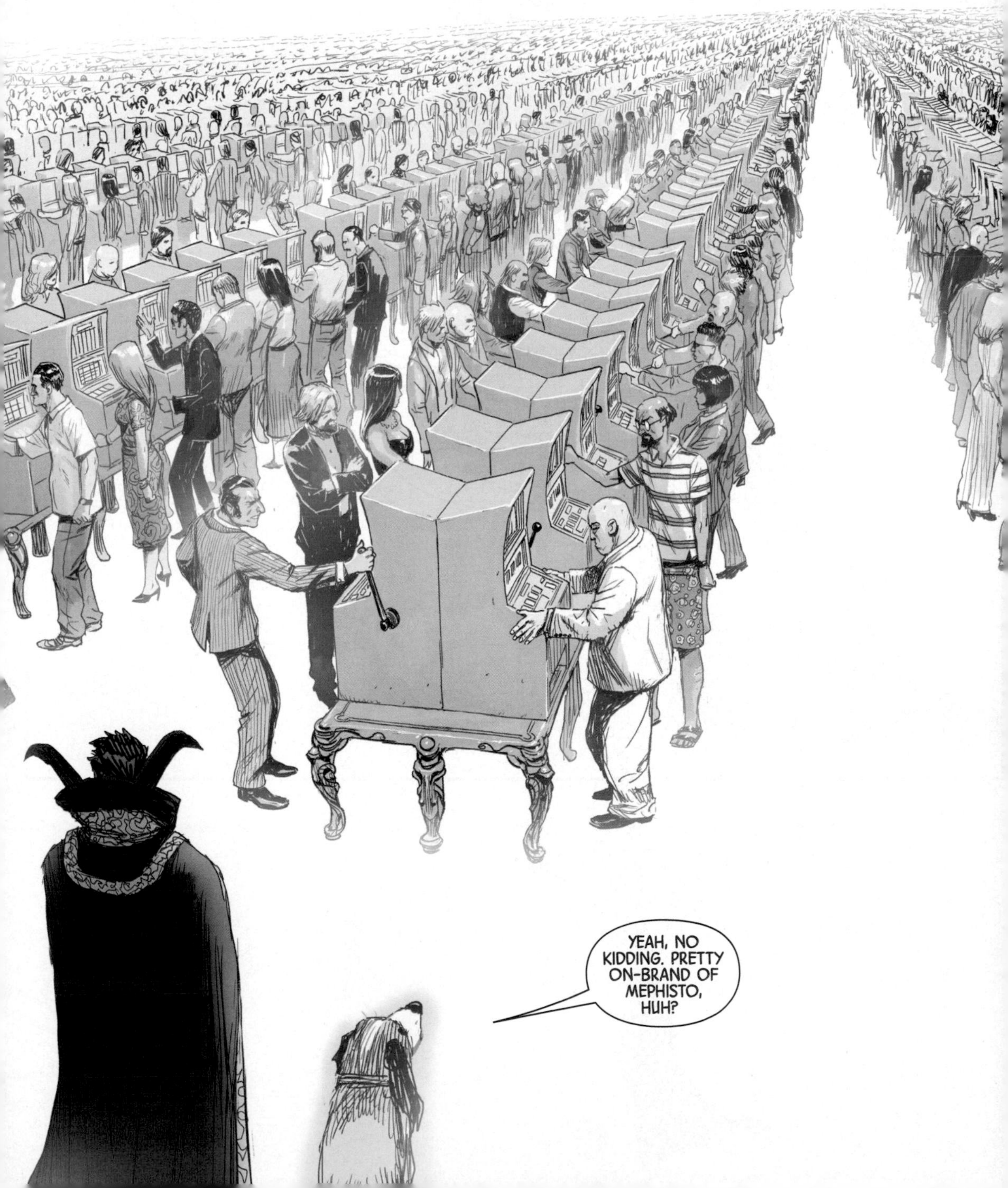
YEAH, NO KIDDING. PRETTY ON-BRAND OF MEPHISTO, HUH?

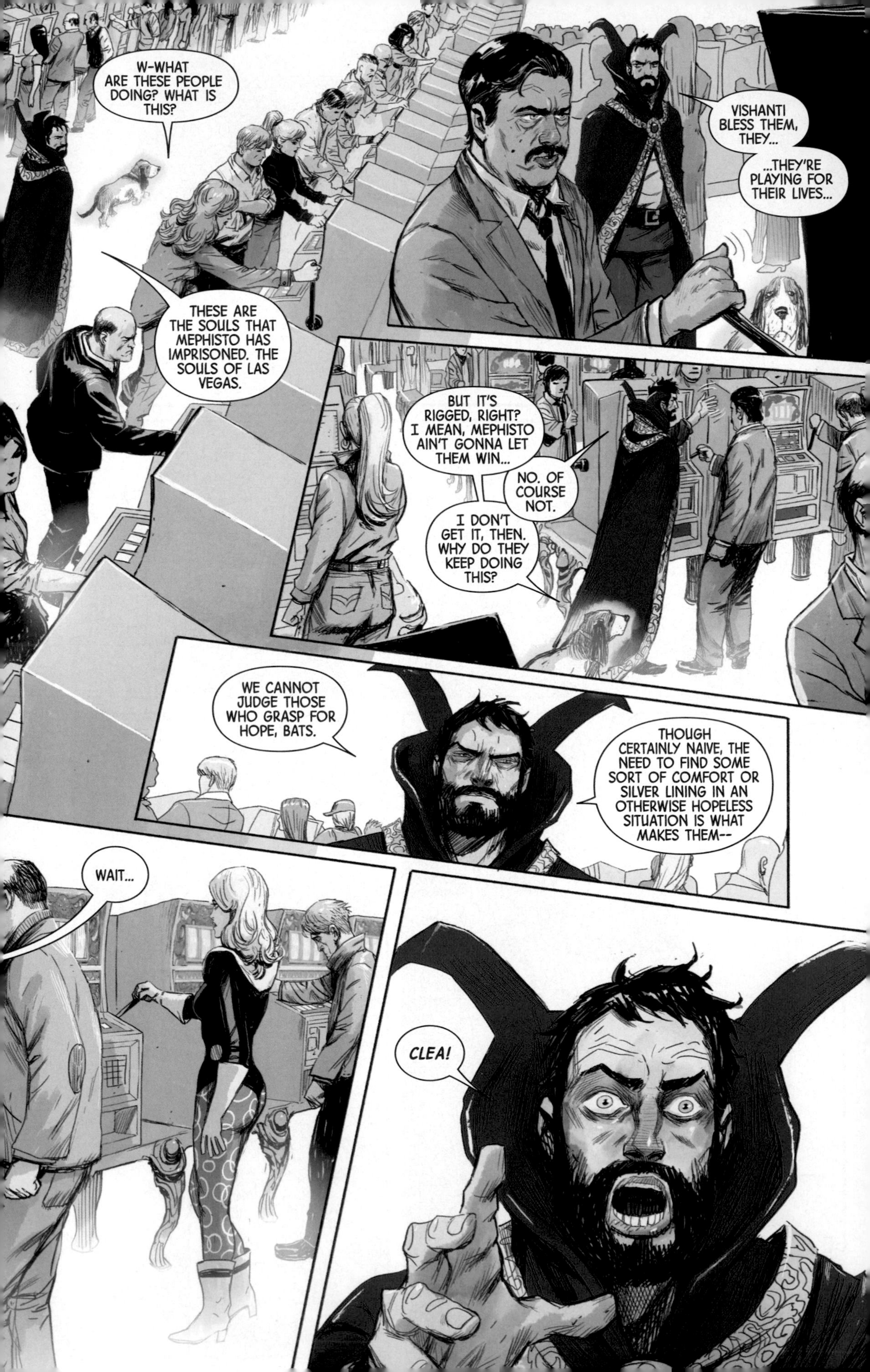

W-WHAT ARE THESE PEOPLE DOING? WHAT IS THIS?
VISHANTI BLESS THEM, THEY...
...THEY'RE PLAYING FOR THEIR LIVES...
THESE ARE THE SOULS THAT MEPHISTO HAS IMPRISONED. THE SOULS OF LAS VEGAS.
BUT IT'S RIGGED, RIGHT? I MEAN, MEPHISTO AIN'T GONNA LET THEM WIN...
NO. OF COURSE NOT.
I DON'T GET IT, THEN. WHY DO THEY KEEP DOING THIS?
WE CANNOT JUDGE THOSE WHO GRASP FOR HOPE, BATS.
THOUGH CERTAINLY NAIVE, THE NEED TO FIND SOME SORT OF COMFORT OR SILVER LINING IN AN OTHERWISE HOPELESS SITUATION IS WHAT MAKES THEM--
WAIT...
CLEA!

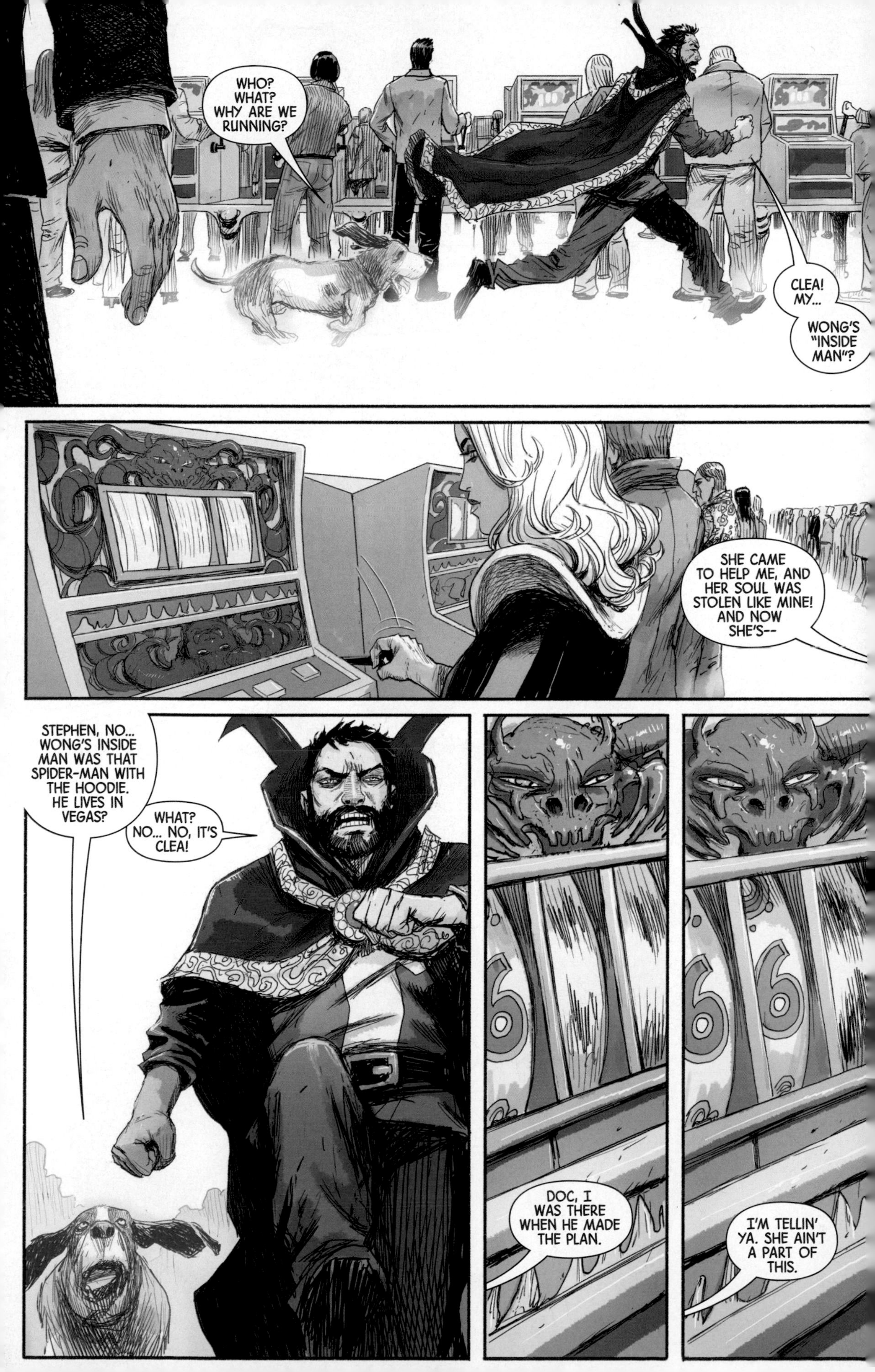
WHO? WHAT? WHY ARE WE RUNNING?
CLEA! MY...
WONG'S "INSIDE MAN"?
SHE CAME TO HELP ME, AND HER SOUL WAS STOLEN LIKE MINE! AND NOW SHE'S--
STEPHEN, NO... WONG'S INSIDE MAN WAS THAT SPIDER-MAN WITH THE HOODIE. HE LIVES IN VEGAS?
WHAT? NO... NO, IT'S CLEA!
DOC, I WAS THERE WHEN HE MADE THE PLAN.
I'M TELLIN' YA. SHE AIN'T A PART OF THIS.

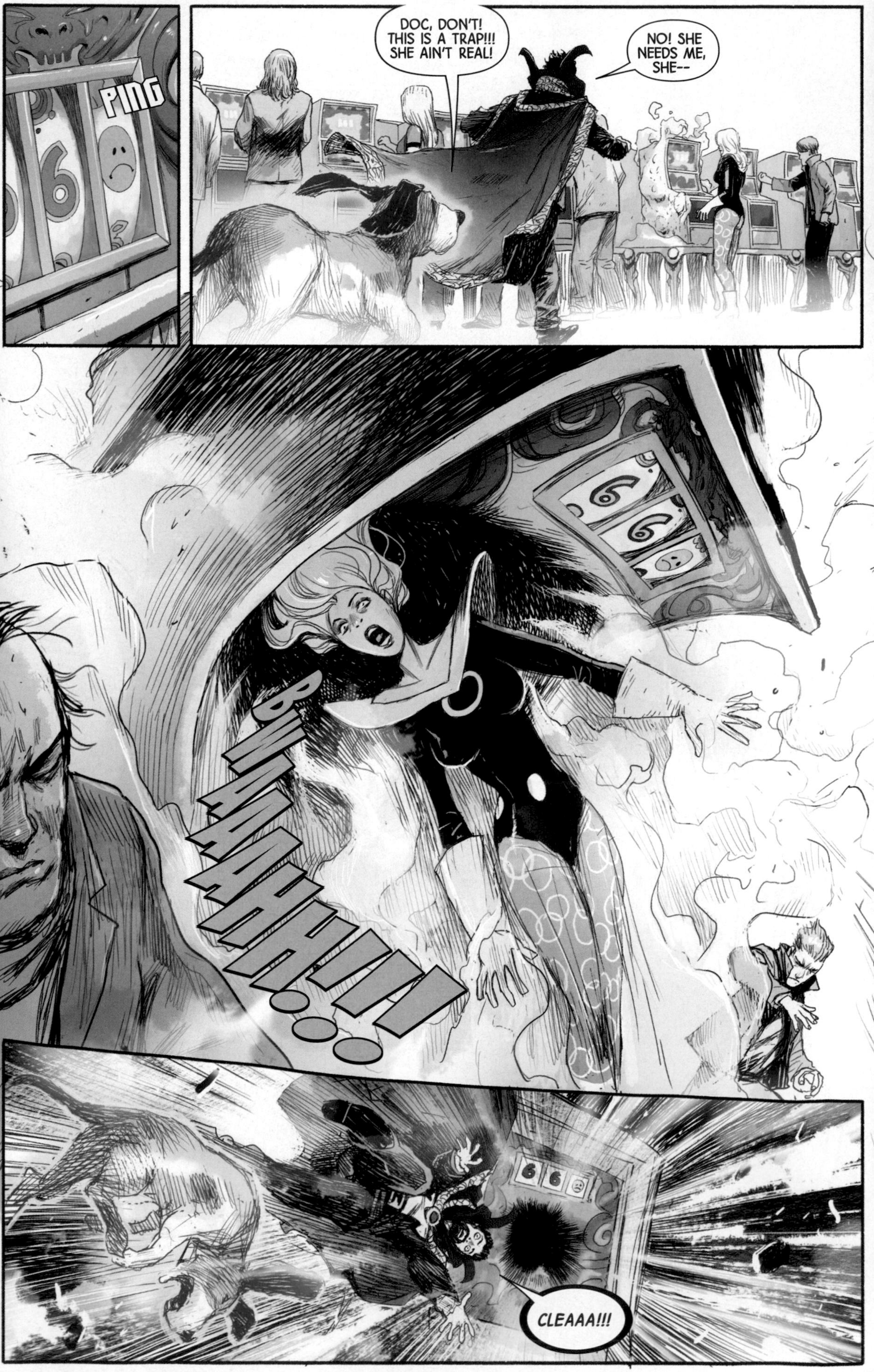
PING
DOC, DON'T! THIS IS A TRAP!!! SHE AIN'T REAL!
NO! SHE NEEDS ME, SHE--
BWAAAAAHH!!!...
CLEAAA!!!

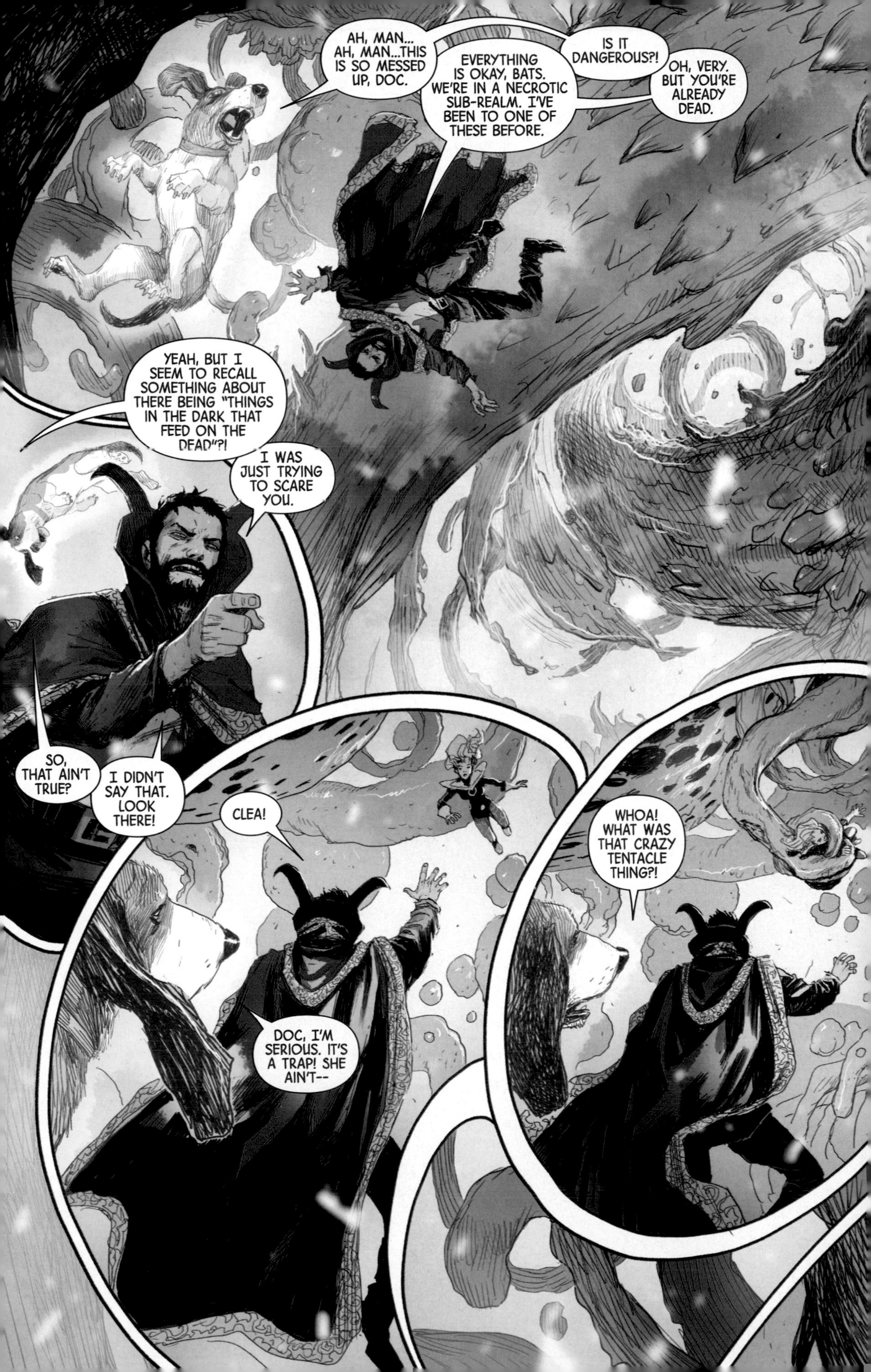
AH, MAN... AH, MAN...THIS IS SO MESSED UP, DOC.
EVERYTHING IS OKAY, BATS. WE'RE IN A NECROTIC SUB-REALM. I'VE BEEN TO ONE OF THESE BEFORE.
IS IT DANGEROUS?!
OH, VERY. BUT YOU'RE ALREADY DEAD.
YEAH, BUT I SEEM TO RECALL SOMETHING ABOUT THERE BEING "THINGS IN THE DARK THAT FEED ON THE DEAD"?!
I WAS JUST TRYING TO SCARE YOU.
SO, THAT AIN'T TRUE?
I DIDN'T SAY THAT. LOOK THERE!
CLEA!
DOC, I'M SERIOUS. IT'S A TRAP! SHE AIN'T--
WHOA! WHAT WAS THAT CRAZY TENTACLE THING?!

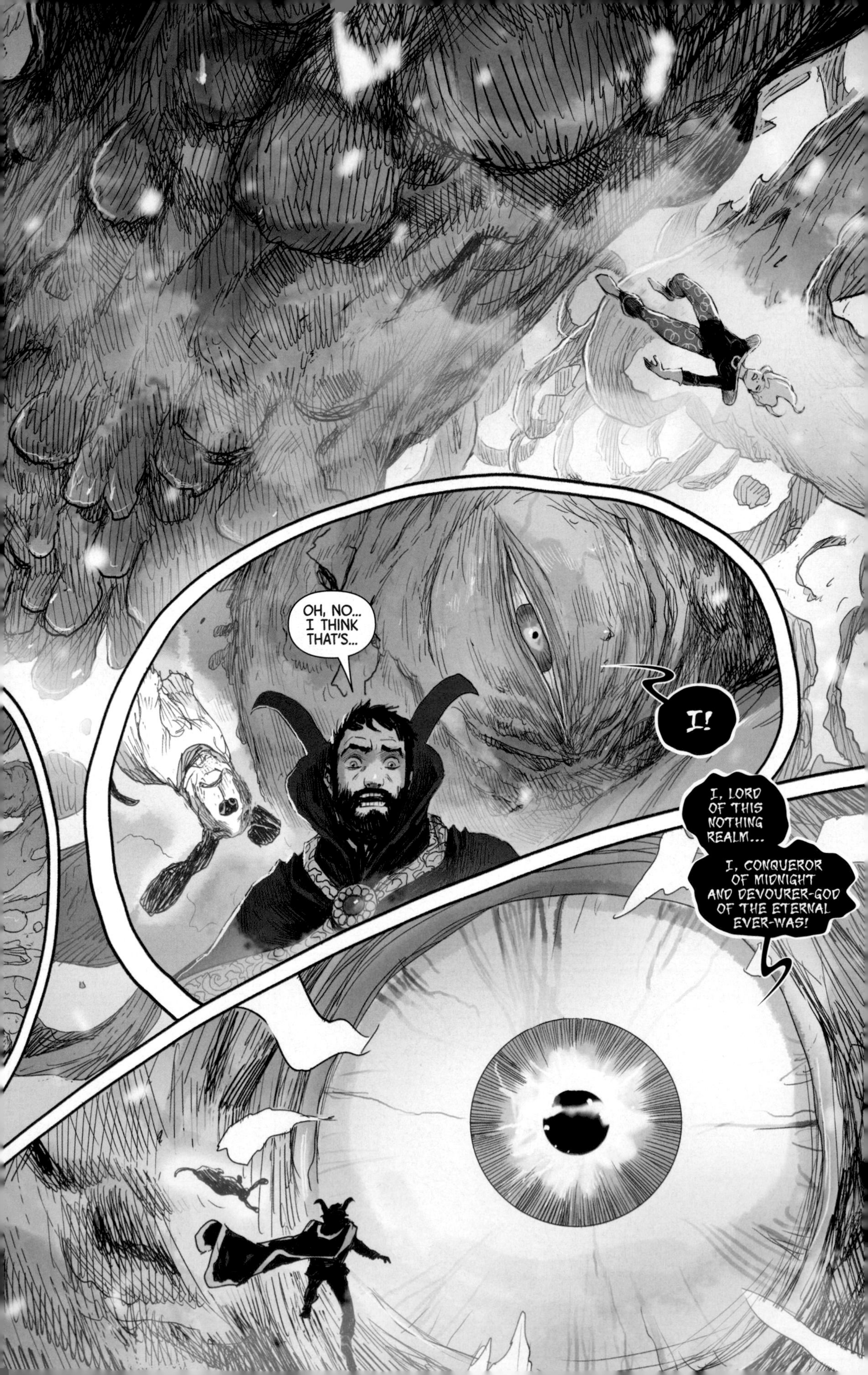

OH, NO... I THINK THAT'S...
I!
I, LORD OF THIS NOTHING REALM...
I, CONQUEROR OF MIDNIGHT AND DEVOURER-GOD OF THE ETERNAL EVER-WAS!

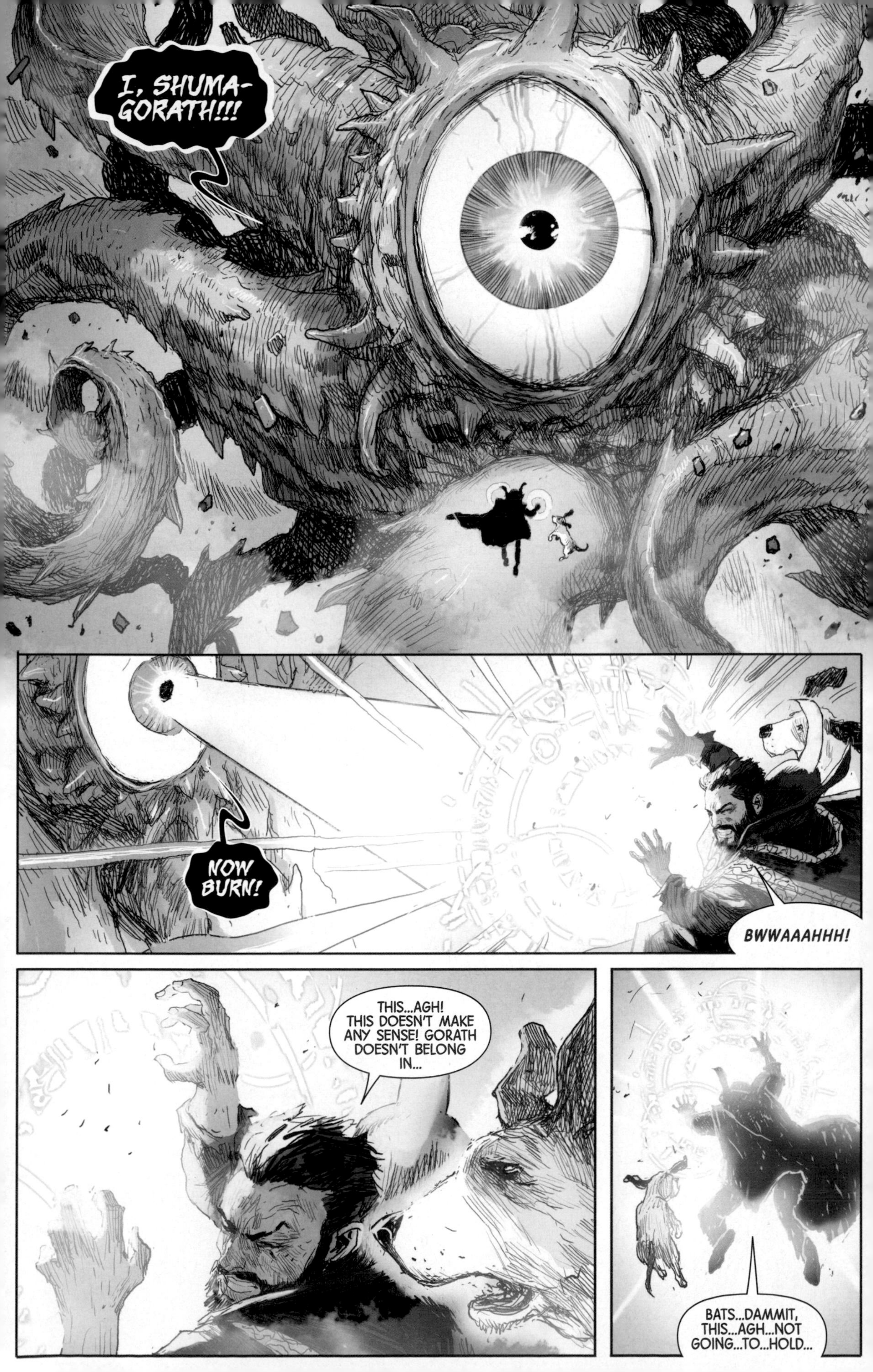
I, SHUMA-GORATH!!!
NOW BURN!
BWWAAAHHH!
THIS...AGH! THIS DOESN'T MAKE ANY SENSE! GORATH DOESN'T BELONG IN...
BATS...DAMMIT, THIS...AGH...NOT GOING...TO...HOLD...

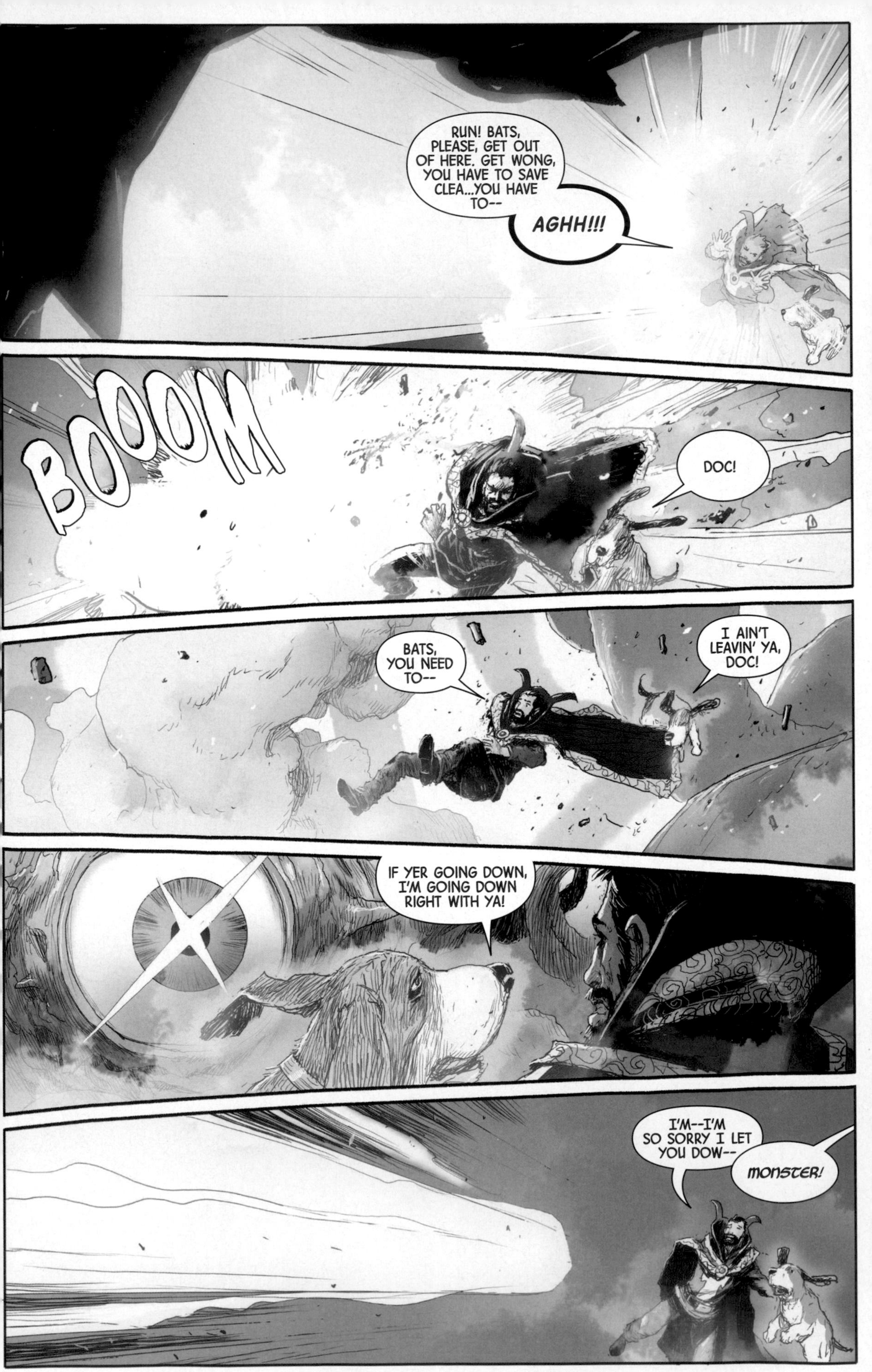
RUN! BATS, PLEASE, GET OUT OF HERE. GET WONG, YOU HAVE TO SAVE CLEA...YOU HAVE TO--
AGHH!!!
BOOOM
DOC!
BATS, YOU NEED TO--
I AIN'T LEAVIN' YA, DOC!
IF YER GOING DOWN, I'M GOING DOWN RIGHT WITH YA!
I'M--I'M SO SORRY I LET YOU DOW--
MONSTER!

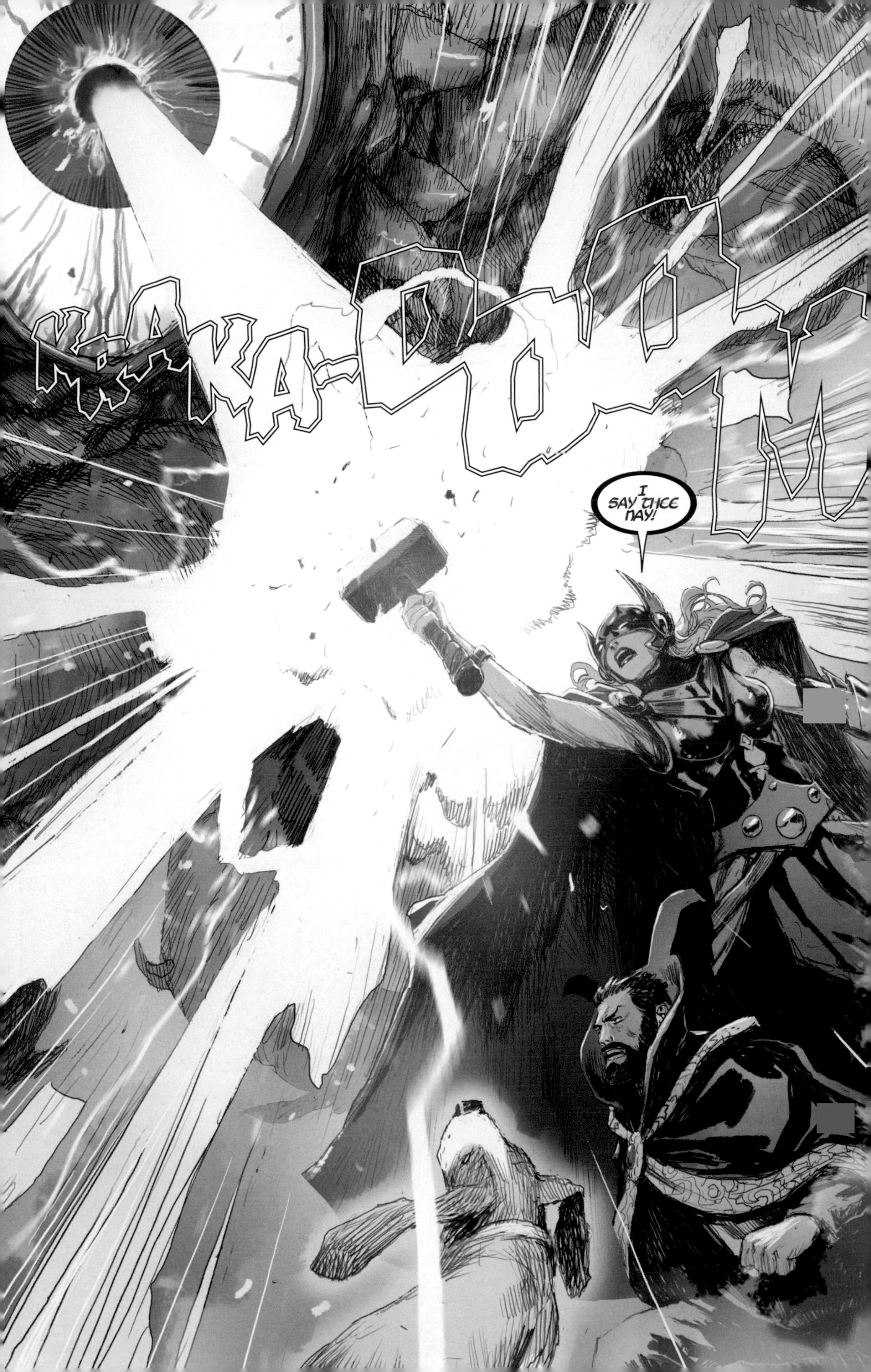

K-KA-DOOOM
I SAY THEE NAY!

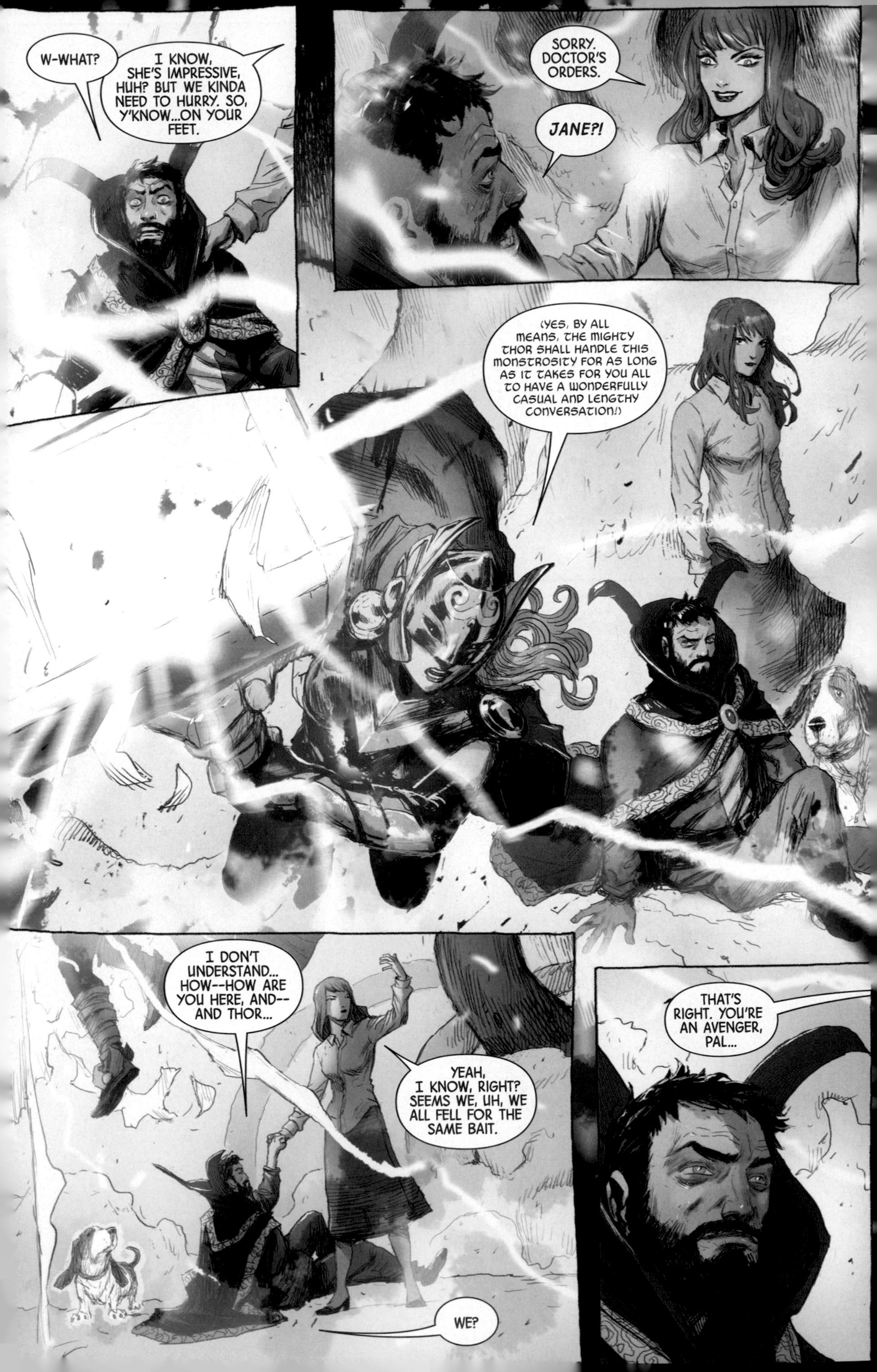
W-WHAT?
I KNOW, SHE'S IMPRESSIVE, HUH? BUT WE KINDA NEED TO HURRY. SO, Y'KNOW...ON YOUR FEET.
SORRY. DOCTOR'S ORDERS.
JANE?!
(YES, BY ALL MEANS, THE MIGHTY THOR SHALL HANDLE THIS MONSTROSITY FOR AS LONG AS IT TAKES FOR YOU ALL TO HAVE A WONDERFULLY CASUAL AND LENGTHY CONVERSATION!)
I DON'T UNDERSTAND... HOW--HOW ARE YOU HERE, AND--AND THOR...
YEAH, I KNOW, RIGHT? SEEMS WE, UH, WE ALL FELL FOR THE SAME BAIT.
WE?
THAT'S RIGHT. YOU'RE AN AVENGER, PAL...

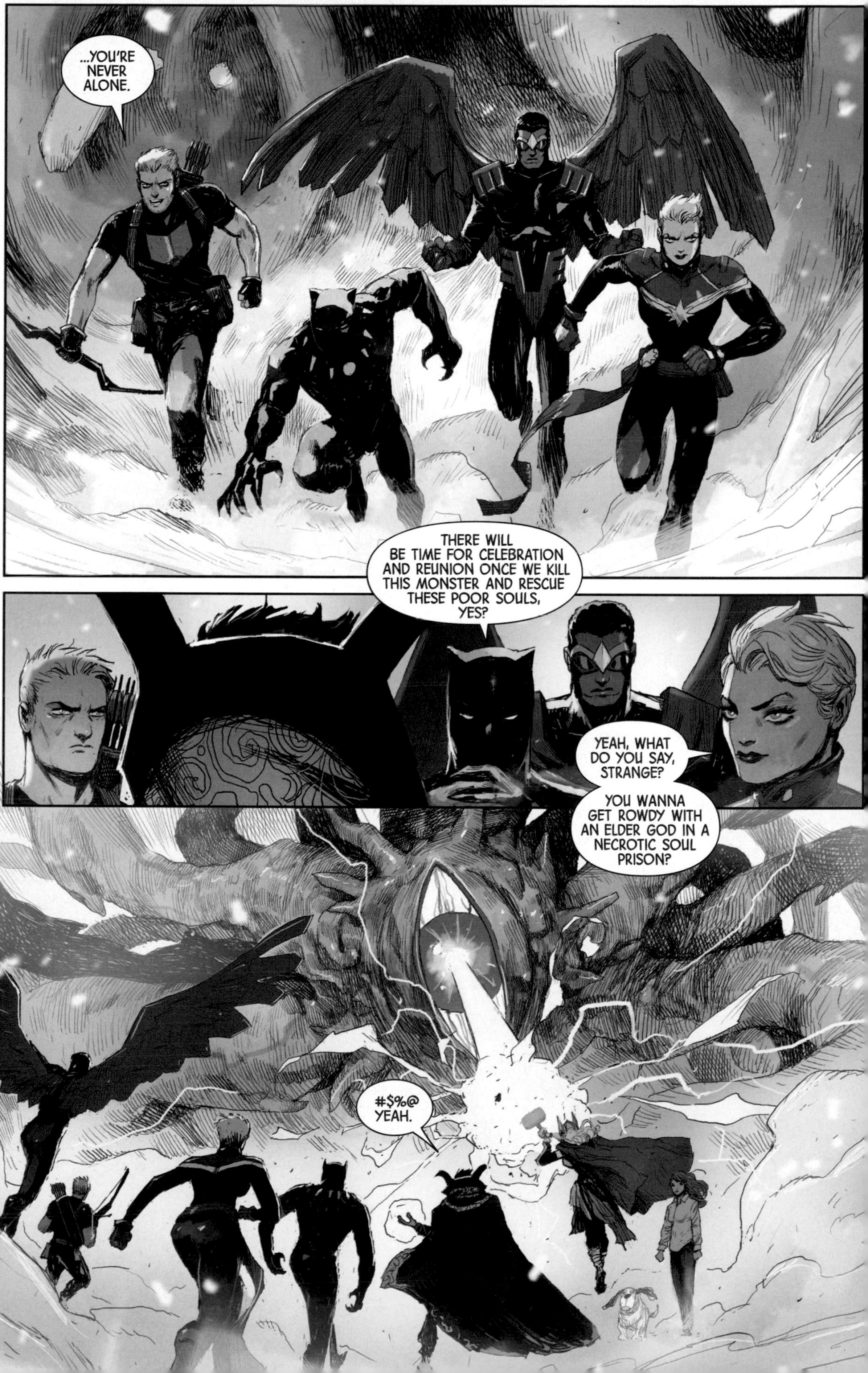
...YOU'RE NEVER ALONE.
THERE WILL BE TIME FOR CELEBRATION AND REUNION ONCE WE KILL THIS MONSTER AND RESCUE THESE POOR SOULS, YES?
YEAH, WHAT DO YOU SAY, STRANGE?
YOU WANNA GET ROWDY WITH AN ELDER GOD IN A NECROTIC SOUL PRISON?
#$%@ YEAH.

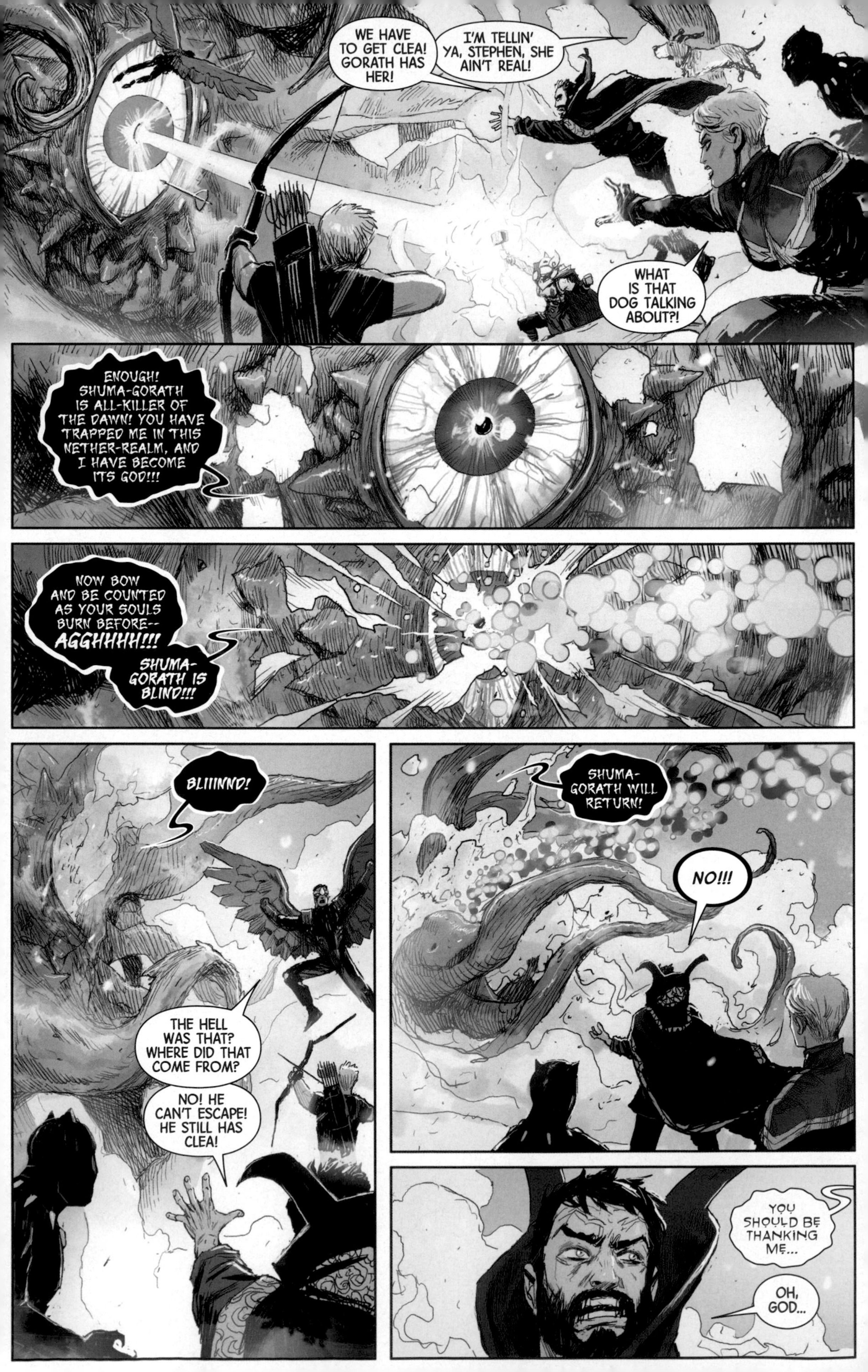
WE HAVE TO GET CLEA! GORATH HAS HER!
I'M TELLIN' YA, STEPHEN, SHE AIN'T REAL!
WHAT IS THAT DOG TALKING ABOUT?!
ENOUGH! SHUMA-GORATH IS ALL-KILLER OF THE DAWN! YOU HAVE TRAPPED ME IN THIS NETHER-REALM, AND I HAVE BECOME ITS GOD!!!
NOW BOW AND BE COUNTED AS YOUR SOULS BURN BEFORE-- AGGHHHH!!!
SHUMA-GORATH IS BLIND!!!
BLIIINND!
THE HELL WAS THAT? WHERE DID THAT COME FROM?
NO! HE CAN'T ESCAPE! HE STILL HAS CLEA!
SHUMA-GORATH WILL RETURN!
NO!!!
YOU SHOULD BE THANKING ME...
OH, GOD...

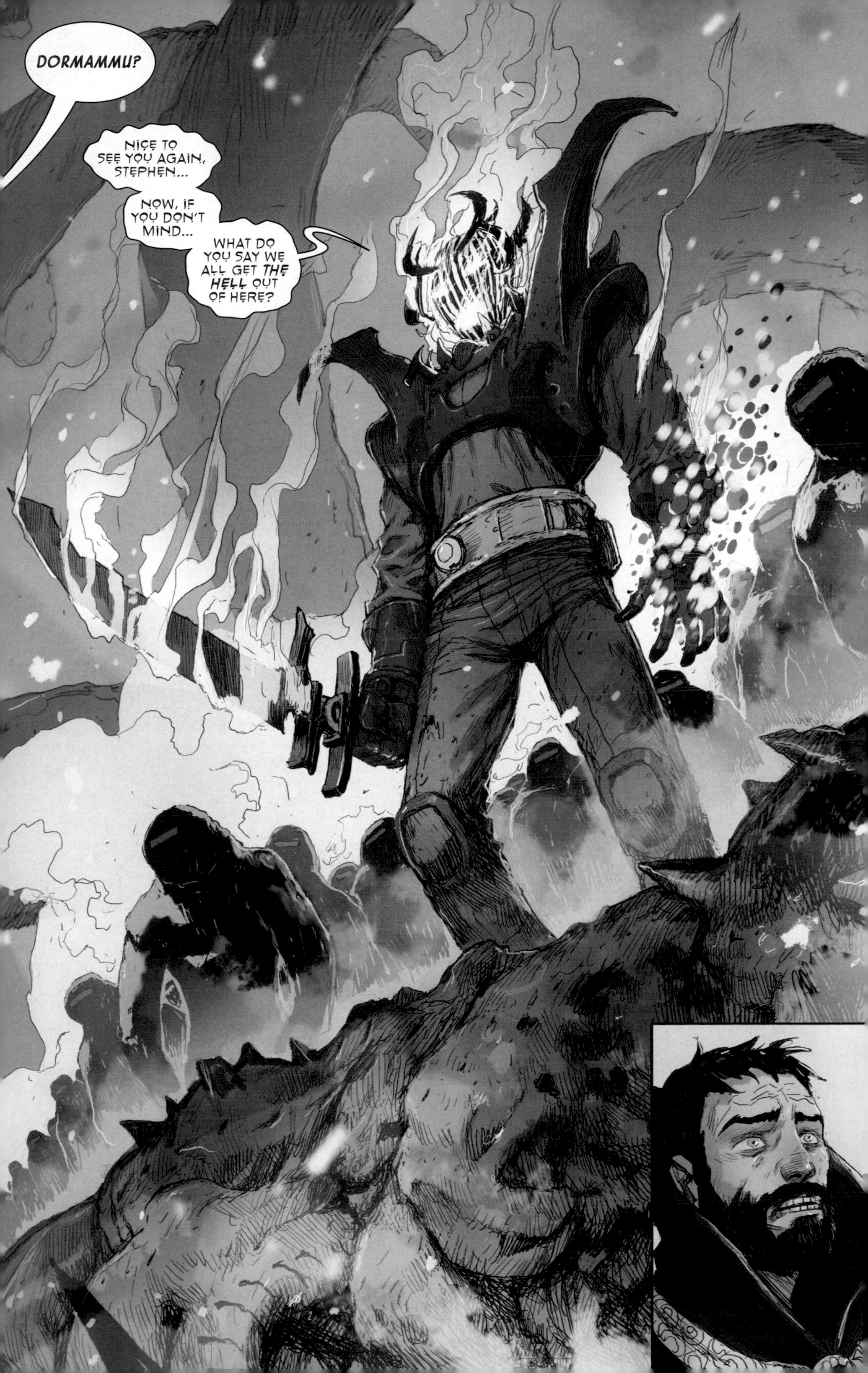
DORMAMMU?
NICE TO SEE YOU AGAIN, STEPHEN...
NOW, IF YOU DON'T MIND...
WHAT DO YOU SAY WE ALL GET THE HELL OUT OF HERE?

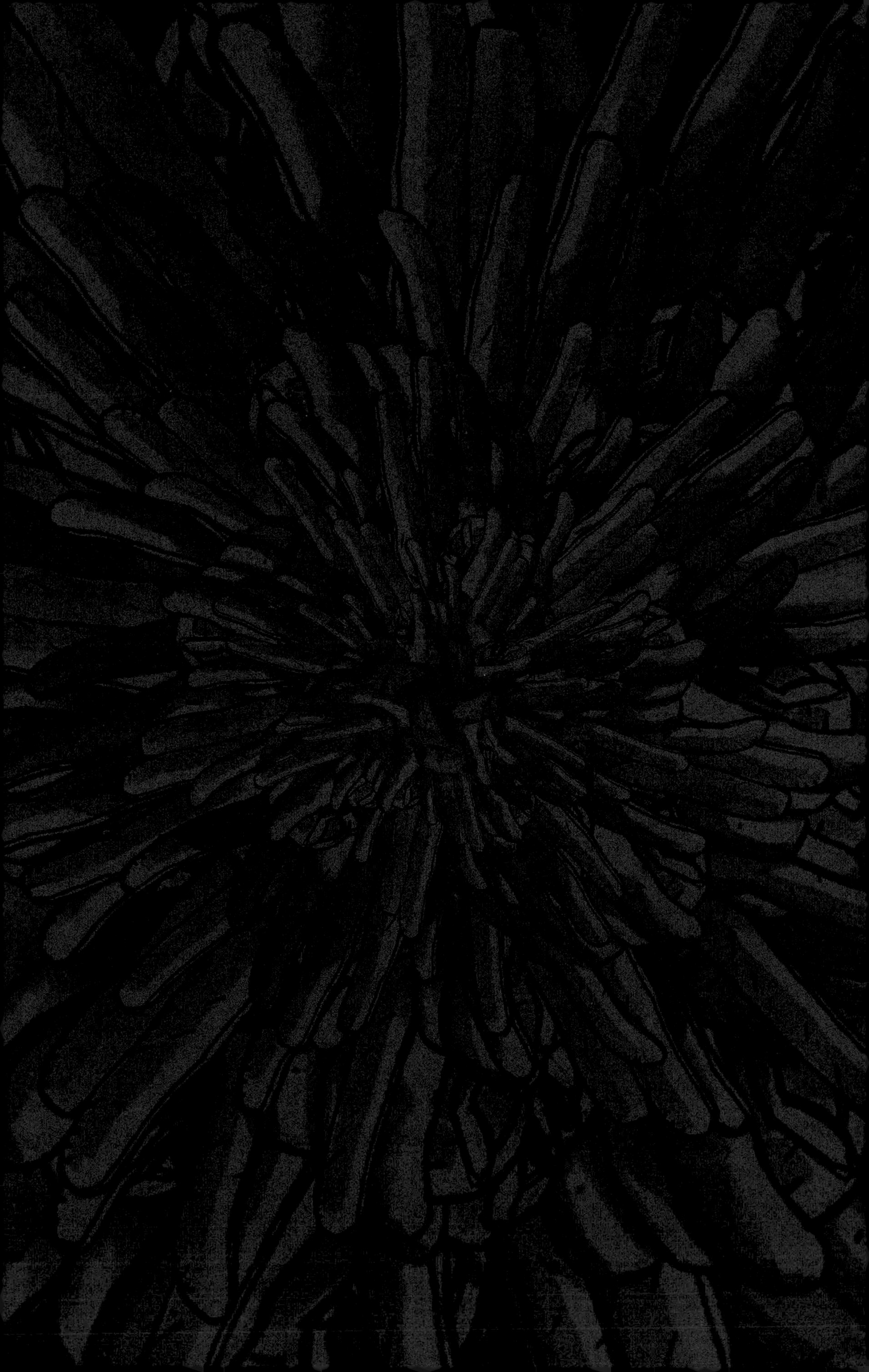

THE EVENTS OF THIS ISSUE TAKE PLACE CONCURRENTLY WITH THOSE IN *DOCTOR STRANGE: DAMNATION* #4.

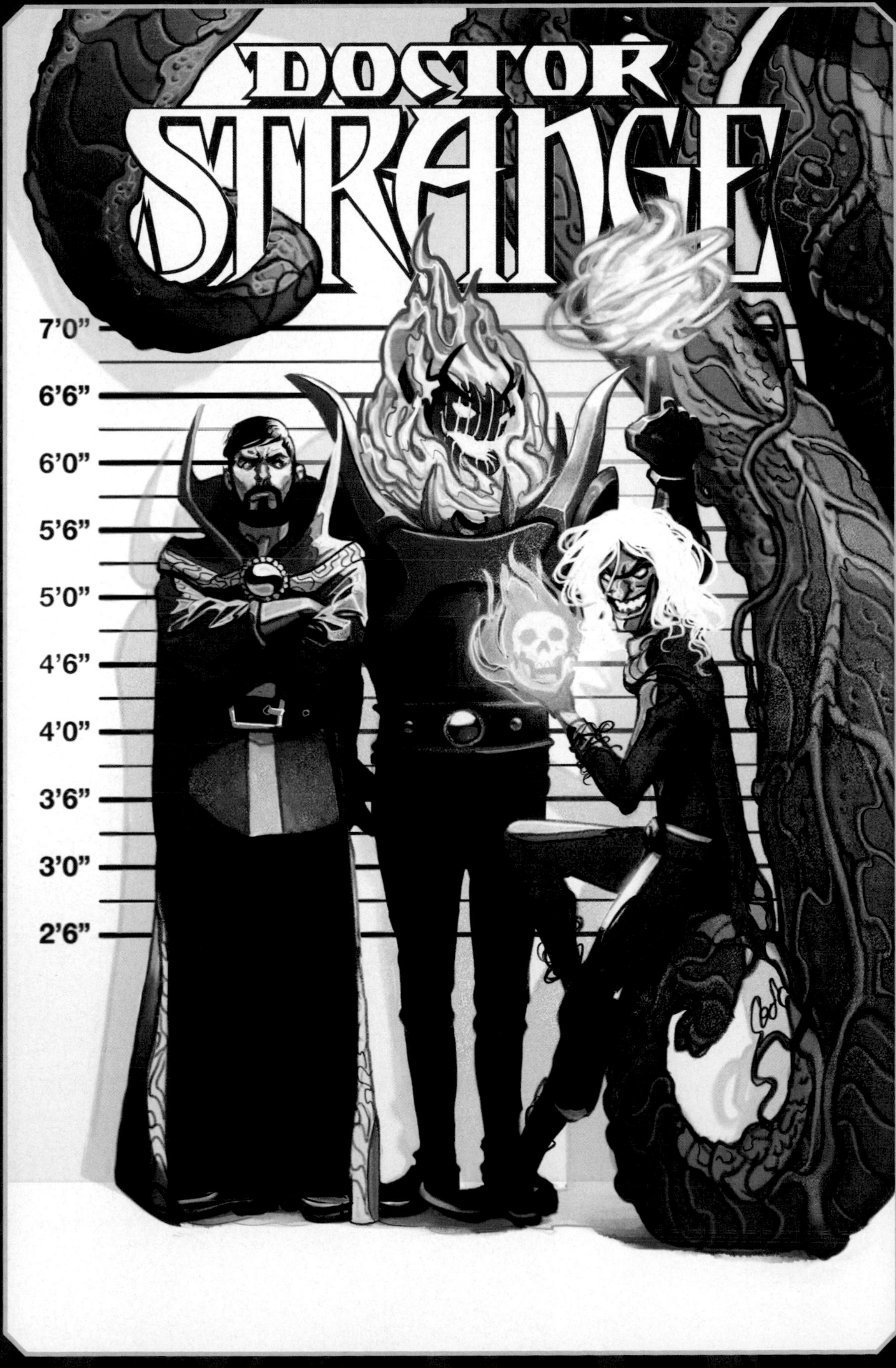
DOCTOR STRANGE
7'0"
6'6"
6'0"
5'6"
5'0"
4'6"
4'0"
3'6"
3'0"
2'6"

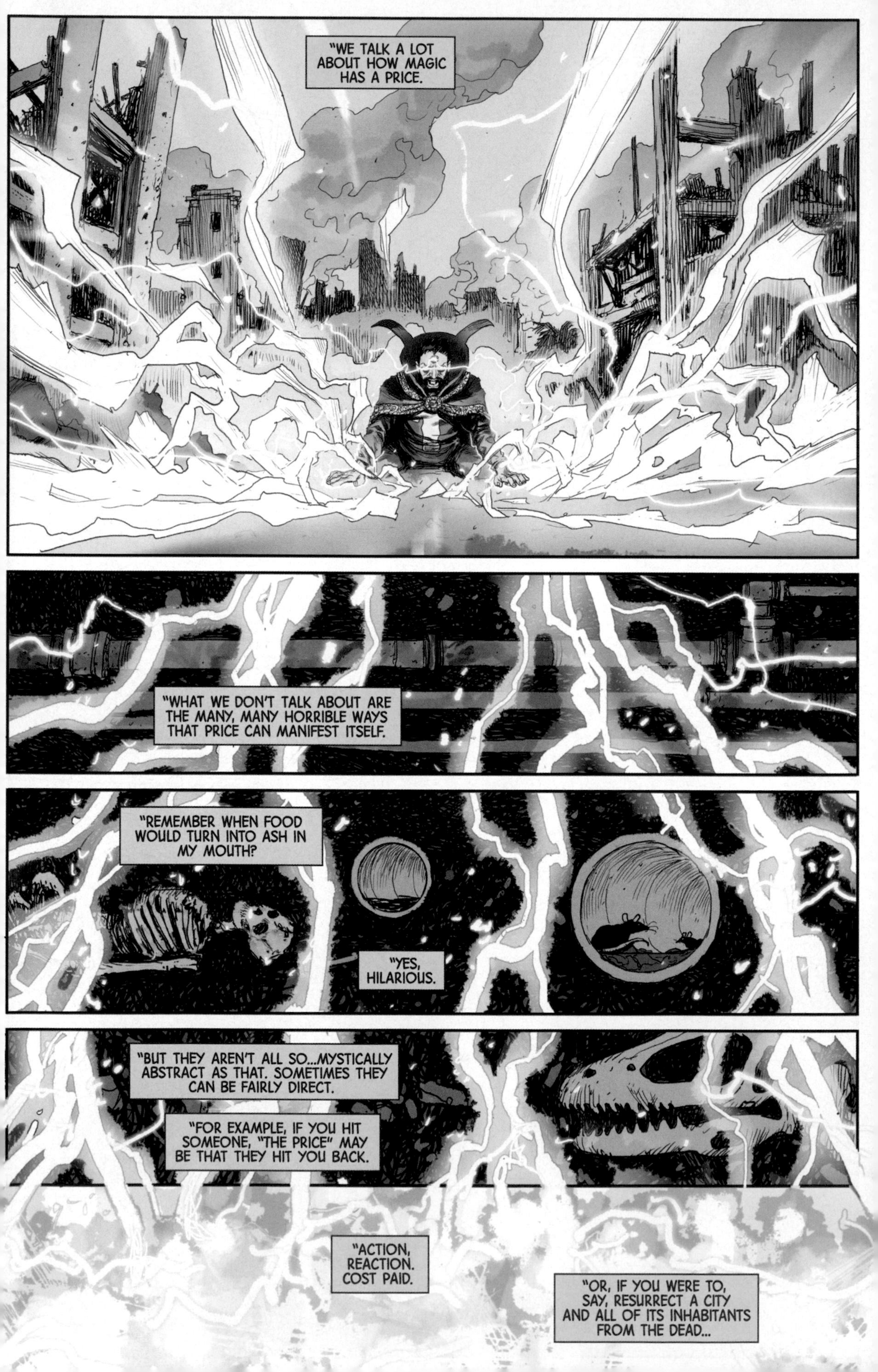
"WE TALK A LOT ABOUT HOW MAGIC HAS A PRICE.
"WHAT WE DON'T TALK ABOUT ARE THE MANY, MANY HORRIBLE WAYS THAT PRICE CAN MANIFEST ITSELF.
"REMEMBER WHEN FOOD WOULD TURN INTO ASH IN MY MOUTH?
"YES, HILARIOUS.
"BUT THEY AREN'T ALL SO...MYSTICALLY ABSTRACT AS THAT. SOMETIMES THEY CAN BE FAIRLY DIRECT.
"FOR EXAMPLE, IF YOU HIT SOMEONE, "THE PRICE" MAY BE THAT THEY HIT YOU BACK.
"ACTION, REACTION. COST PAID.
"OR, IF YOU WERE TO, SAY, RESURRECT A CITY AND ALL OF ITS INHABITANTS FROM THE DEAD...

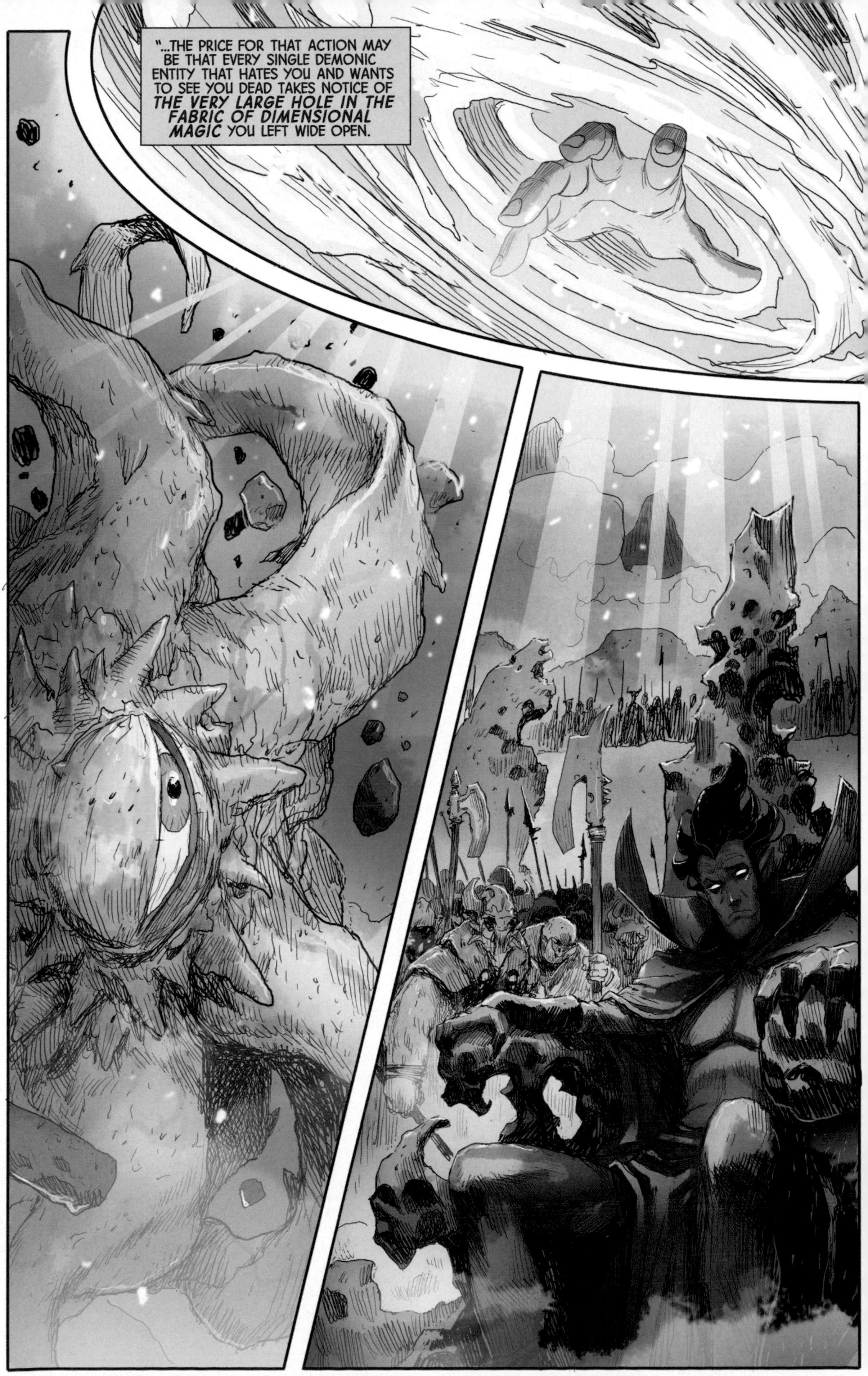
"...THE PRICE FOR THAT ACTION MAY BE THAT EVERY SINGLE DEMONIC ENTITY THAT HATES YOU AND WANTS TO SEE YOU DEAD TAKES NOTICE OF *THE VERY LARGE HOLE IN THE FABRIC OF DIMENSIONAL MAGIC* YOU LEFT WIDE OPEN.

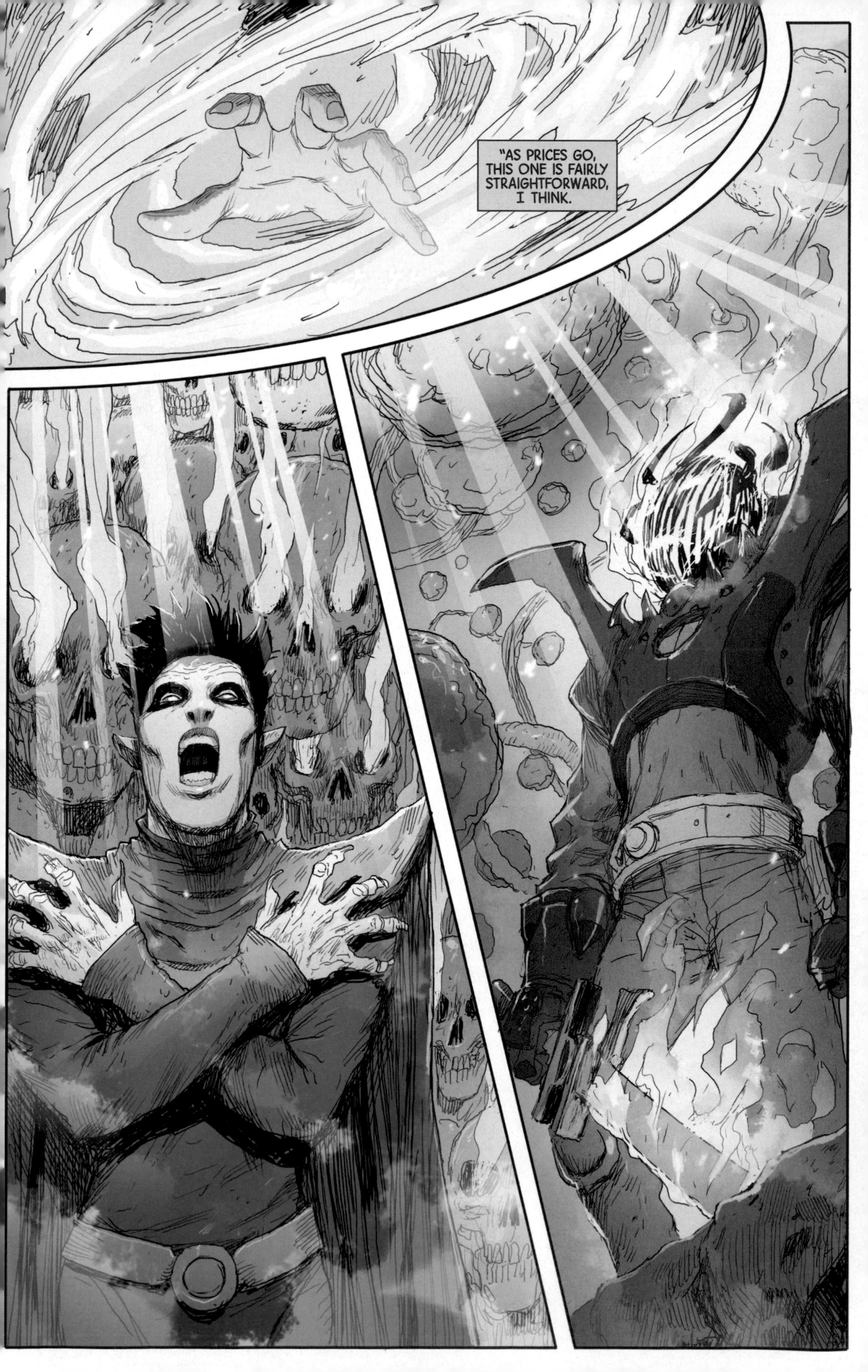
"AS PRICES GO, THIS ONE IS FAIRLY STRAIGHTFORWARD, I THINK.

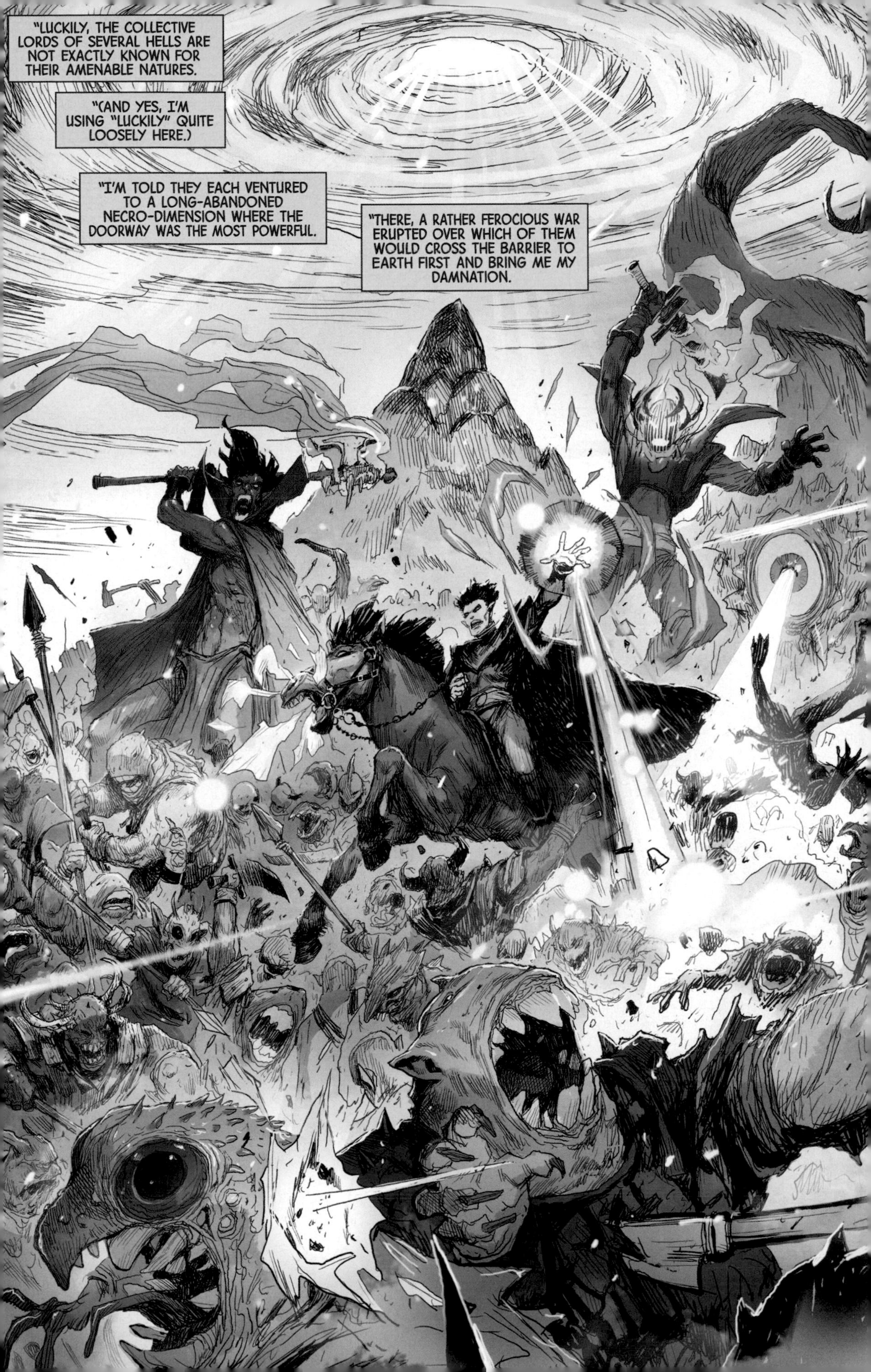
"LUCKILY, THE COLLECTIVE LORDS OF SEVERAL HELLS ARE NOT EXACTLY KNOWN FOR THEIR AMENABLE NATURES.
"(AND YES, I'M USING "LUCKILY" QUITE LOOSELY HERE.)
"I'M TOLD THEY EACH VENTURED TO A LONG-ABANDONED NECRO-DIMENSION WHERE THE DOORWAY WAS THE MOST POWERFUL.
"THERE, A RATHER FEROCIOUS WAR ERUPTED OVER WHICH OF THEM WOULD CROSS THE BARRIER TO EARTH FIRST AND BRING ME MY DAMNATION.

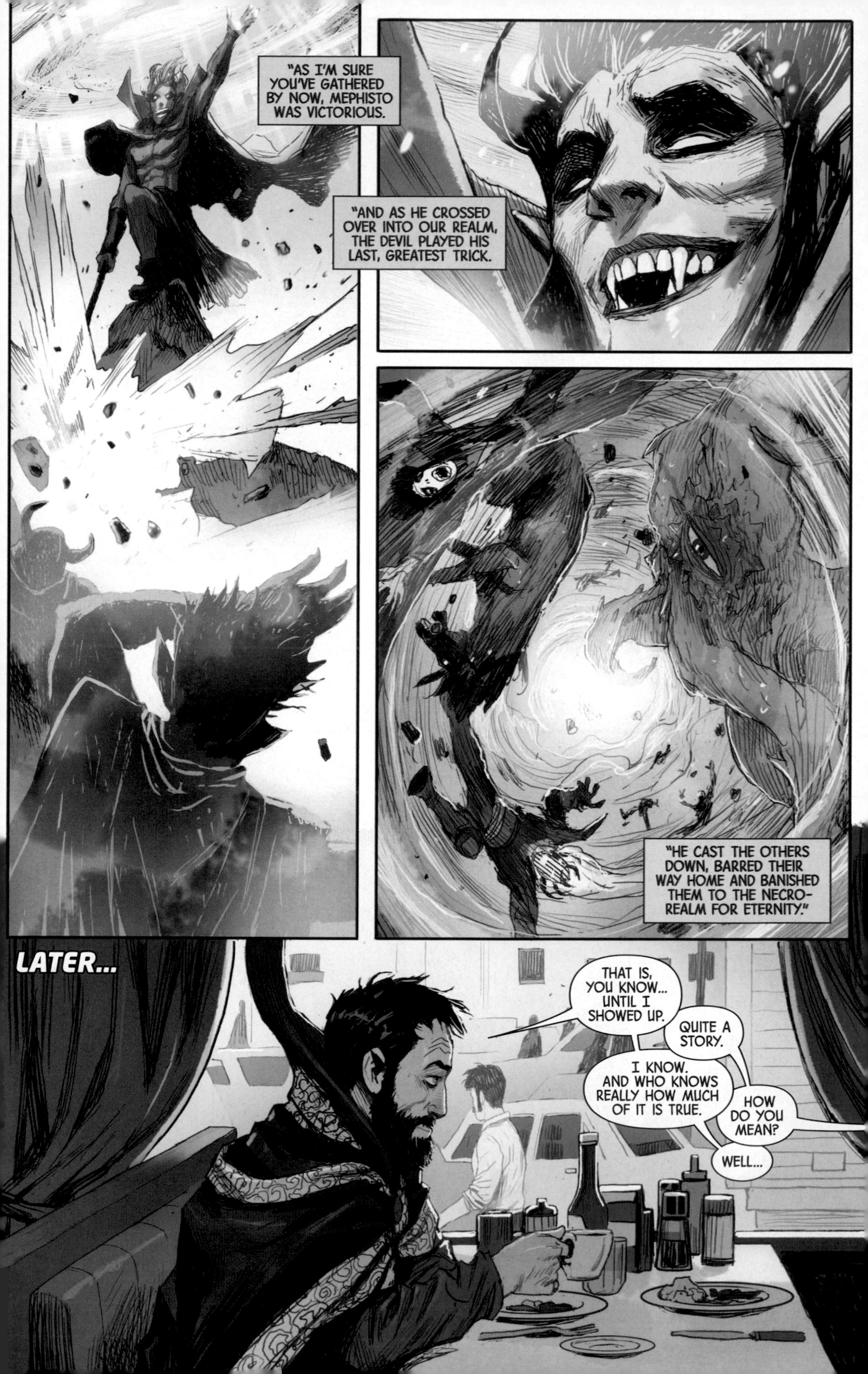
"AS I'M SURE YOU'VE GATHERED BY NOW, MEPHISTO WAS VICTORIOUS.
"AND AS HE CROSSED OVER INTO OUR REALM, THE DEVIL PLAYED HIS LAST, GREATEST TRICK.
"HE CAST THE OTHERS DOWN, BARRED THEIR WAY HOME AND BANISHED THEM TO THE NECRO-REALM FOR ETERNITY."
LATER...
THAT IS, YOU KNOW... UNTIL I SHOWED UP.
QUITE A STORY.
I KNOW. AND WHO KNOWS REALLY HOW MUCH OF IT IS TRUE.
HOW DO YOU MEAN?
WELL...

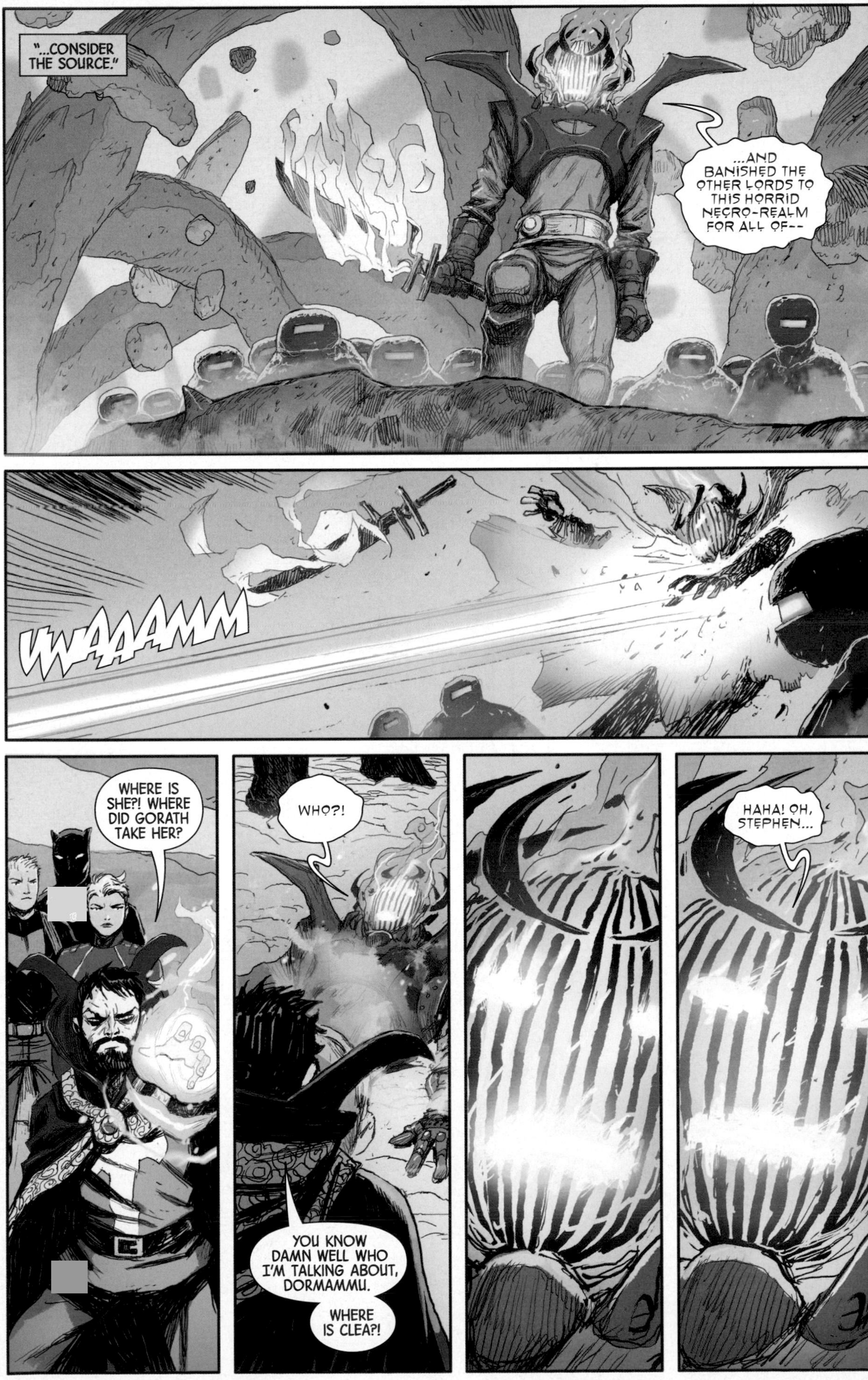
"...CONSIDER THE SOURCE."
...AND BANISHED THE OTHER LORDS TO THIS HORRID NECRO-REALM FOR ALL OF--
WWAAAMM
WHERE IS SHE?! WHERE DID GORATH TAKE HER?
WHO?!
YOU KNOW DAMN WELL WHO I'M TALKING ABOUT, DORMAMMU.
WHERE IS CLEA?!
HAHA! OH, STEPHEN...

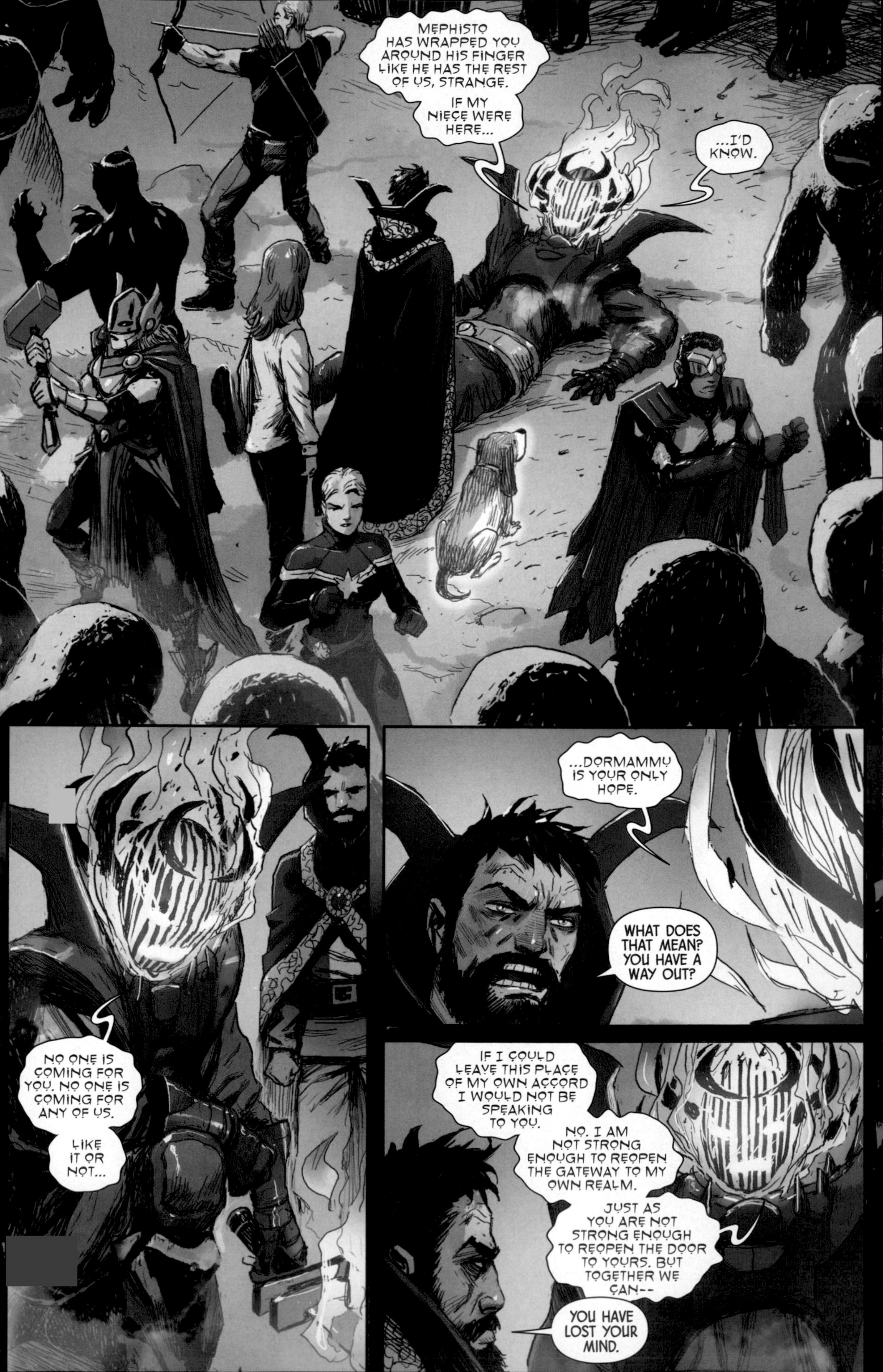
MEPHISTO HAS WRAPPED YOU AROUND HIS FINGER LIKE HE HAS THE REST OF US, STRANGE.
IF MY NIECE WERE HERE...
...I'D KNOW.
NO ONE IS COMING FOR YOU. NO ONE IS COMING FOR ANY OF US.
LIKE IT OR NOT...
...DORMAMMU IS YOUR ONLY HOPE.
WHAT DOES THAT MEAN? YOU HAVE A WAY OUT?
IF I COULD LEAVE THIS PLACE OF MY OWN ACCORD I WOULD NOT BE SPEAKING TO YOU.
NO. I AM NOT STRONG ENOUGH TO REOPEN THE GATEWAY TO MY OWN REALM.
JUST AS YOU ARE NOT STRONG ENOUGH TO REOPEN THE DOOR TO YOURS. BUT TOGETHER WE CAN--
YOU HAVE LOST YOUR MIND.

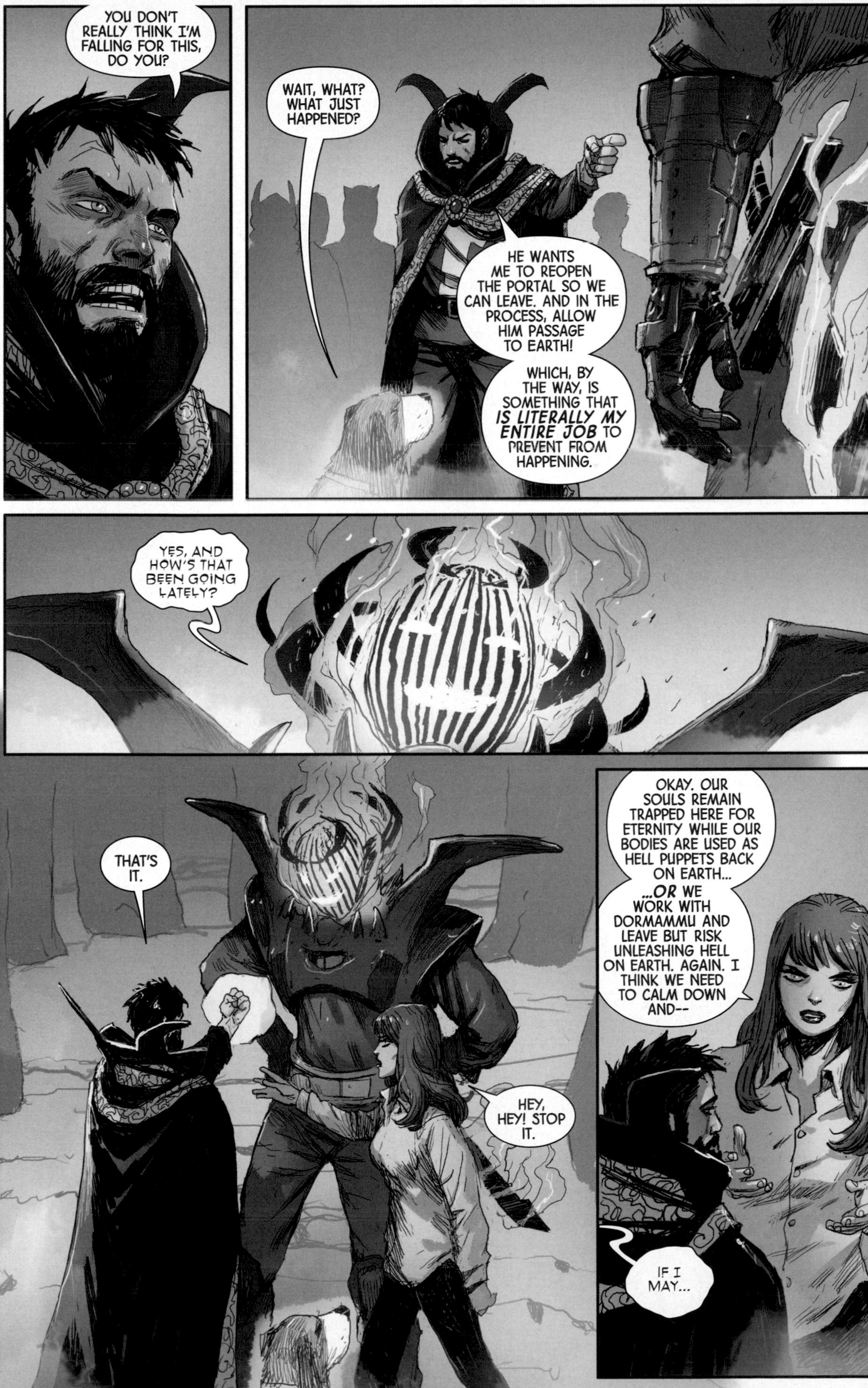
YOU DON'T REALLY THINK I'M FALLING FOR THIS, DO YOU?
WAIT, WHAT? WHAT JUST HAPPENED?
HE WANTS ME TO REOPEN THE PORTAL SO WE CAN LEAVE. AND IN THE PROCESS, ALLOW HIM PASSAGE TO EARTH!
WHICH, BY THE WAY, IS SOMETHING THAT ***IS LITERALLY MY ENTIRE JOB*** TO PREVENT FROM HAPPENING.
YES, AND HOW'S THAT BEEN GOING LATELY?
THAT'S IT.
HEY, HEY! STOP IT.
OKAY. OUR SOULS REMAIN TRAPPED HERE FOR ETERNITY WHILE OUR BODIES ARE USED AS HELL PUPPETS BACK ON EARTH...
...OR WE WORK WITH DORMAMMU AND LEAVE BUT RISK UNLEASHING HELL ON EARTH. AGAIN. I THINK WE NEED TO CALM DOWN AND--
IF I MAY...

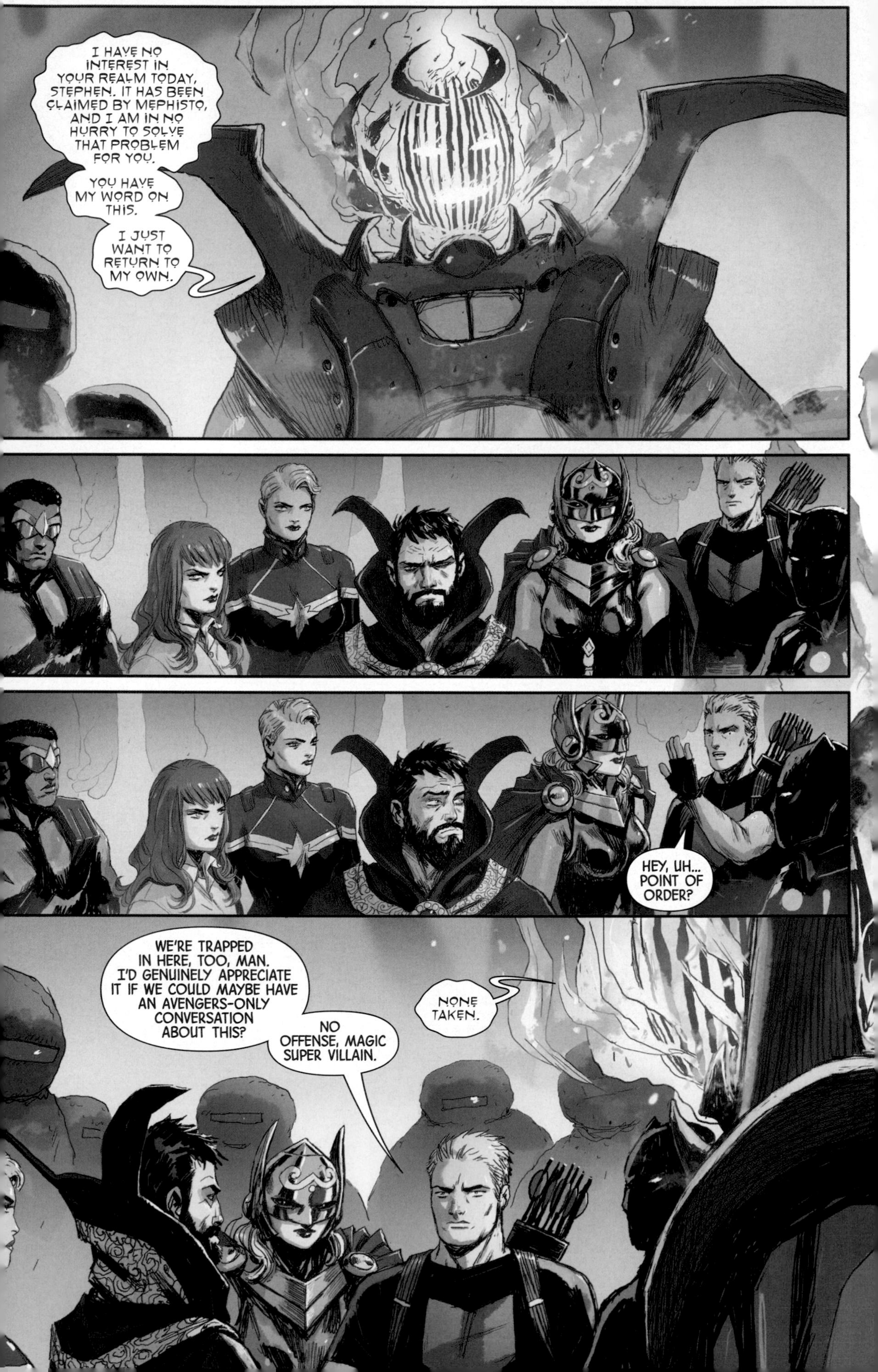
I HAVE NO INTEREST IN YOUR REALM TODAY, STEPHEN. IT HAS BEEN CLAIMED BY MEPHISTO, AND I AM IN NO HURRY TO SOLVE THAT PROBLEM FOR YOU.
YOU HAVE MY WORD ON THIS.
I JUST WANT TO RETURN TO MY OWN.
HEY, UH... POINT OF ORDER?
WE'RE TRAPPED IN HERE, TOO, MAN. I'D GENUINELY APPRECIATE IT IF WE COULD MAYBE HAVE AN AVENGERS-ONLY CONVERSATION ABOUT THIS?
NO OFFENSE, MAGIC SUPER VILLAIN.
NONE TAKEN.

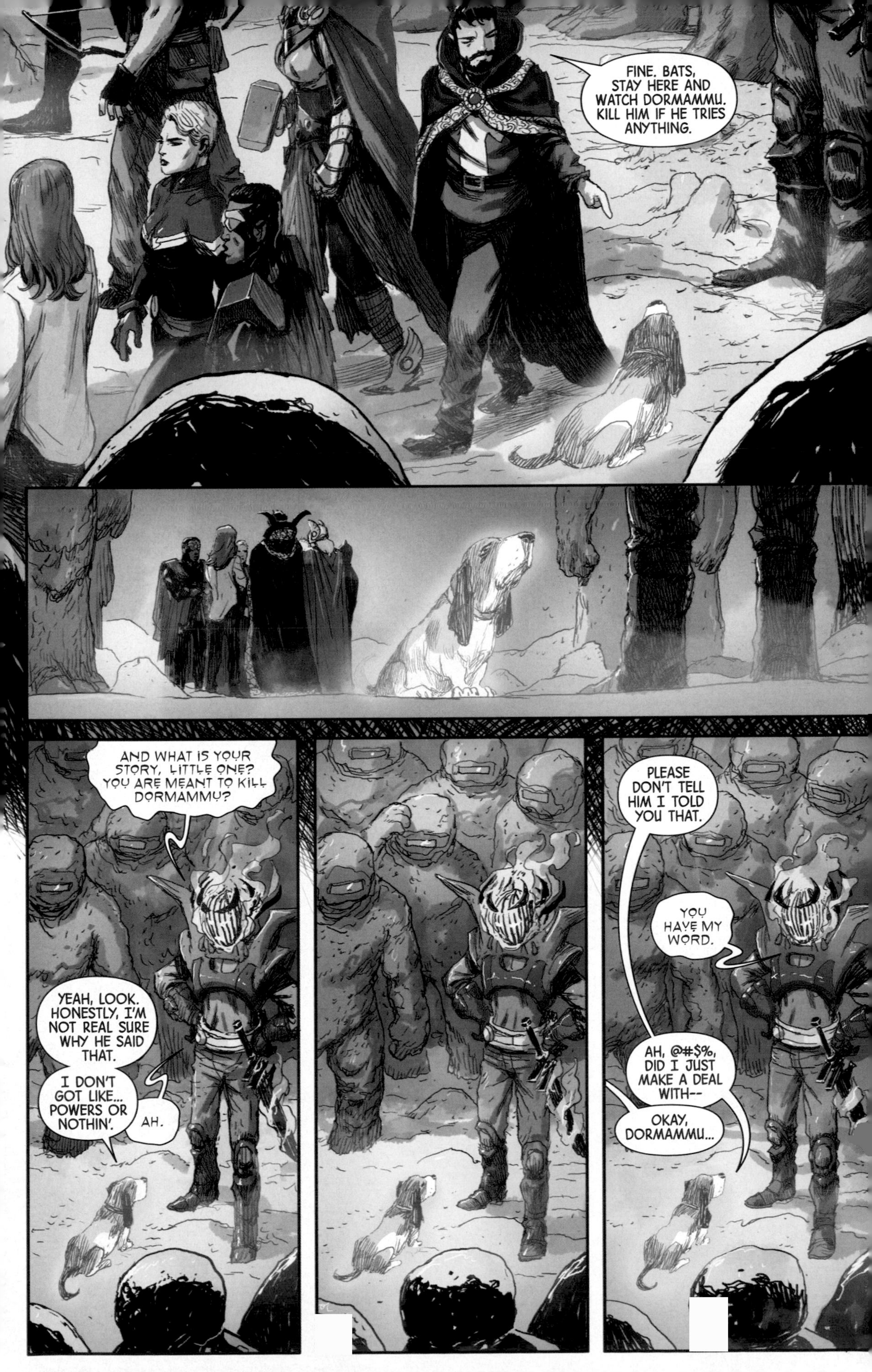
FINE. BATS, STAY HERE AND WATCH DORMAMMU. KILL HIM IF HE TRIES ANYTHING.
AND WHAT IS YOUR STORY, LITTLE ONE? YOU ARE MEANT TO KILL DORMAMMU?
YEAH, LOOK. HONESTLY, I'M NOT REAL SURE WHY HE SAID THAT.
I DON'T GOT LIKE... POWERS OR NOTHIN'.
AH.
PLEASE DON'T TELL HIM I TOLD YOU THAT.
YOU HAVE MY WORD.
AH, @#$%, DID I JUST MAKE A DEAL WITH--
OKAY, DORMAMMU...

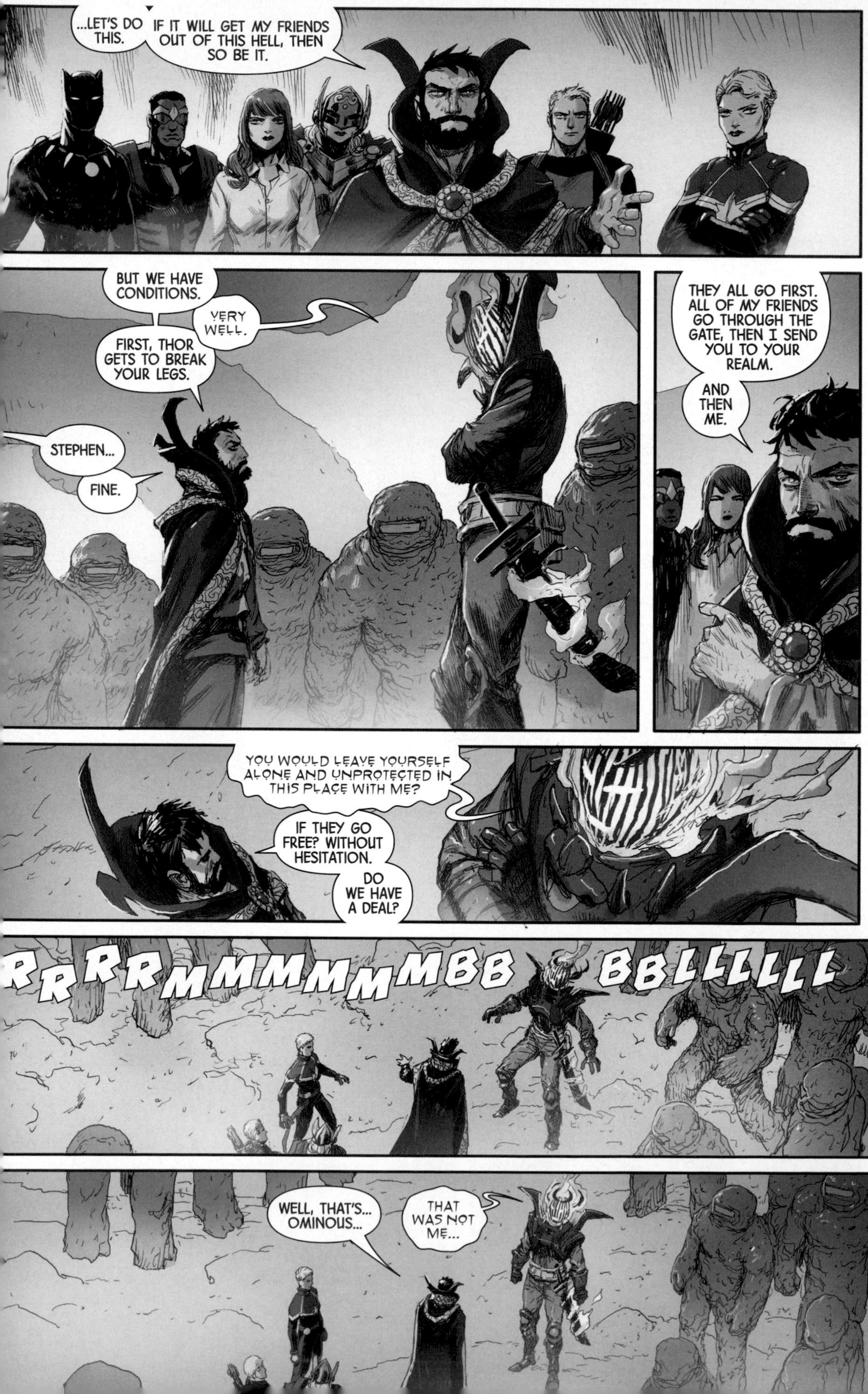

...LET'S DO THIS.
IF IT WILL GET MY FRIENDS OUT OF THIS HELL, THEN SO BE IT.
BUT WE HAVE CONDITIONS.
VERY WELL.
FIRST, THOR GETS TO BREAK YOUR LEGS.
STEPHEN...
FINE.
THEY ALL GO FIRST. ALL OF MY FRIENDS GO THROUGH THE GATE, THEN I SEND YOU TO YOUR REALM.
AND THEN ME.
YOU WOULD LEAVE YOURSELF ALONE AND UNPROTECTED IN THIS PLACE WITH ME?
IF THEY GO FREE? WITHOUT HESITATION.
DO WE HAVE A DEAL?
RRRRMMMMMMMBB BBLLLLLL
WELL, THAT'S... OMINOUS...
THAT WAS NOT ME...

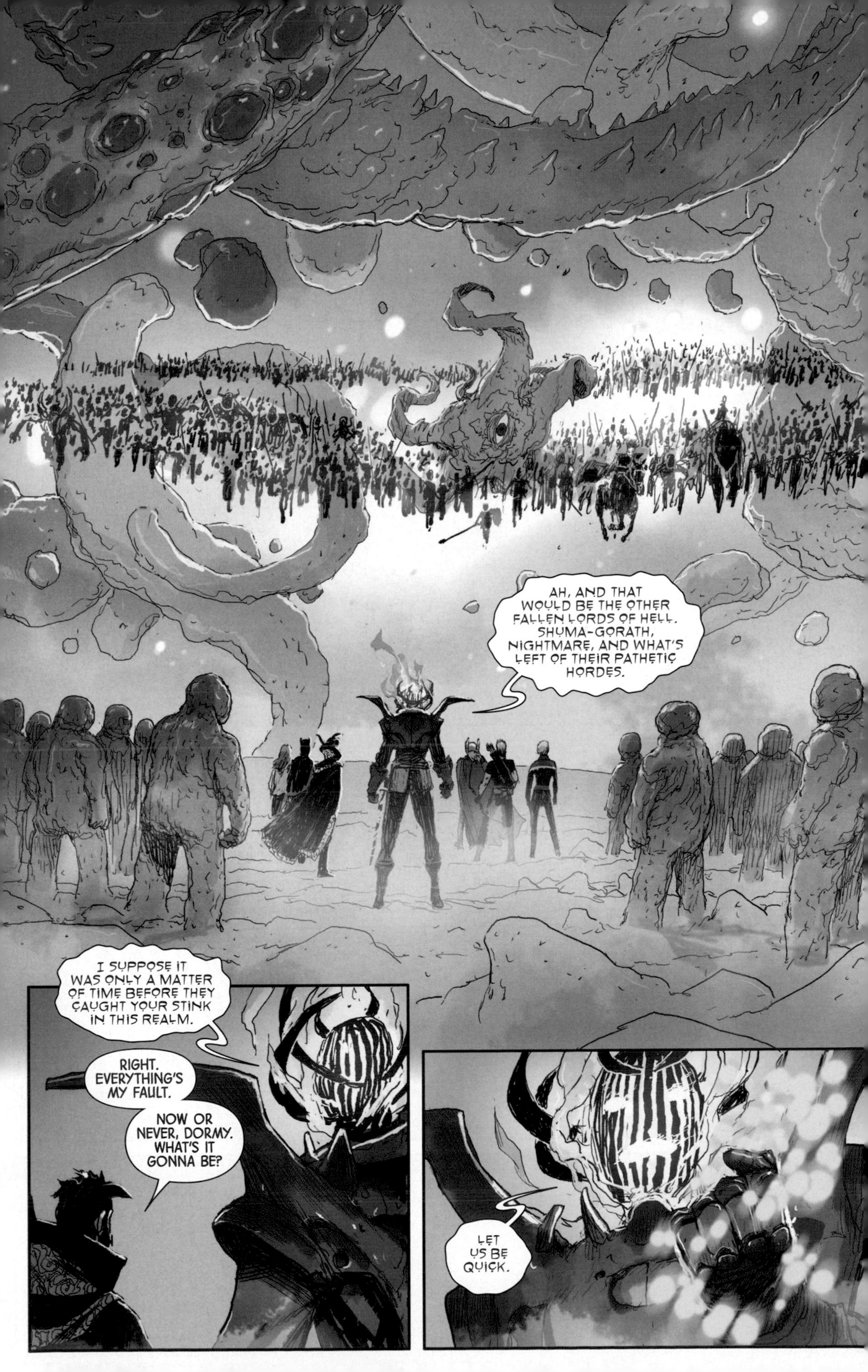
AH, AND THAT WOULD BE THE OTHER FALLEN LORDS OF HELL. SHUMA-GORATH, NIGHTMARE, AND WHAT'S LEFT OF THEIR PATHETIC HORDES.
I SUPPOSE IT WAS ONLY A MATTER OF TIME BEFORE THEY CAUGHT YOUR STINK IN THIS REALM.
RIGHT. EVERYTHING'S MY FAULT.
NOW OR NEVER, DORMY. WHAT'S IT GONNA BE?
LET US BE QUICK.

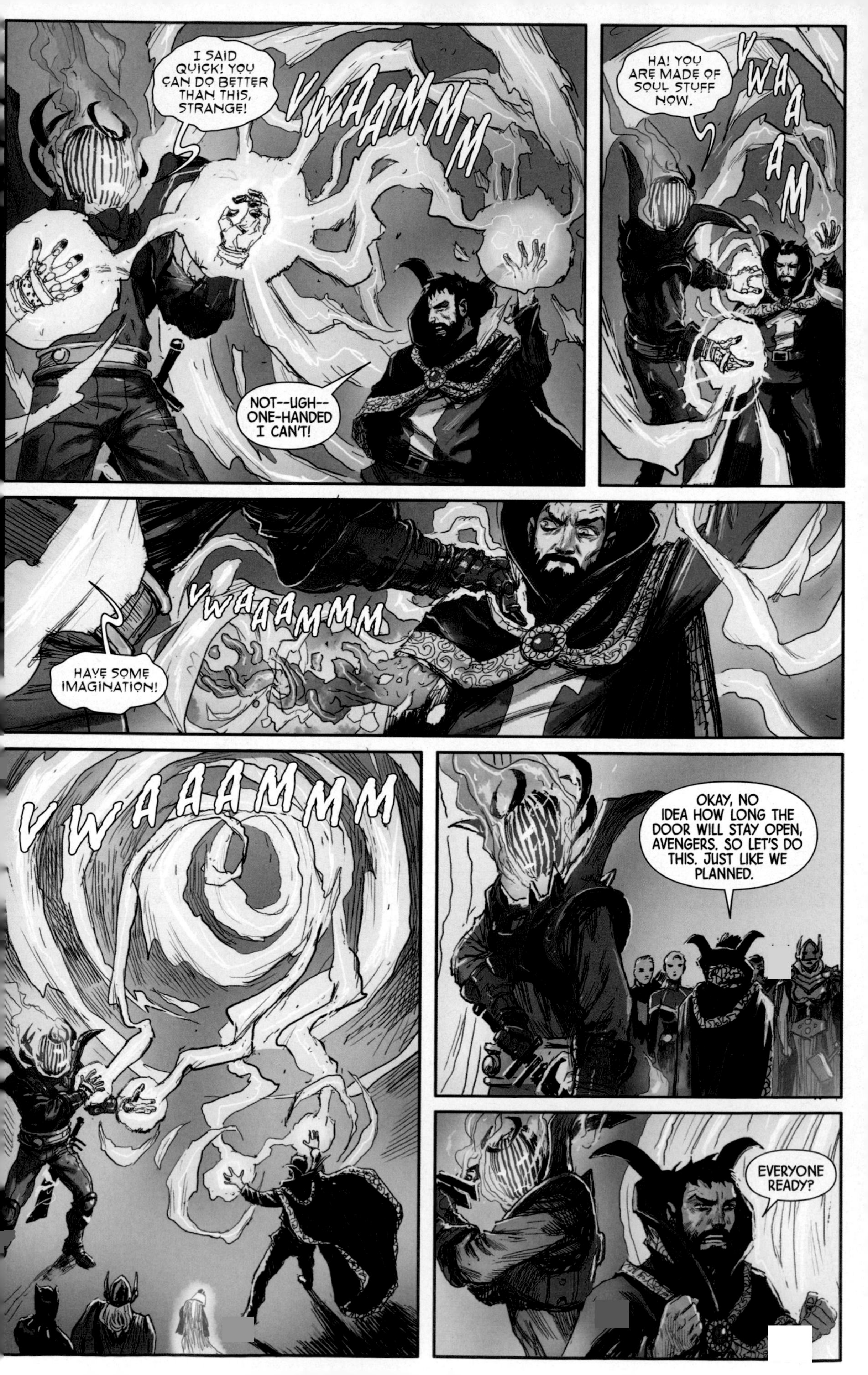
I SAID QUICK! YOU CAN DO BETTER THAN THIS, STRANGE!
VWAAMMM
NOT--UGH--ONE-HANDED I CAN'T!
HA! YOU ARE MADE OF SOUL STUFF NOW.
VWAAAM
VWAAAMMMM
HAVE SOME IMAGINATION!
VWAAAAMMMM
OKAY, NO IDEA HOW LONG THE DOOR WILL STAY OPEN, AVENGERS. SO LET'S DO THIS. JUST LIKE WE PLANNED.
EVERYONE READY?

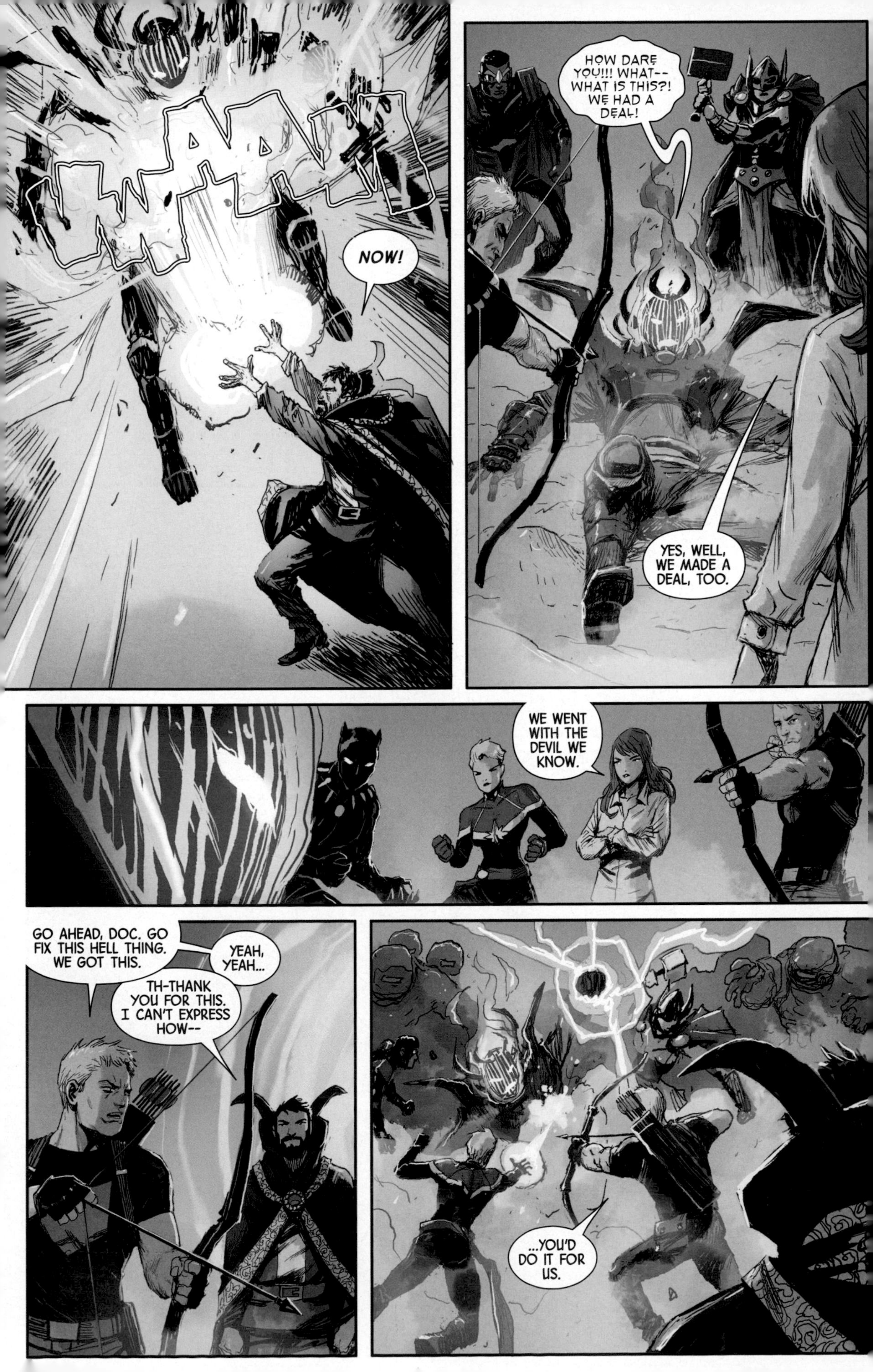
WHAAM
NOW!
HOW DARE YOU!!! WHAT-- WHAT IS THIS?! WE HAD A DEAL!
YES, WELL, WE MADE A DEAL, TOO.
WE WENT WITH THE DEVIL WE KNOW.
GO AHEAD, DOC. GO FIX THIS HELL THING. WE GOT THIS.
YEAH, YEAH...
TH-THANK YOU FOR THIS. I CAN'T EXPRESS HOW--
...YOU'D DO IT FOR US.

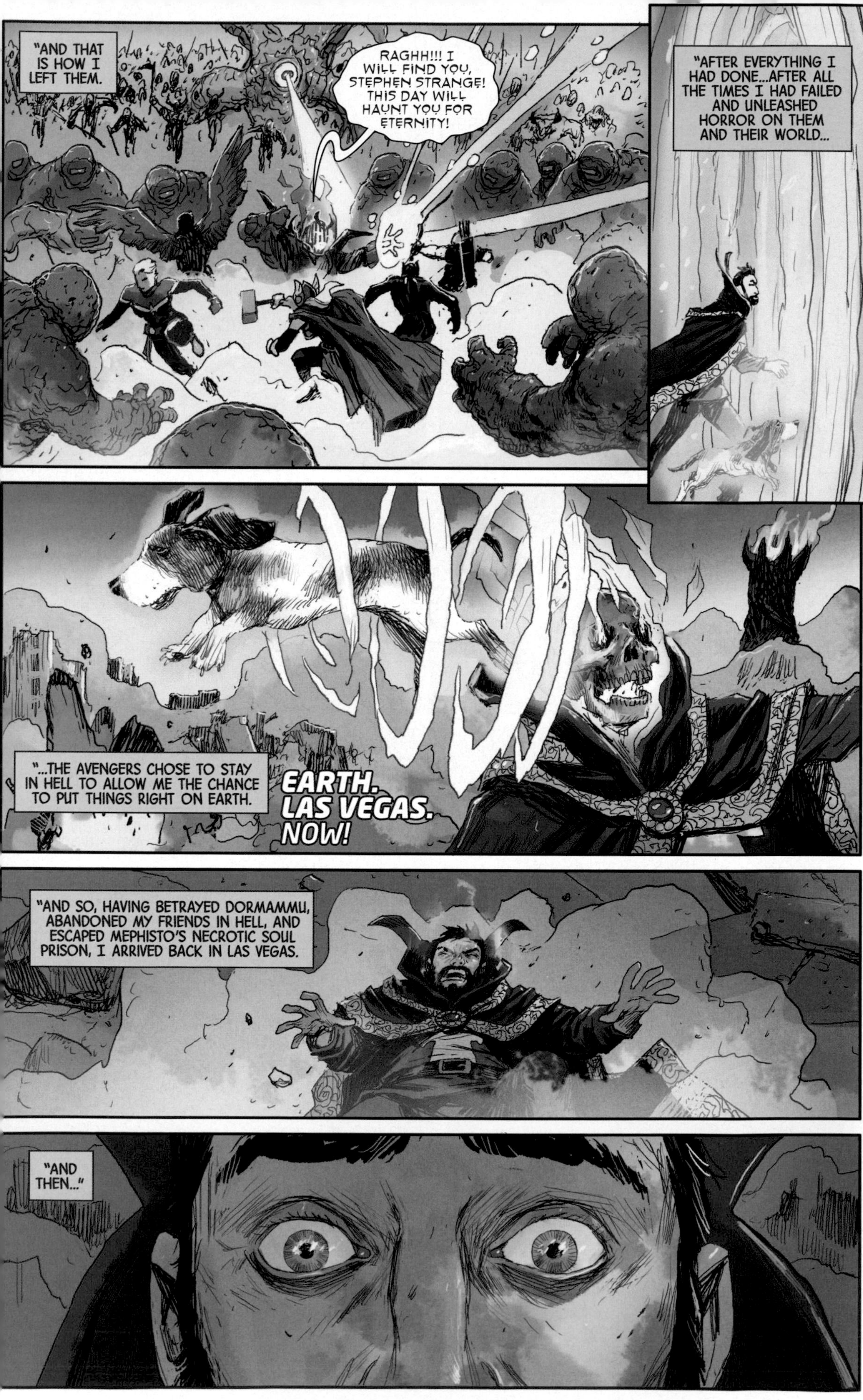
"AND THAT IS HOW I LEFT THEM.
RAGHH!!! I WILL FIND YOU, STEPHEN STRANGE! THIS DAY WILL HAUNT YOU FOR ETERNITY!
"AFTER EVERYTHING I HAD DONE...AFTER ALL THE TIMES I HAD FAILED AND UNLEASHED HORROR ON THEM AND THEIR WORLD...
"...THE AVENGERS CHOSE TO STAY IN HELL TO ALLOW ME THE CHANCE TO PUT THINGS RIGHT ON EARTH.
EARTH. LAS VEGAS. NOW!
"AND SO, HAVING BETRAYED DORMAMMU, ABANDONED MY FRIENDS IN HELL, AND ESCAPED MEPHISTO'S NECROTIC SOUL PRISON, I ARRIVED BACK IN LAS VEGAS.
"AND THEN..."

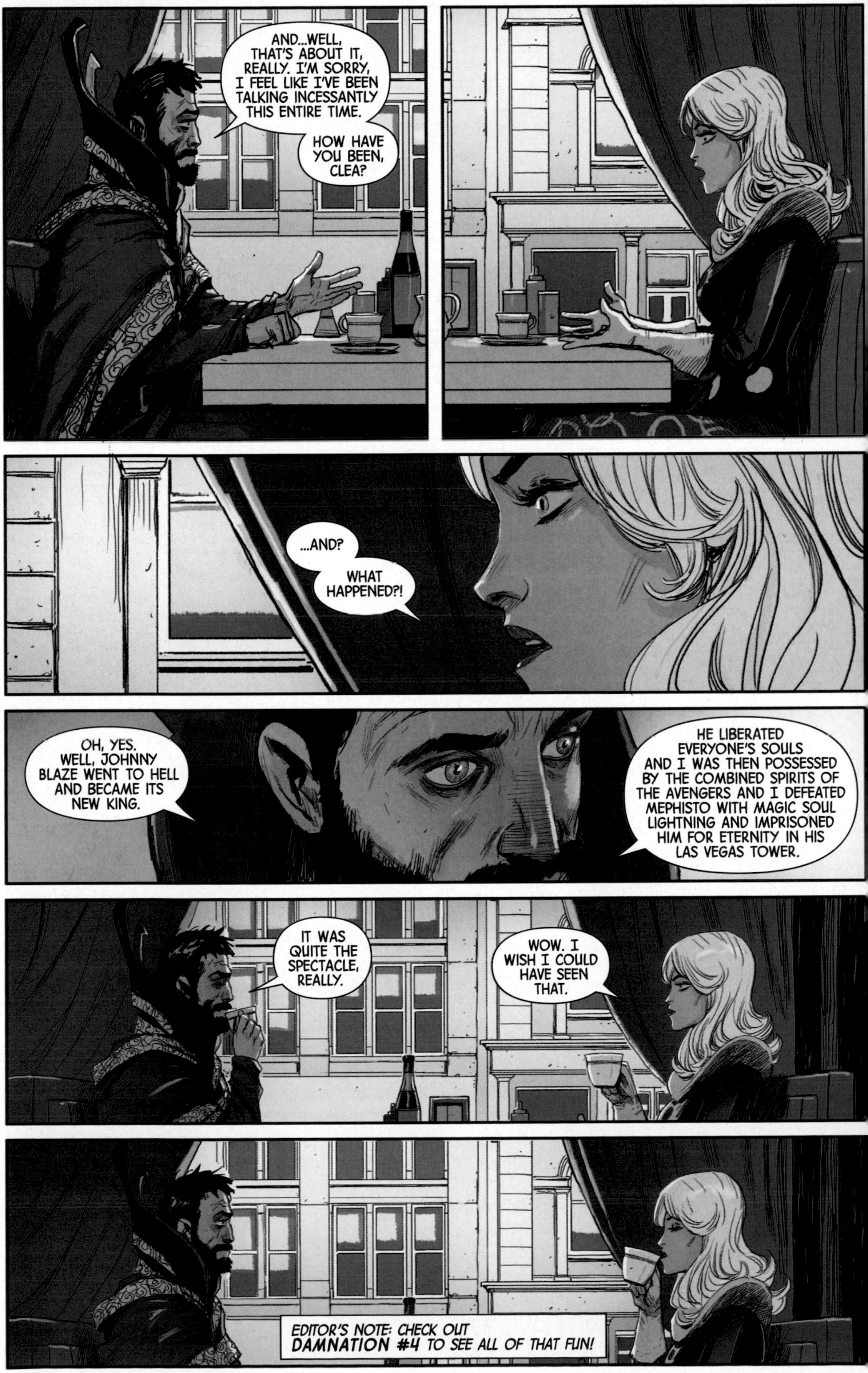
AND...WELL, THAT'S ABOUT IT, REALLY. I'M SORRY, I FEEL LIKE I'VE BEEN TALKING INCESSANTLY THIS ENTIRE TIME.
HOW HAVE YOU BEEN, CLEA?
...AND?
WHAT HAPPENED?!
OH, YES. WELL, JOHNNY BLAZE WENT TO HELL AND BECAME ITS NEW KING.
HE LIBERATED EVERYONE'S SOULS AND I WAS THEN POSSESSED BY THE COMBINED SPIRITS OF THE AVENGERS AND I DEFEATED MEPHISTO WITH MAGIC SOUL LIGHTNING AND IMPRISONED HIM FOR ETERNITY IN HIS LAS VEGAS TOWER.
IT WAS QUITE THE SPECTACLE, REALLY.
WOW. I WISH I COULD HAVE SEEN THAT.
EDITOR'S NOTE: CHECK OUT DAMNATION #4 TO SEE ALL OF THAT FUN!

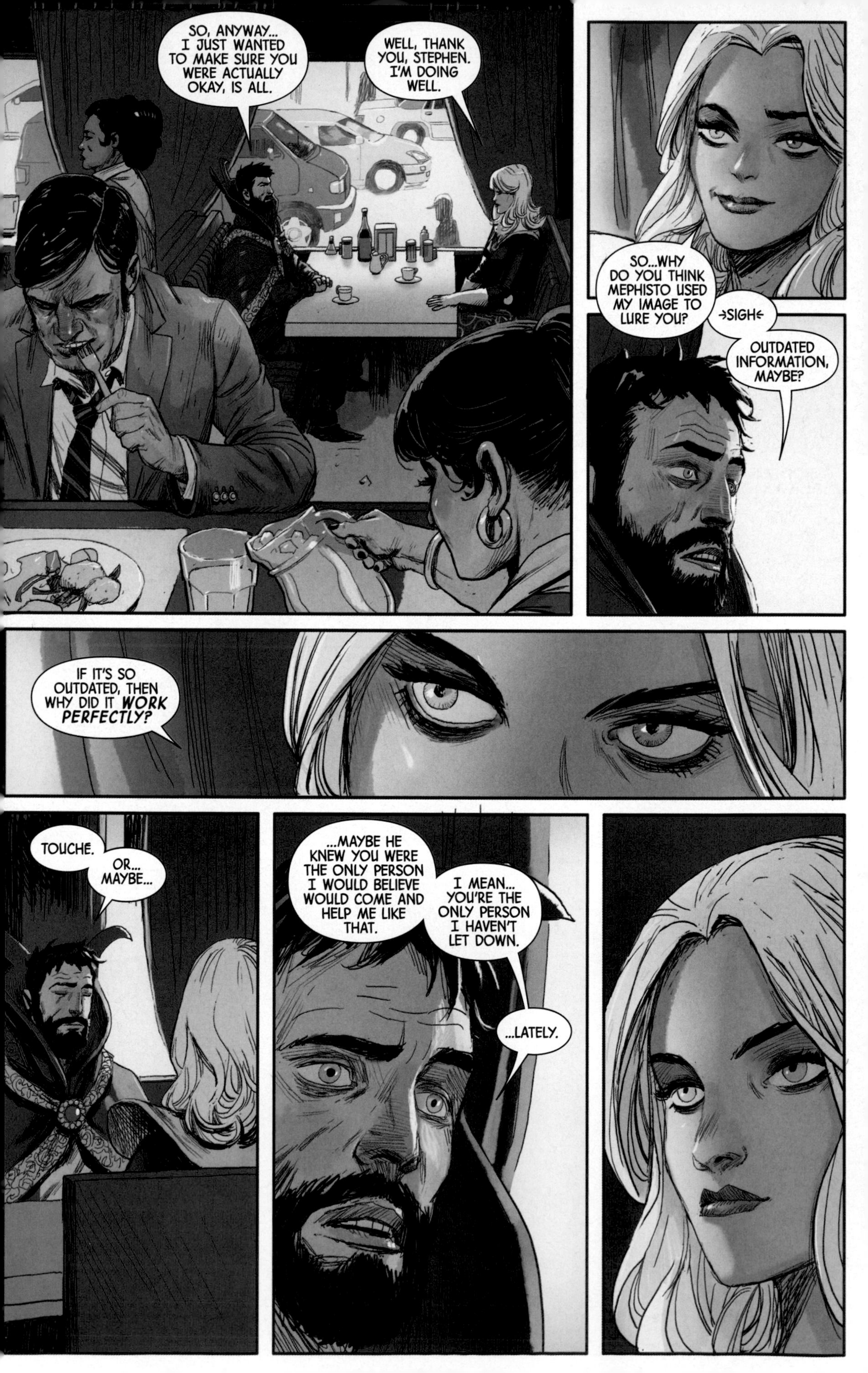
SO, ANYWAY... I JUST WANTED TO MAKE SURE YOU WERE ACTUALLY OKAY, IS ALL.
WELL, THANK YOU, STEPHEN. I'M DOING WELL.
SO...WHY DO YOU THINK MEPHISTO USED MY IMAGE TO LURE YOU?
→SIGH←
OUTDATED INFORMATION, MAYBE?
IF IT'S SO OUTDATED, THEN WHY DID IT *WORK PERFECTLY?*
TOUCHE.
OR... MAYBE...
...MAYBE HE KNEW YOU WERE THE ONLY PERSON I WOULD BELIEVE WOULD COME AND HELP ME LIKE THAT.
I MEAN... YOU'RE THE ONLY PERSON I HAVEN'T LET DOWN.
...LATELY.

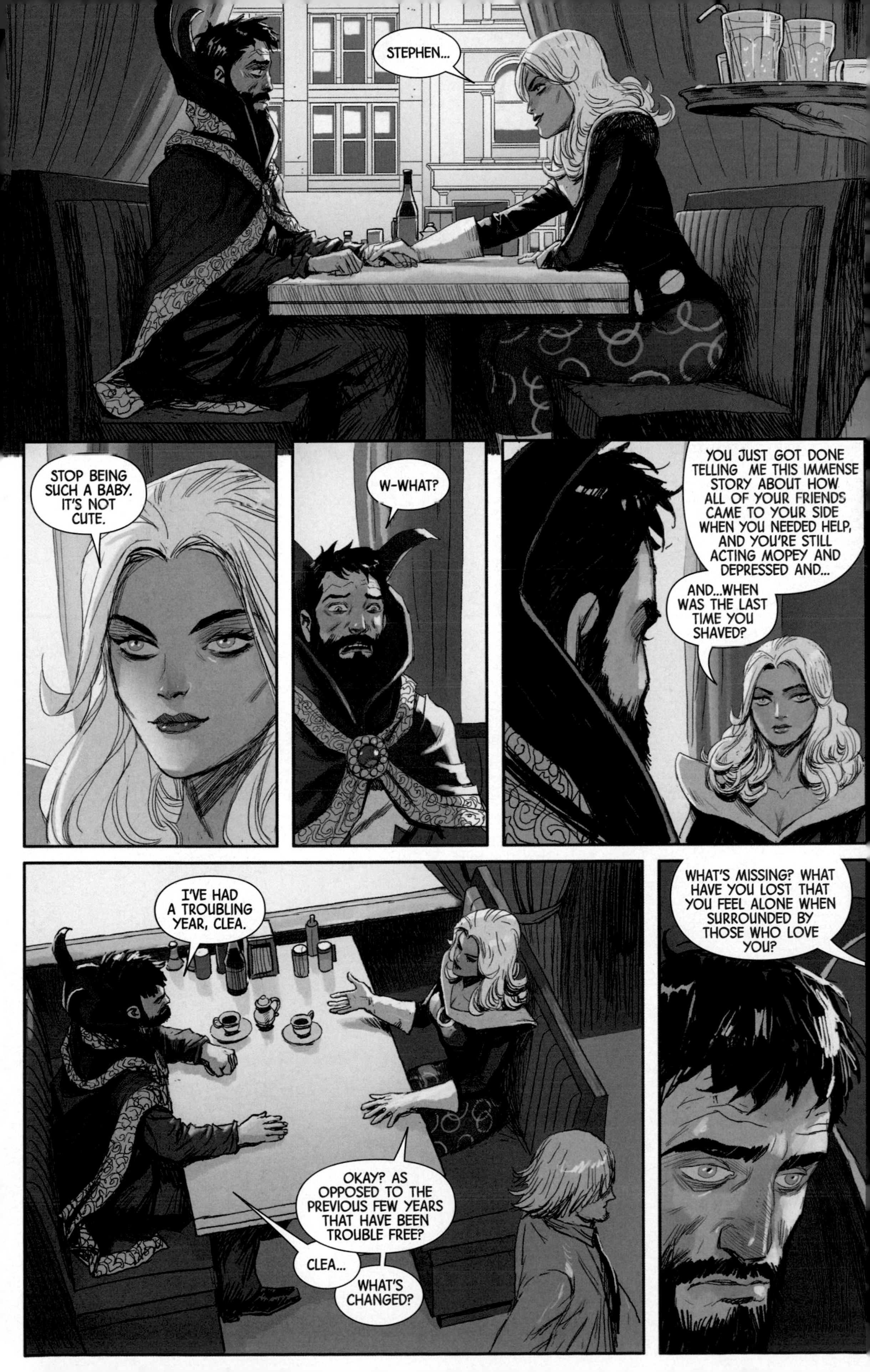
STEPHEN...
STOP BEING SUCH A BABY. IT'S NOT CUTE.
W-WHAT?
YOU JUST GOT DONE TELLING ME THIS IMMENSE STORY ABOUT HOW ALL OF YOUR FRIENDS CAME TO YOUR SIDE WHEN YOU NEEDED HELP, AND YOU'RE STILL ACTING MOPEY AND DEPRESSED AND...
AND...WHEN WAS THE LAST TIME YOU SHAVED?
I'VE HAD A TROUBLING YEAR, CLEA.
OKAY? AS OPPOSED TO THE PREVIOUS FEW YEARS THAT HAVE BEEN TROUBLE FREE?
CLEA...
WHAT'S CHANGED?
WHAT'S MISSING? WHAT HAVE YOU LOST THAT YOU FEEL ALONE WHEN SURROUNDED BY THOSE WHO LOVE YOU?

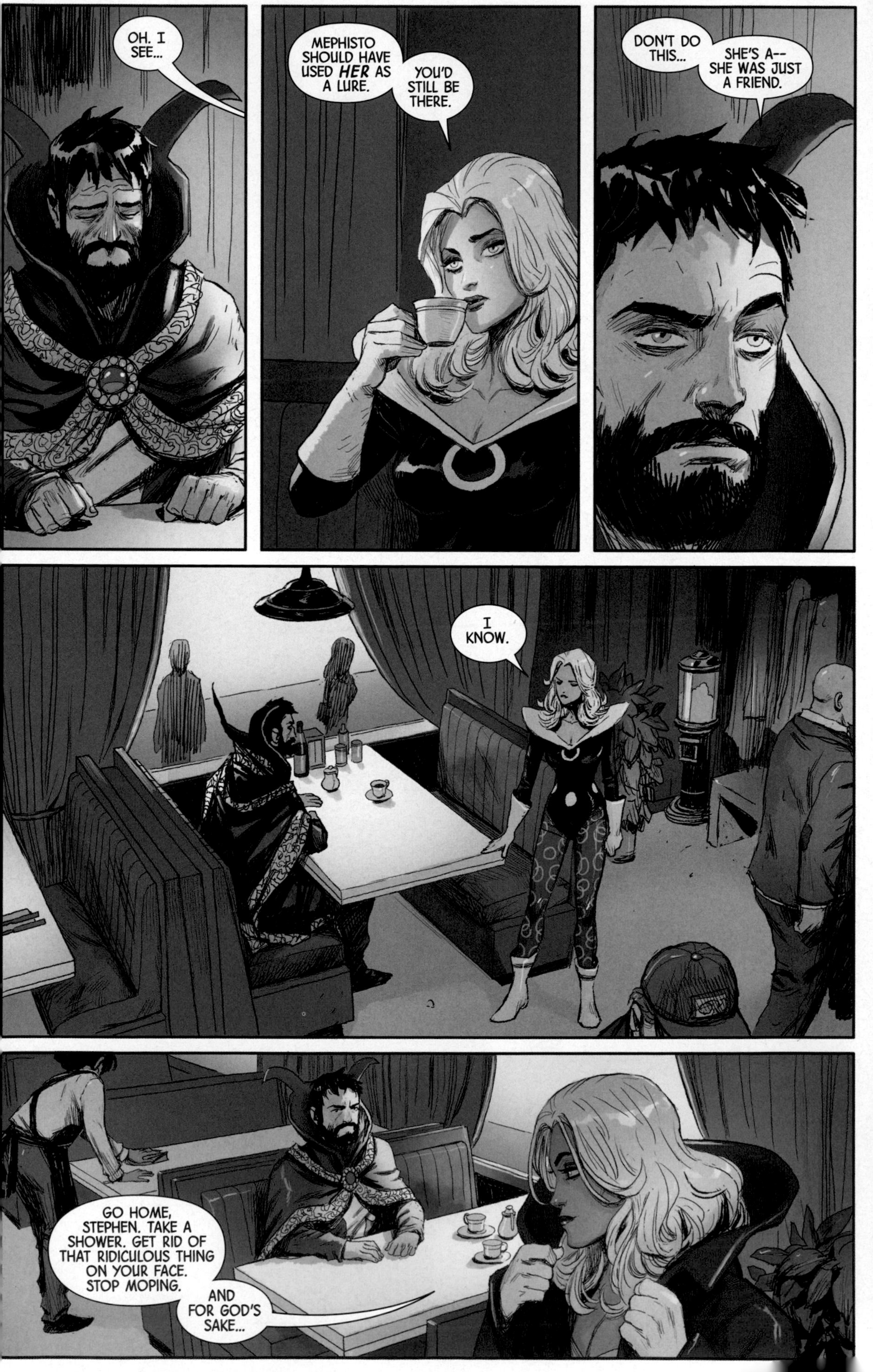
OH. I SEE...
MEPHISTO SHOULD HAVE USED *HER* AS A LURE.
YOU'D STILL BE THERE.
DON'T DO THIS...
SHE'S A-- SHE WAS JUST A FRIEND.
I KNOW.
GO HOME, STEPHEN. TAKE A SHOWER. GET RID OF THAT RIDICULOUS THING ON YOUR FACE. STOP MOPING.
AND FOR GOD'S SAKE...

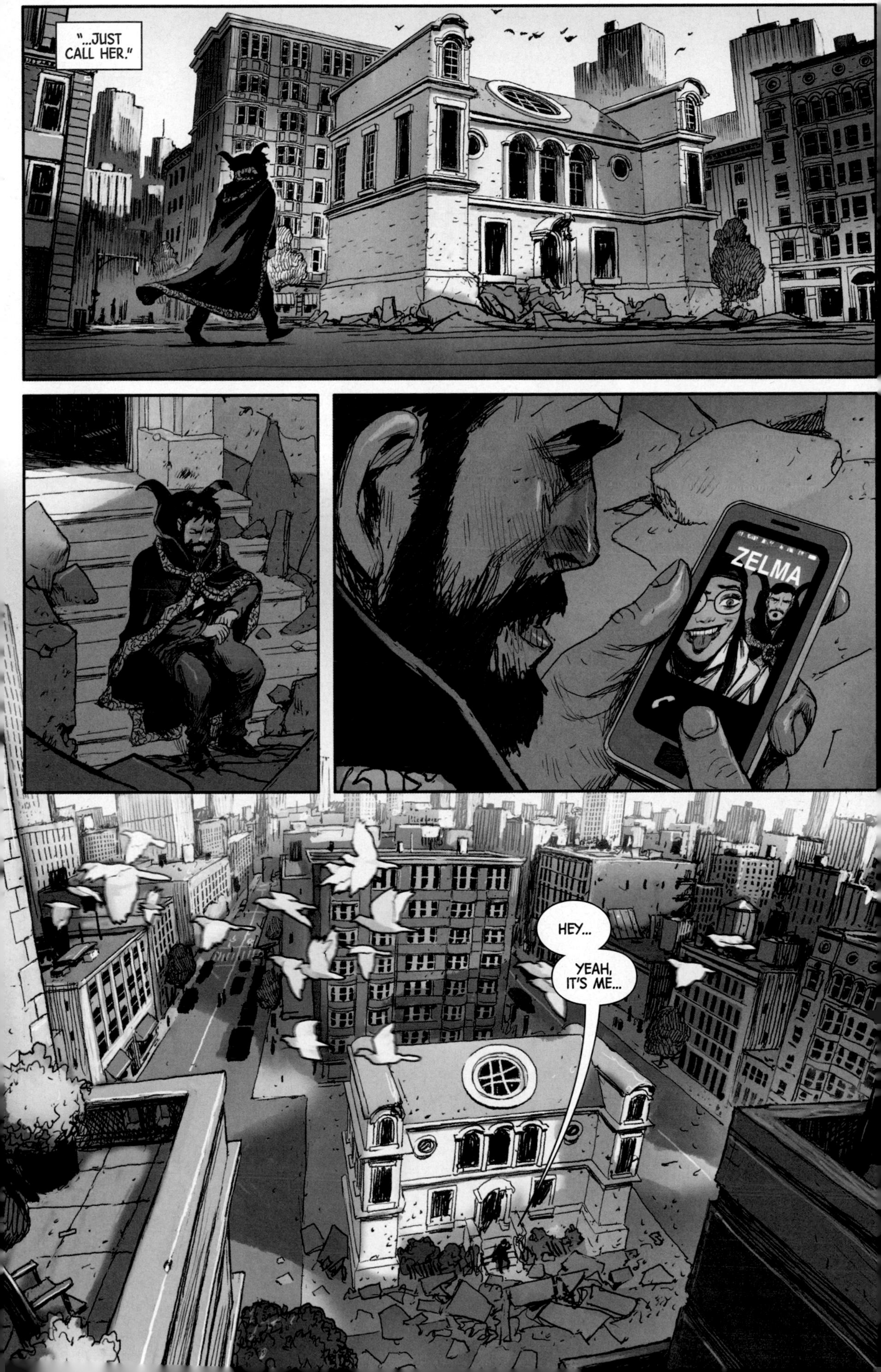
"...JUST CALL HER."
ZELMA
HEY...
YEAH, IT'S ME...

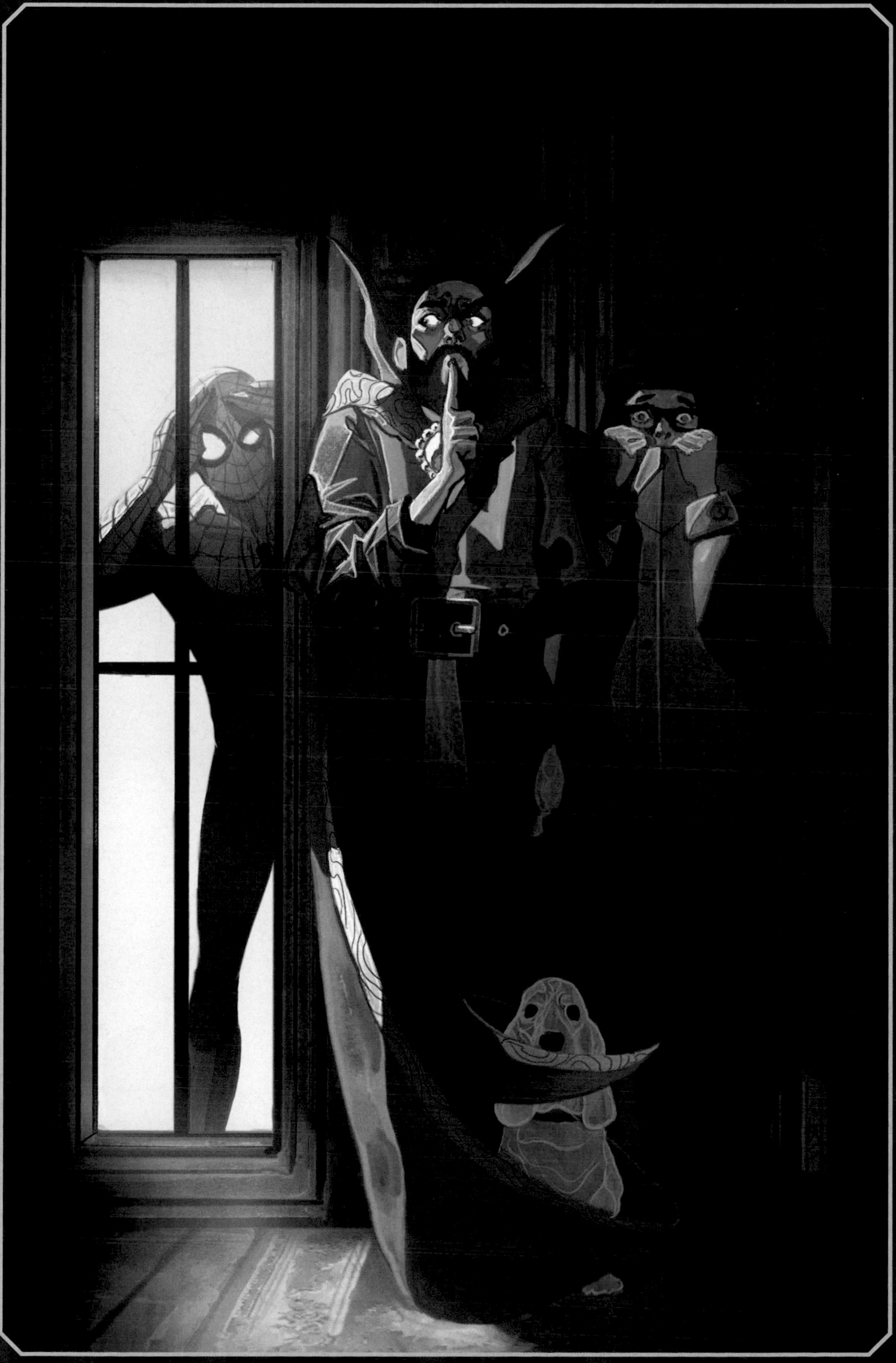

390

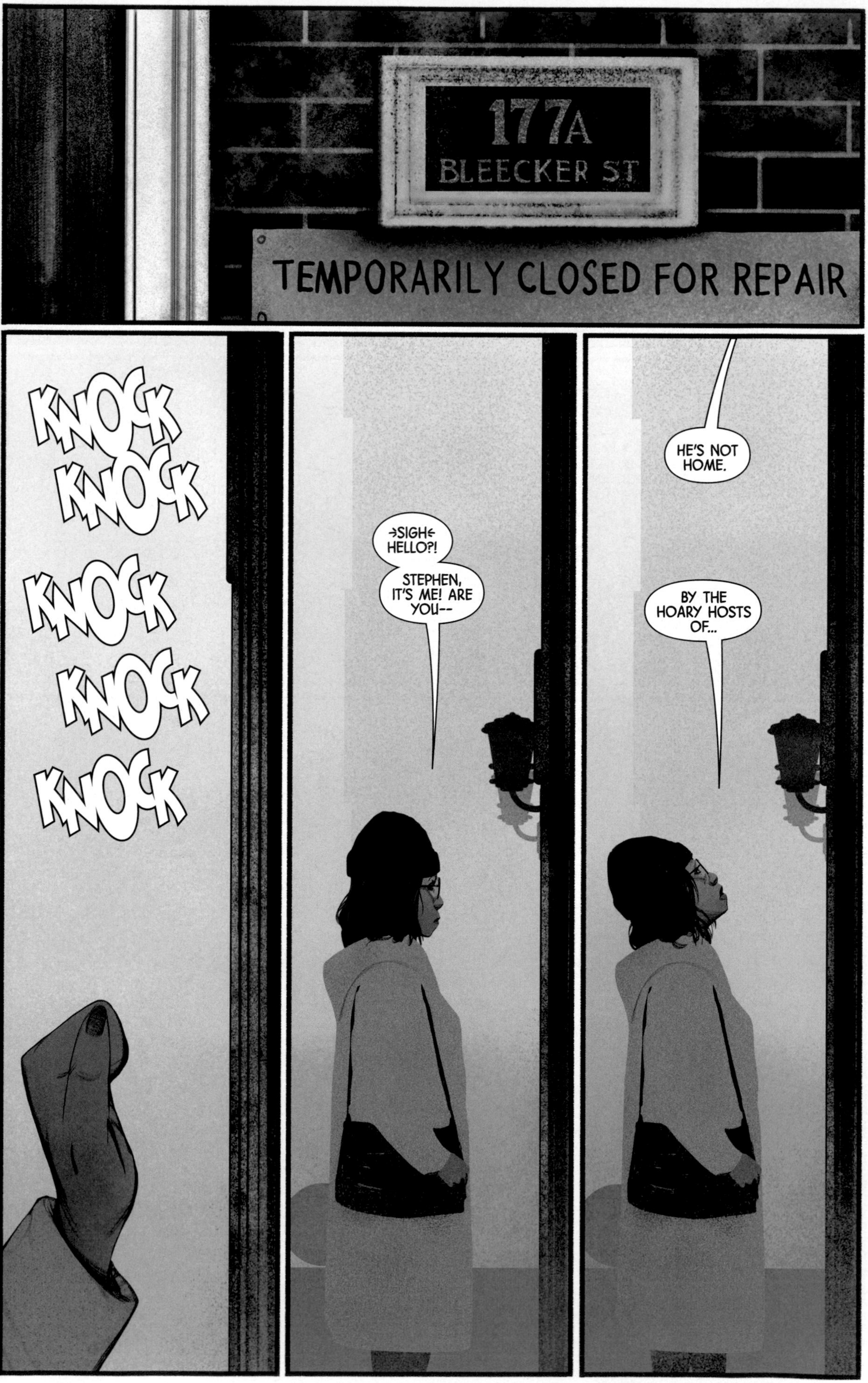
177A
BLEECKER ST
TEMPORARILY CLOSED FOR REPAIR
KNOCK
KNOCK
KNOCK
KNOCK
KNOCK
→SIGH← HELLO?!
STEPHEN, IT'S ME! ARE YOU--
HE'S NOT HOME.
BY THE HOARY HOSTS OF...

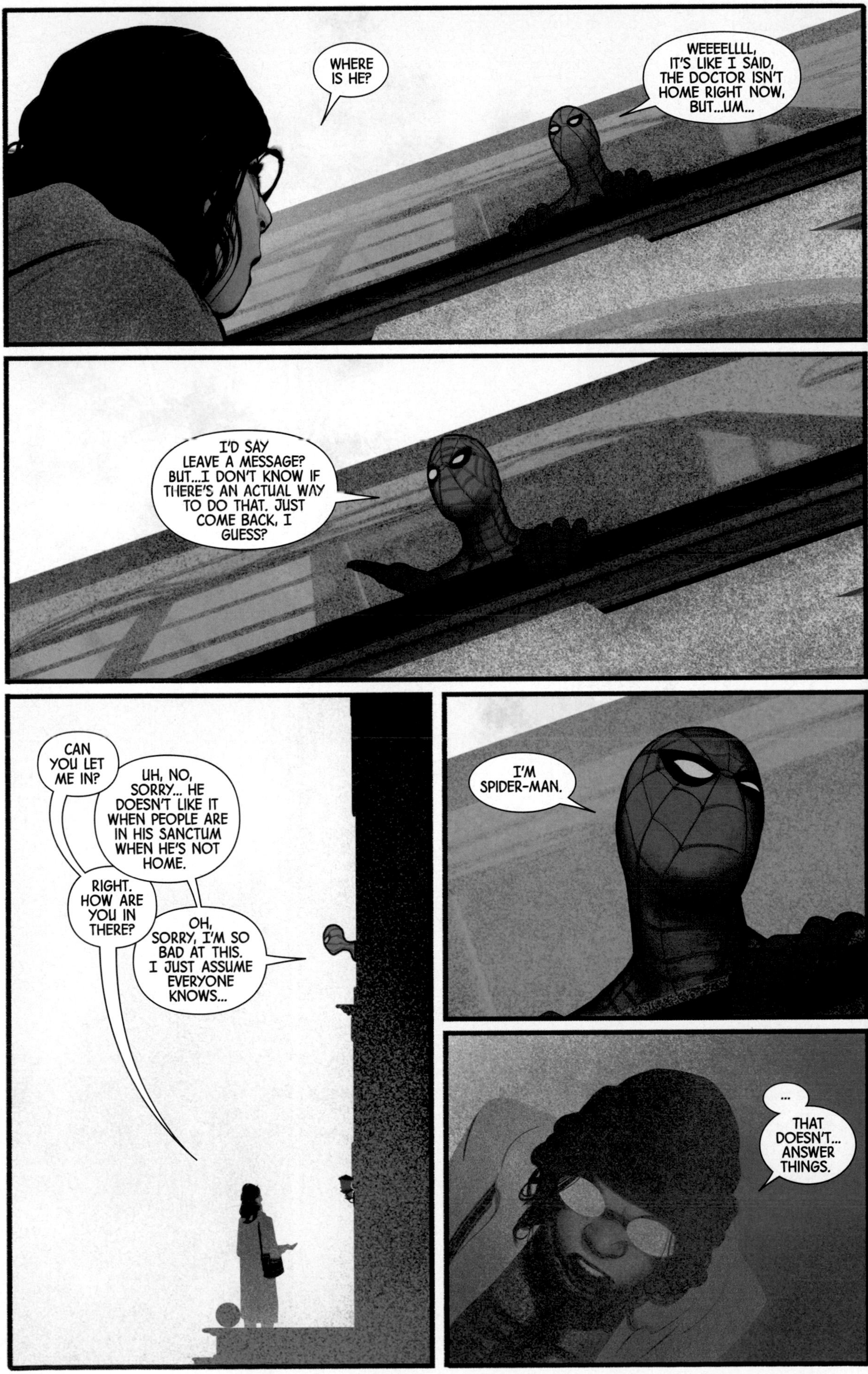
WHERE IS HE?
WEEEELLLL, IT'S LIKE I SAID, THE DOCTOR ISN'T HOME RIGHT NOW, BUT...UM...
I'D SAY LEAVE A MESSAGE? BUT...I DON'T KNOW IF THERE'S AN ACTUAL WAY TO DO THAT. JUST COME BACK, I GUESS?
CAN YOU LET ME IN?
UH, NO, SORRY... HE DOESN'T LIKE IT WHEN PEOPLE ARE IN HIS SANCTUM WHEN HE'S NOT HOME.
RIGHT. HOW ARE YOU IN THERE?
OH, SORRY, I'M SO BAD AT THIS. I JUST ASSUME EVERYONE KNOWS...
I'M SPIDER-MAN.
...
THAT DOESN'T... ANSWER THINGS.

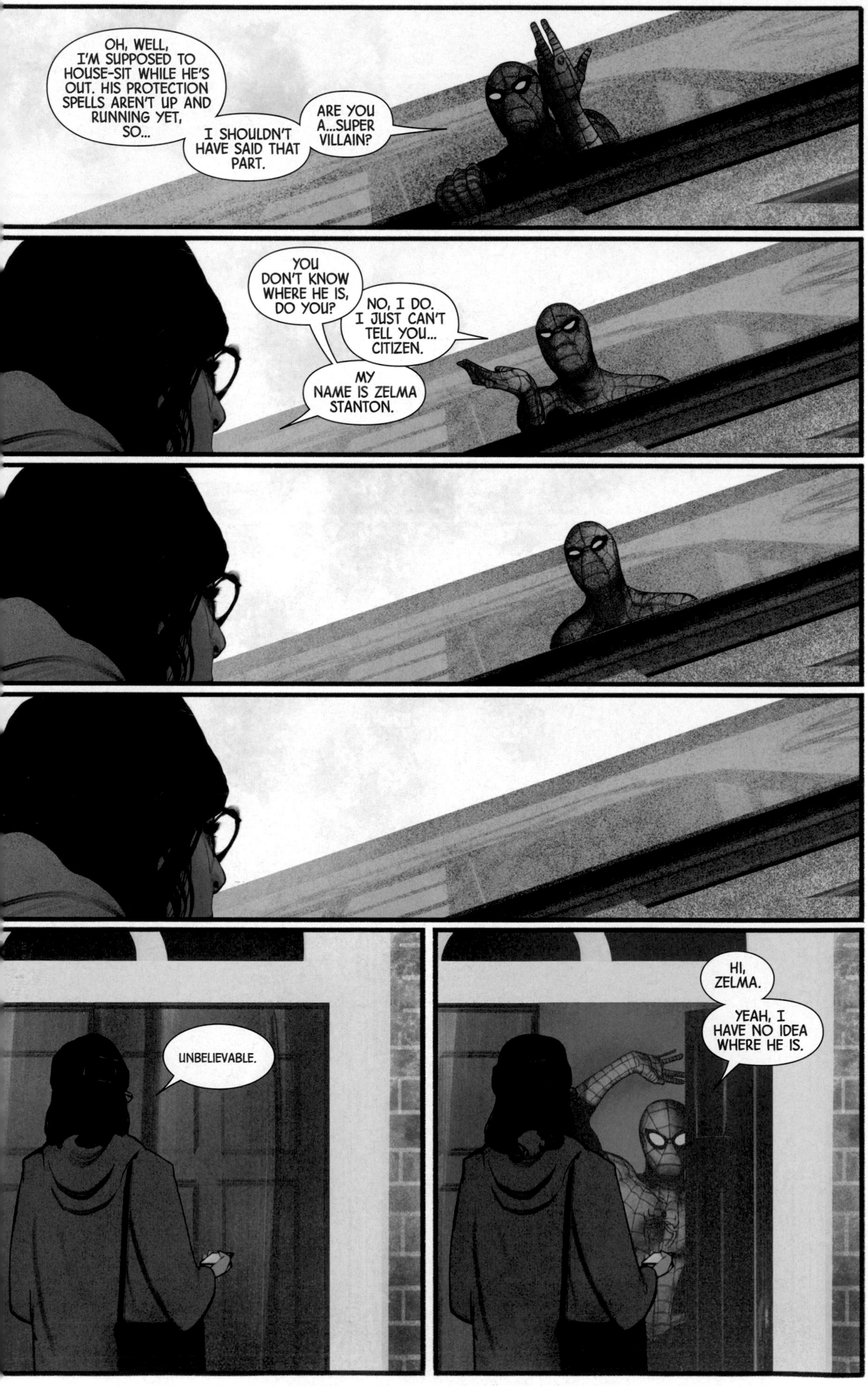
OH, WELL, I'M SUPPOSED TO HOUSE-SIT WHILE HE'S OUT. HIS PROTECTION SPELLS AREN'T UP AND RUNNING YET, SO...
I SHOULDN'T HAVE SAID THAT PART.
ARE YOU A...SUPER VILLAIN?
YOU DON'T KNOW WHERE HE IS, DO YOU?
NO, I DO. I JUST CAN'T TELL YOU... CITIZEN.
MY NAME IS ZELMA STANTON.
UNBELIEVABLE.
HI, ZELMA.
YEAH, I HAVE NO IDEA WHERE HE IS.

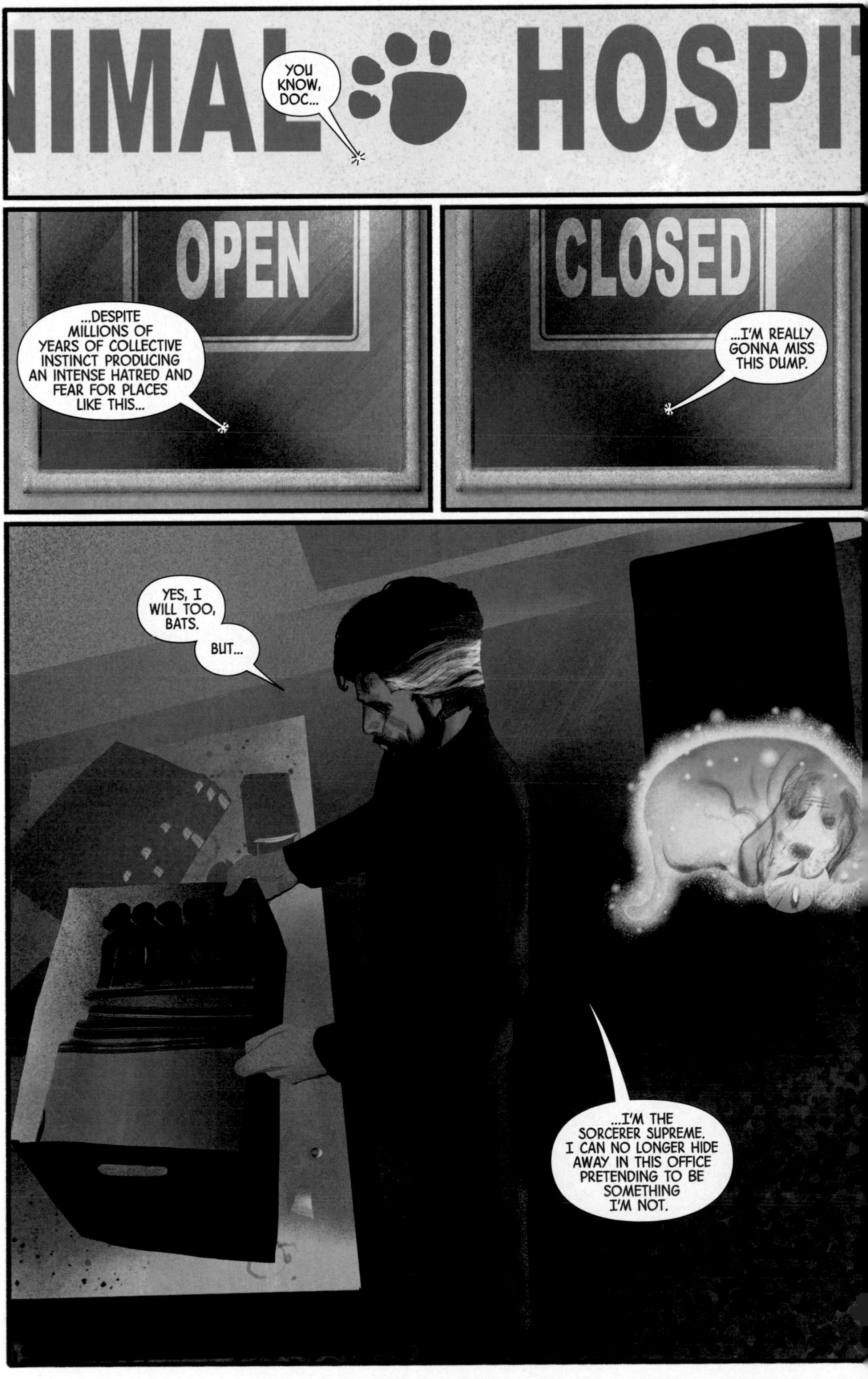
NIMAL HOSPIT
YOU KNOW, DOC...
OPEN
...DESPITE MILLIONS OF YEARS OF COLLECTIVE INSTINCT PRODUCING AN INTENSE HATRED AND FEAR FOR PLACES LIKE THIS...
CLOSED
...I'M REALLY GONNA MISS THIS DUMP.
YES, I WILL TOO, BATS.
BUT...
...I'M THE SORCERER SUPREME. I CAN NO LONGER HIDE AWAY IN THIS OFFICE PRETENDING TO BE SOMETHING I'M NOT.

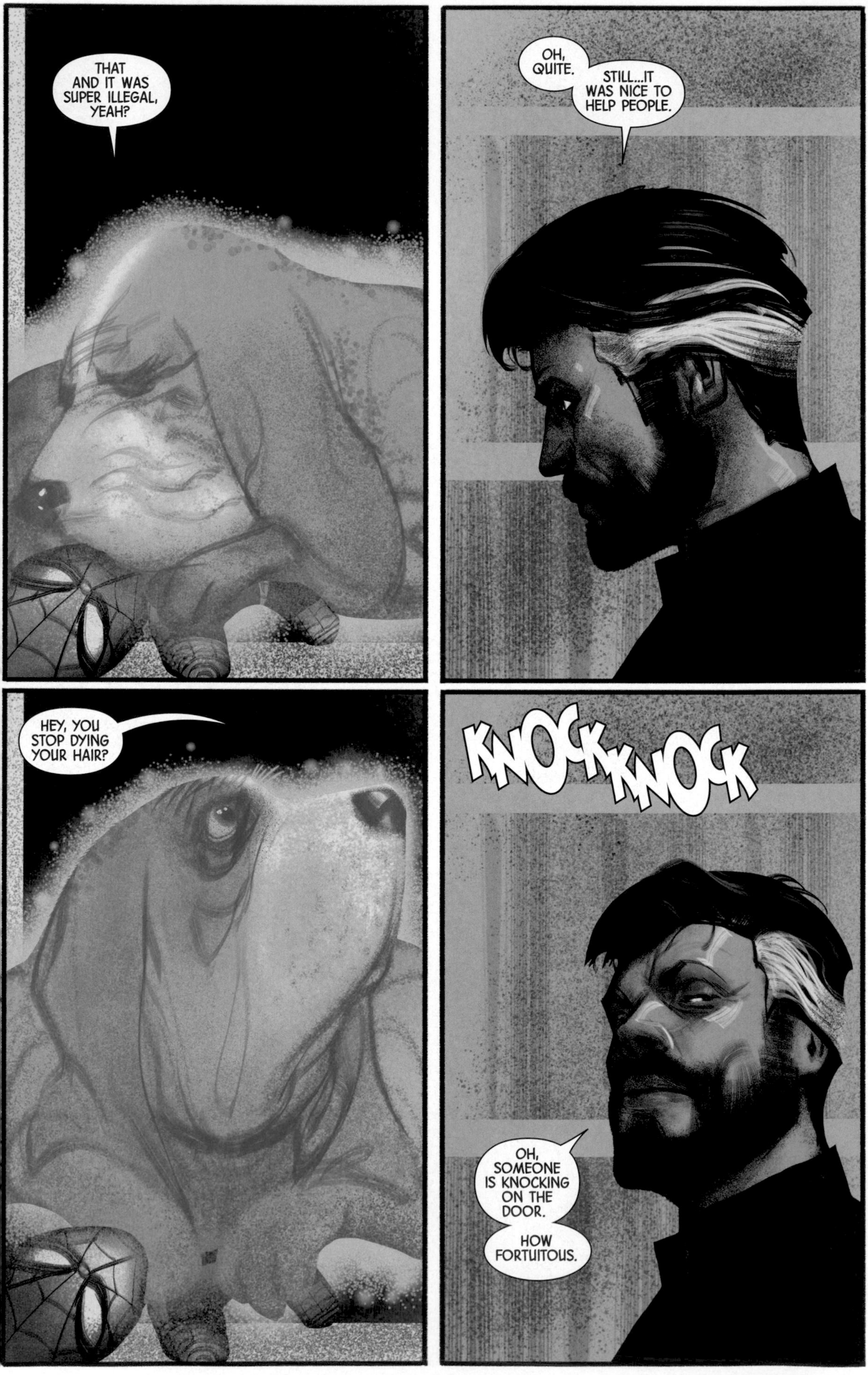
THAT AND IT WAS SUPER ILLEGAL, YEAH?
OH, QUITE.
STILL...IT WAS NICE TO HELP PEOPLE.
HEY, YOU STOP DYING YOUR HAIR?
KNOCK KNOCK
OH, SOMEONE IS KNOCKING ON THE DOOR.
HOW FORTUITOUS.

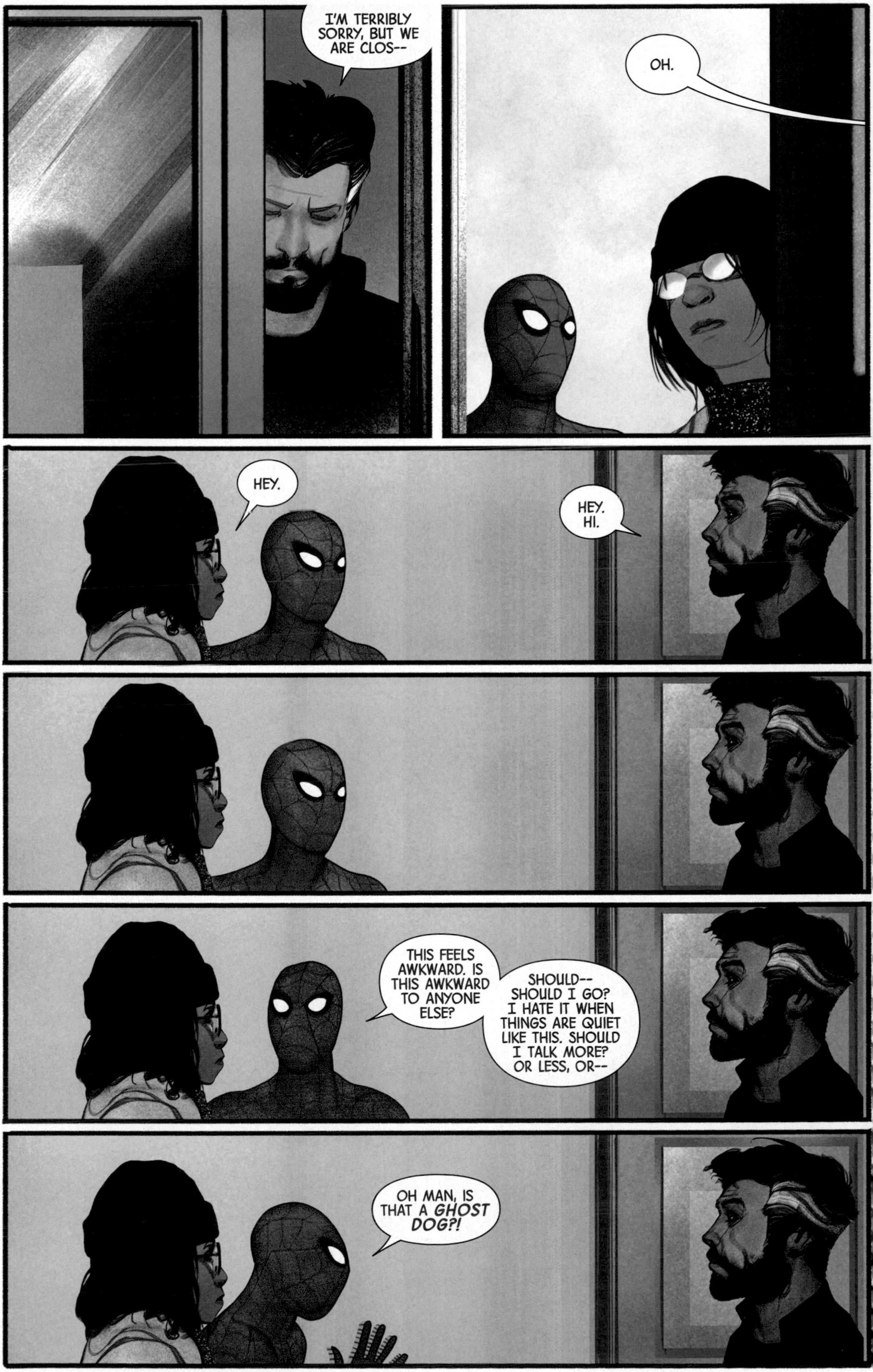
I'M TERRIBLY SORRY, BUT WE ARE CLOS--
OH.
HEY.
HEY. HI.
THIS FEELS AWKWARD. IS THIS AWKWARD TO ANYONE ELSE?
SHOULD-- SHOULD I GO? I HATE IT WHEN THINGS ARE QUIET LIKE THIS. SHOULD I TALK MORE? OR LESS, OR--
OH MAN, IS THAT A *GHOST DOG?!*

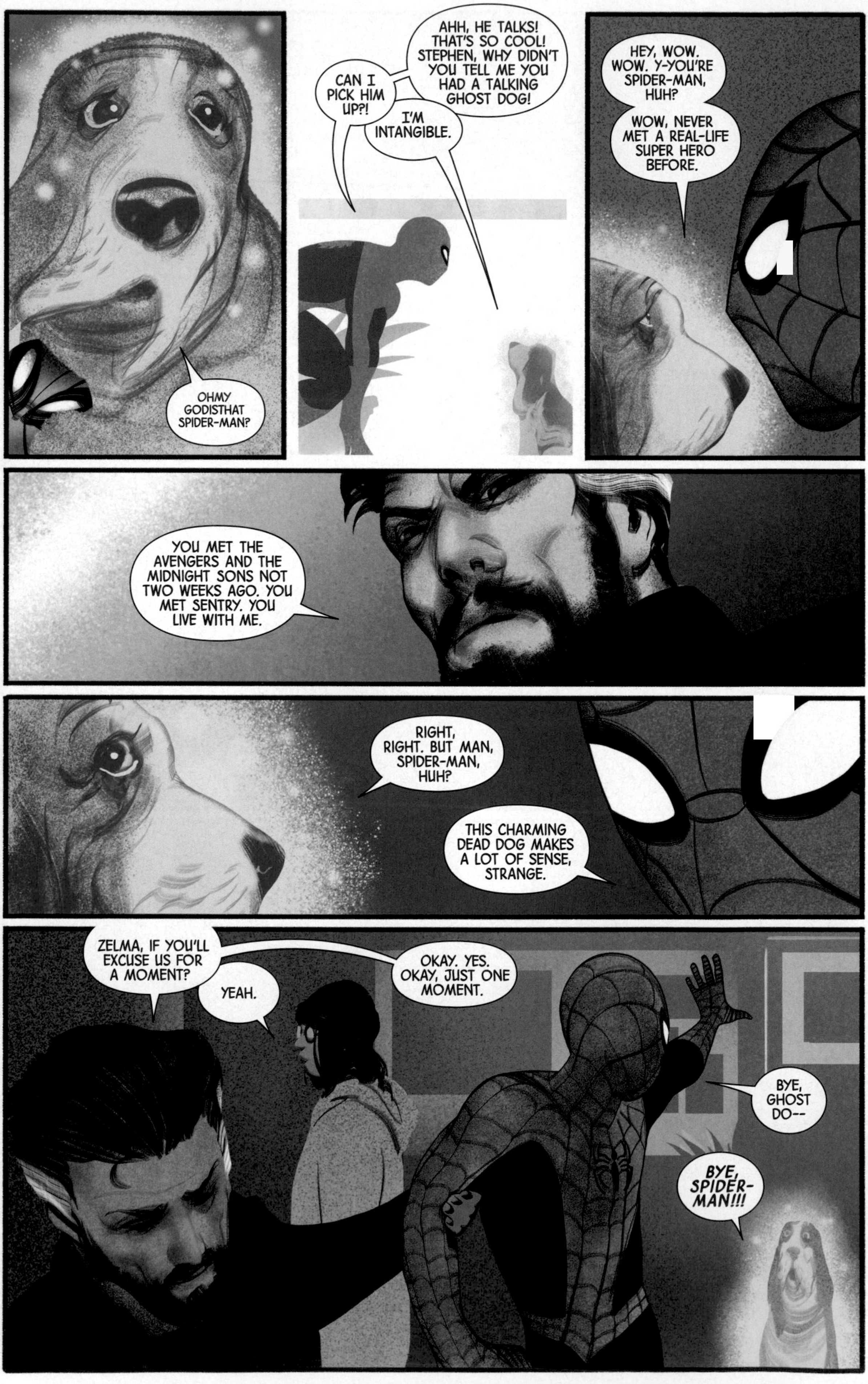
OHMY GODISTHAT SPIDER-MAN?
CAN I PICK HIM UP?!
AHH, HE TALKS! THAT'S SO COOL! STEPHEN, WHY DIDN'T YOU TELL ME YOU HAD A TALKING GHOST DOG!
I'M INTANGIBLE.
HEY, WOW. WOW. Y-YOU'RE SPIDER-MAN, HUH?
WOW, NEVER MET A REAL-LIFE SUPER HERO BEFORE.
YOU MET THE AVENGERS AND THE MIDNIGHT SONS NOT TWO WEEKS AGO. YOU MET SENTRY. YOU LIVE WITH ME.
RIGHT, RIGHT. BUT MAN, SPIDER-MAN, HUH?
THIS CHARMING DEAD DOG MAKES A LOT OF SENSE, STRANGE.
ZELMA, IF YOU'LL EXCUSE US FOR A MOMENT?
YEAH.
OKAY. YES. OKAY, JUST ONE MOMENT.
BYE, GHOST DO--
BYE, SPIDER-MAN!!!

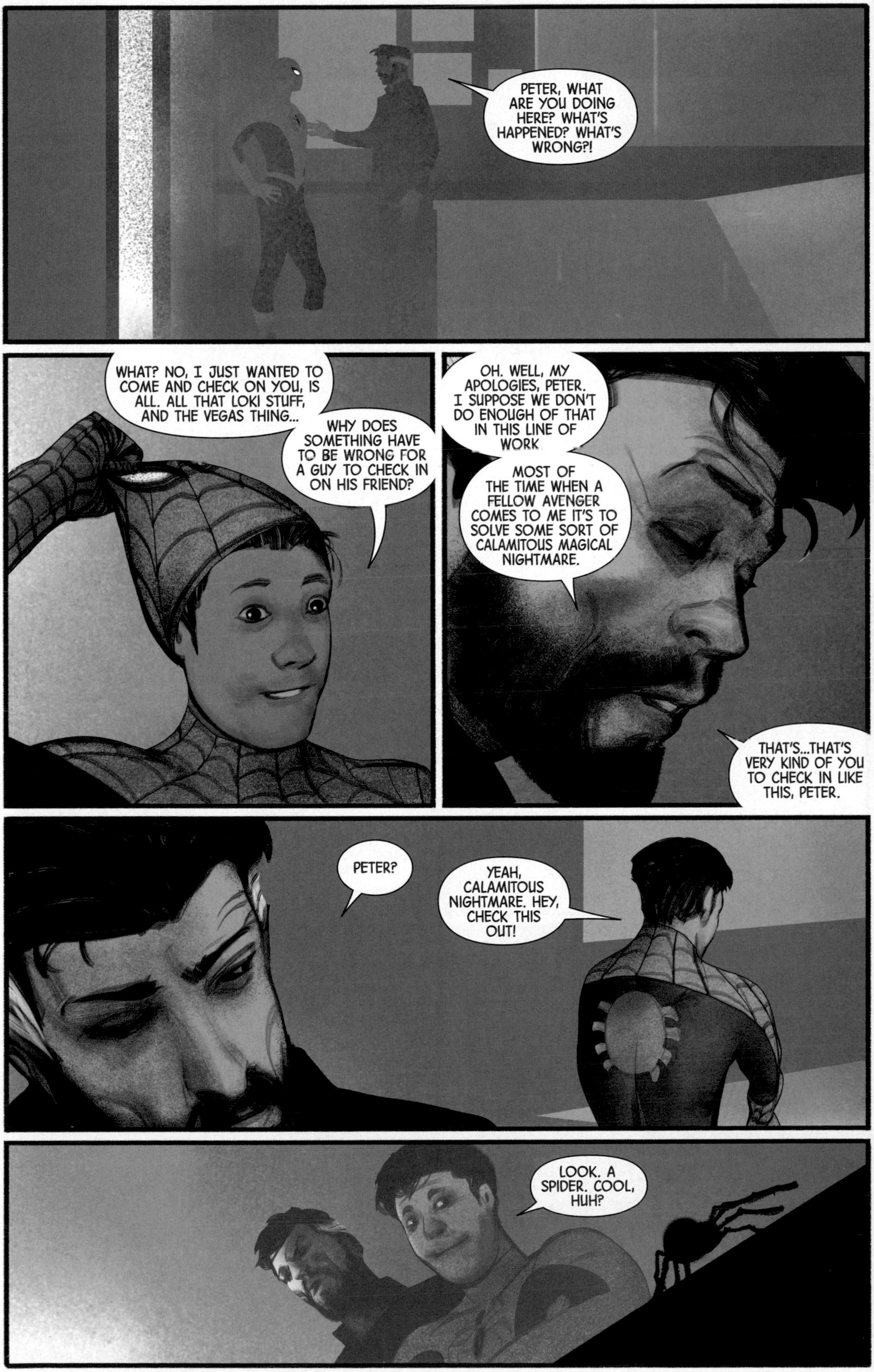
PETER, WHAT ARE YOU DOING HERE? WHAT'S HAPPENED? WHAT'S WRONG?!
WHAT? NO, I JUST WANTED TO COME AND CHECK ON YOU, IS ALL. ALL THAT LOKI STUFF, AND THE VEGAS THING...
WHY DOES SOMETHING HAVE TO BE WRONG FOR A GUY TO CHECK IN ON HIS FRIEND?
OH. WELL, MY APOLOGIES, PETER. I SUPPOSE WE DON'T DO ENOUGH OF THAT IN THIS LINE OF WORK.
MOST OF THE TIME WHEN A FELLOW AVENGER COMES TO ME IT'S TO SOLVE SOME SORT OF CALAMITOUS MAGICAL NIGHTMARE.
THAT'S...THAT'S VERY KIND OF YOU TO CHECK IN LIKE THIS, PETER.
PETER?
YEAH, CALAMITOUS NIGHTMARE. HEY, CHECK THIS OUT!
LOOK. A SPIDER. COOL, HUH?

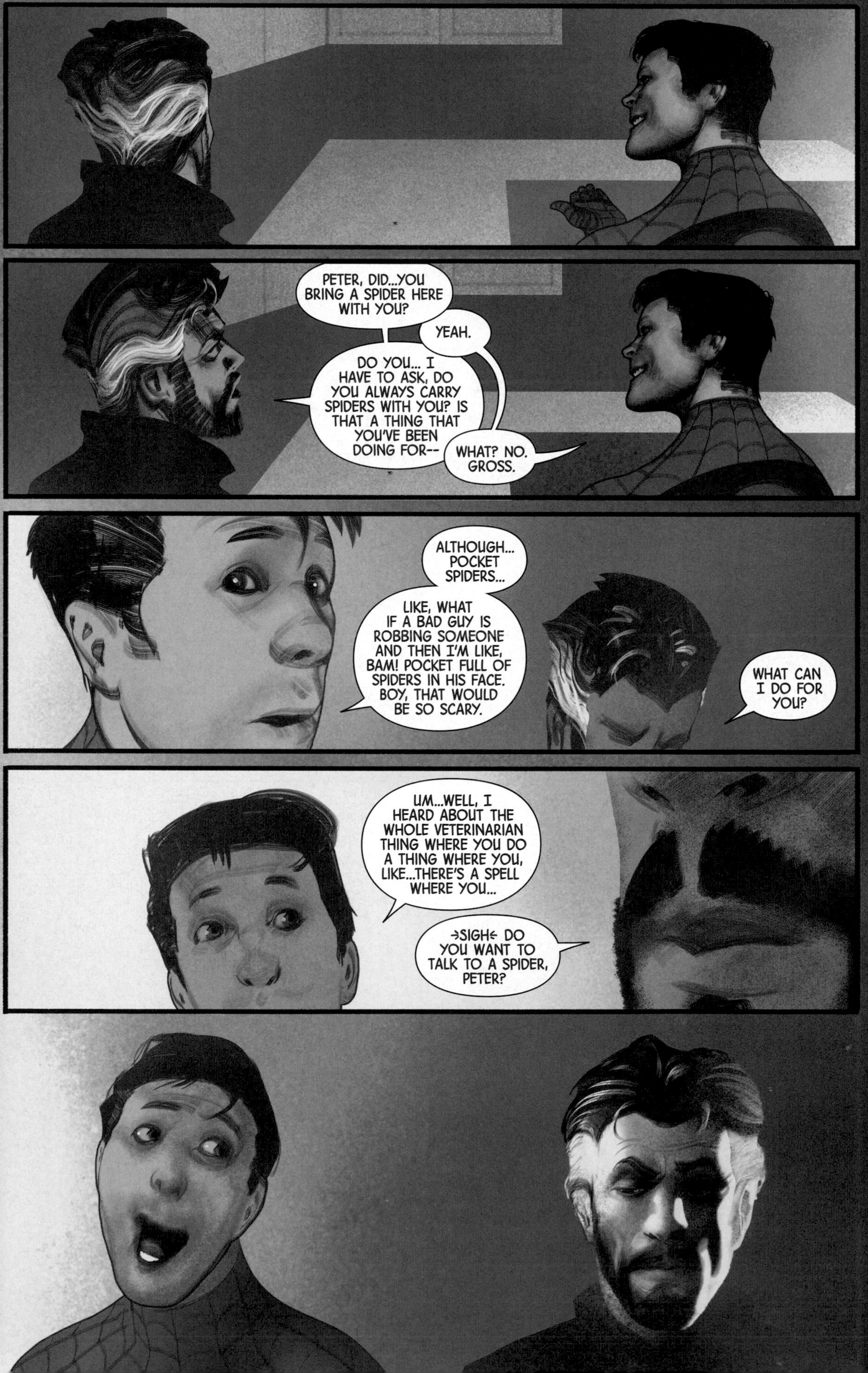
PETER, DID...YOU BRING A SPIDER HERE WITH YOU?
YEAH.
DO YOU... I HAVE TO ASK, DO YOU ALWAYS CARRY SPIDERS WITH YOU? IS THAT A THING THAT YOU'VE BEEN DOING FOR--
WHAT? NO. GROSS.
ALTHOUGH... POCKET SPIDERS...
LIKE, WHAT IF A BAD GUY IS ROBBING SOMEONE AND THEN I'M LIKE, BAM! POCKET FULL OF SPIDERS IN HIS FACE. BOY, THAT WOULD BE SO SCARY.
WHAT CAN I DO FOR YOU?
UM...WELL, I HEARD ABOUT THE WHOLE VETERINARIAN THING WHERE YOU DO A THING WHERE YOU, LIKE...THERE'S A SPELL WHERE YOU...
→SIGH← DO YOU WANT TO TALK TO A SPIDER, PETER?

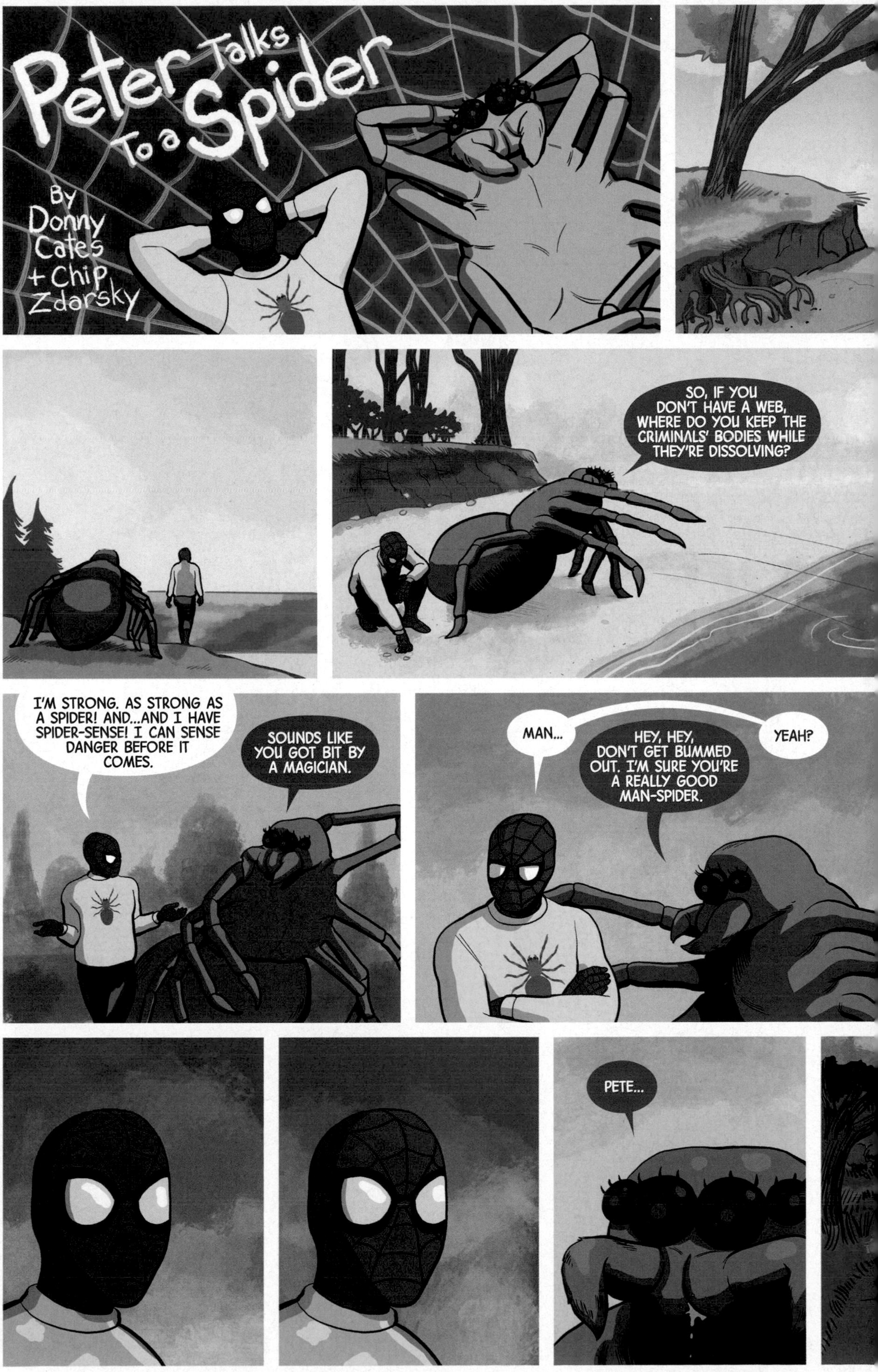
Peter Talks To a Spider
By Donny Cates + Chip Zdarsky
SO, IF YOU DON'T HAVE A WEB, WHERE DO YOU KEEP THE CRIMINALS' BODIES WHILE THEY'RE DISSOLVING?
I'M STRONG. AS STRONG AS A SPIDER! AND...AND I HAVE SPIDER-SENSE! I CAN SENSE DANGER BEFORE IT COMES.
SOUNDS LIKE YOU GOT BIT BY A MAGICIAN.
MAN...
YEAH?
HEY, HEY, DON'T GET BUMMED OUT. I'M SURE YOU'RE A REALLY GOOD MAN-SPIDER.
PETE...

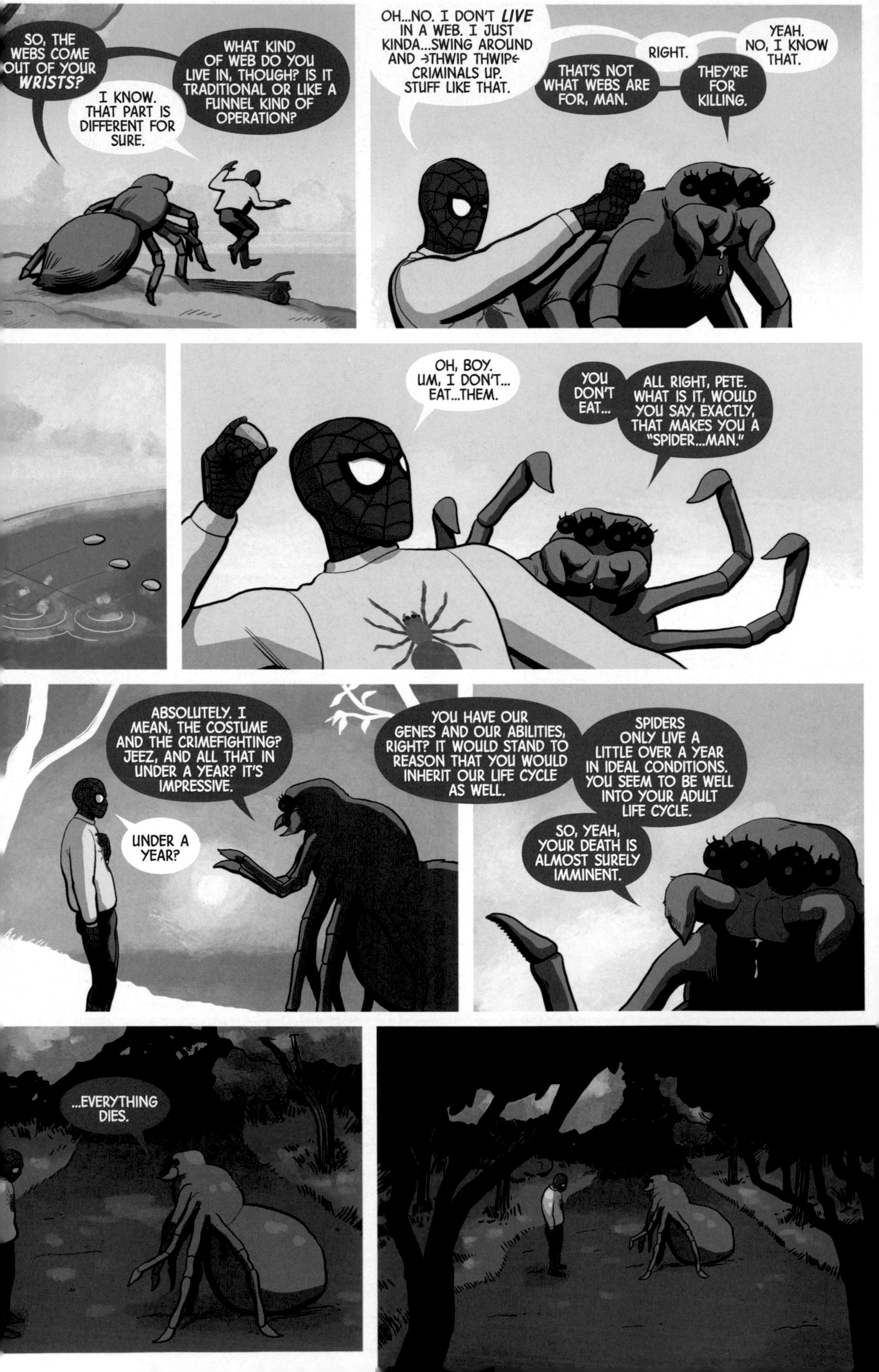

SO, THE WEBS COME OUT OF YOUR *WRISTS?*
WHAT KIND OF WEB DO YOU LIVE IN, THOUGH? IS IT TRADITIONAL OR LIKE A FUNNEL KIND OF OPERATION?
I KNOW. THAT PART IS DIFFERENT FOR SURE.
OH...NO. I DON'T *LIVE* IN A WEB. I JUST KINDA...SWING AROUND AND →THWIP THWIP← CRIMINALS UP. STUFF LIKE THAT.
THAT'S NOT WHAT WEBS ARE FOR, MAN.
RIGHT.
THEY'RE FOR KILLING.
YEAH. NO, I KNOW THAT.
OH, BOY. UM, I DON'T... EAT...THEM.
YOU DON'T EAT...
ALL RIGHT, PETE. WHAT IS IT, WOULD YOU SAY, EXACTLY, THAT MAKES YOU A "SPIDER...MAN."
ABSOLUTELY. I MEAN, THE COSTUME AND THE CRIMEFIGHTING? JEEZ, AND ALL THAT IN UNDER A YEAR? IT'S IMPRESSIVE.
UNDER A YEAR?
YOU HAVE OUR GENES AND OUR ABILITIES, RIGHT? IT WOULD STAND TO REASON THAT YOU WOULD INHERIT OUR LIFE CYCLE AS WELL.
SPIDERS ONLY LIVE A LITTLE OVER A YEAR IN IDEAL CONDITIONS. YOU SEEM TO BE WELL INTO YOUR ADULT LIFE CYCLE.
SO, YEAH, YOUR DEATH IS ALMOST SURELY IMMINENT.
...EVERYTHING DIES.

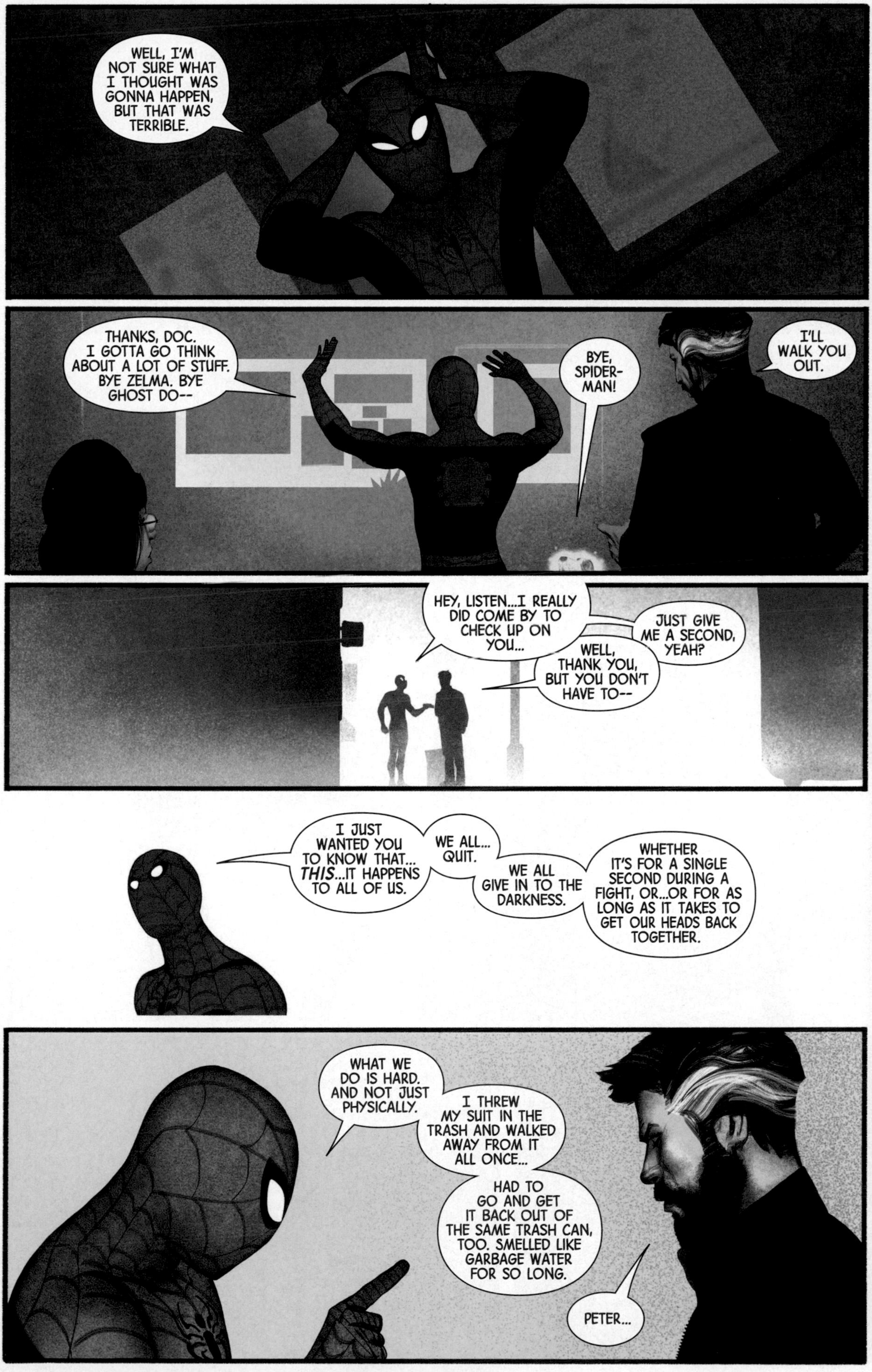
WELL, I'M NOT SURE WHAT I THOUGHT WAS GONNA HAPPEN, BUT THAT WAS TERRIBLE.
THANKS, DOC. I GOTTA GO THINK ABOUT A LOT OF STUFF. BYE ZELMA. BYE GHOST DO--
BYE, SPIDER-MAN!
I'LL WALK YOU OUT.
HEY, LISTEN...I REALLY DID COME BY TO CHECK UP ON YOU...
WELL, THANK YOU, BUT YOU DON'T HAVE TO--
JUST GIVE ME A SECOND, YEAH?
I JUST WANTED YOU TO KNOW THAT... *THIS*...IT HAPPENS TO ALL OF US.
WE ALL... QUIT.
WE ALL GIVE IN TO THE DARKNESS.
WHETHER IT'S FOR A SINGLE SECOND DURING A FIGHT, OR...OR FOR AS LONG AS IT TAKES TO GET OUR HEADS BACK TOGETHER.
WHAT WE DO IS HARD. AND NOT JUST PHYSICALLY.
I THREW MY SUIT IN THE TRASH AND WALKED AWAY FROM IT ALL ONCE...
HAD TO GO AND GET IT BACK OUT OF THE SAME TRASH CAN, TOO. SMELLED LIKE GARBAGE WATER FOR SO LONG.
PETER...

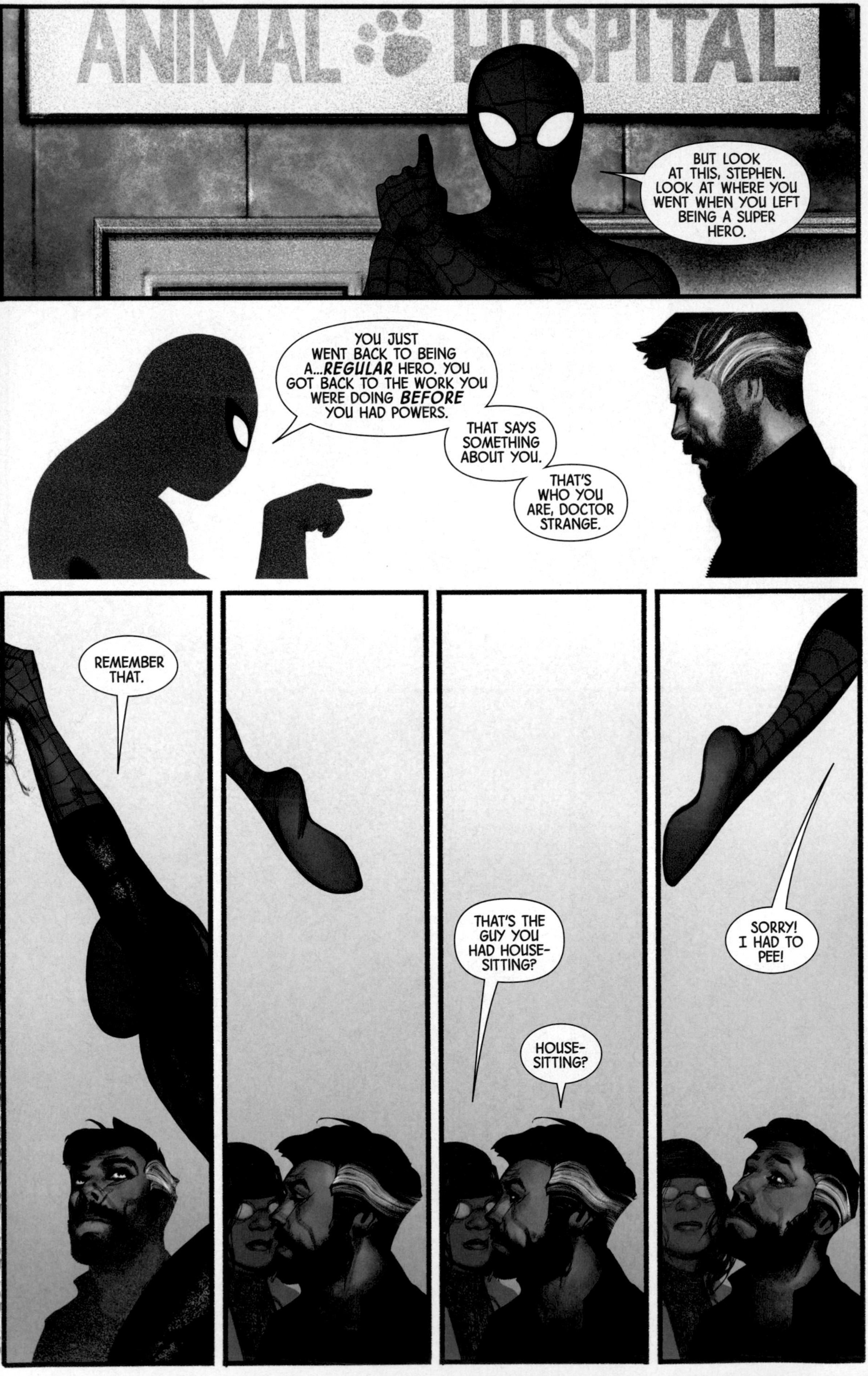
ANIMAL HOSPITAL
BUT LOOK AT THIS, STEPHEN. LOOK AT WHERE YOU WENT WHEN YOU LEFT BEING A SUPER HERO.
YOU JUST WENT BACK TO BEING A...*REGULAR* HERO. YOU GOT BACK TO THE WORK YOU WERE DOING *BEFORE* YOU HAD POWERS.
THAT SAYS SOMETHING ABOUT YOU.
THAT'S WHO YOU ARE, DOCTOR STRANGE.
REMEMBER THAT.
THAT'S THE GUY YOU HAD HOUSE-SITTING?
HOUSE-SITTING?
SORRY! I HAD TO PEE!

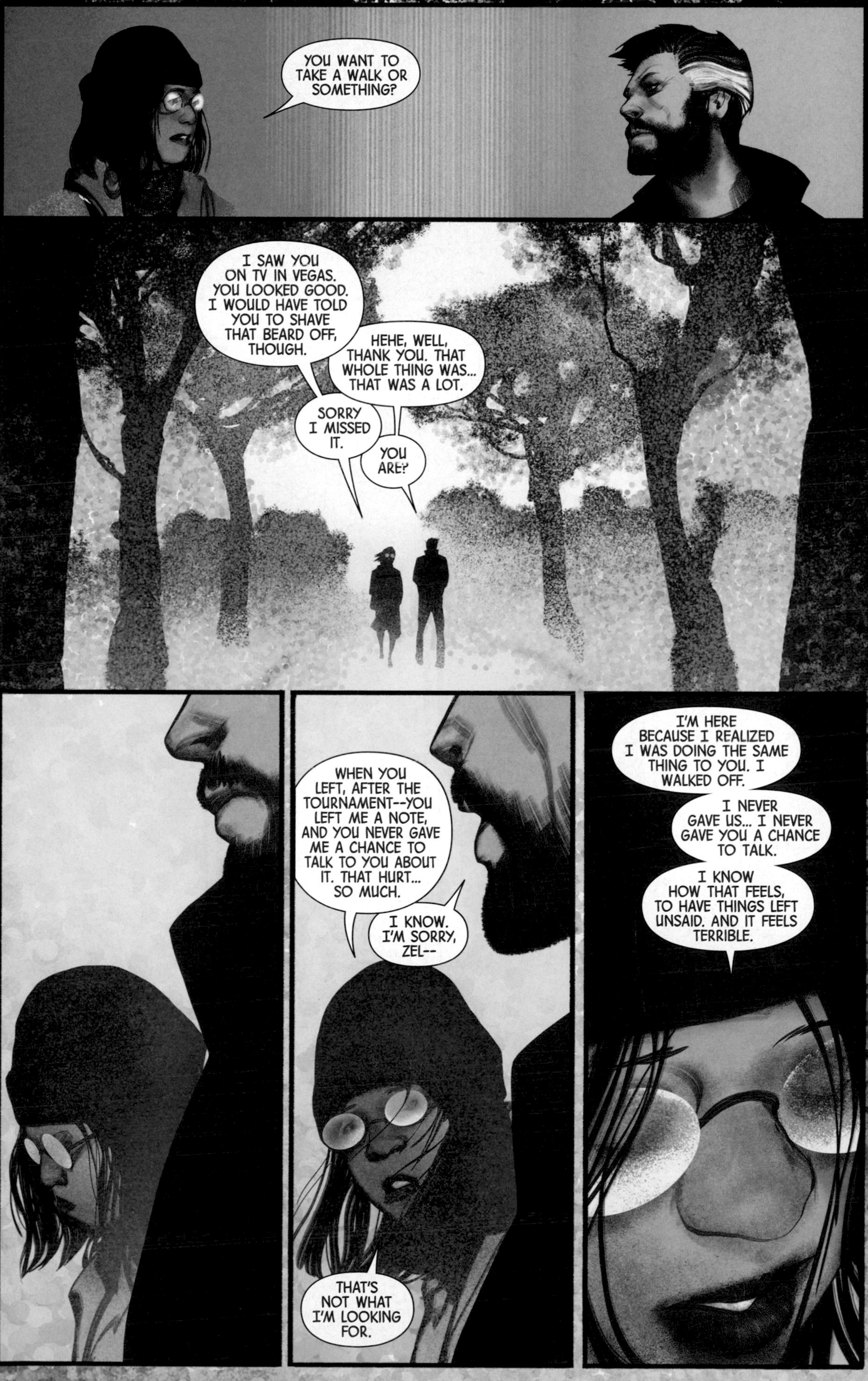
YOU WANT TO TAKE A WALK OR SOMETHING?
I SAW YOU ON TV IN VEGAS. YOU LOOKED GOOD. I WOULD HAVE TOLD YOU TO SHAVE THAT BEARD OFF, THOUGH.
HEHE, WELL, THANK YOU. THAT WHOLE THING WAS... THAT WAS A LOT.
SORRY I MISSED IT.
YOU ARE?
WHEN YOU LEFT, AFTER THE TOURNAMENT--YOU LEFT ME A NOTE, AND YOU NEVER GAVE ME A CHANCE TO TALK TO YOU ABOUT IT. THAT HURT... SO MUCH.
I KNOW. I'M SORRY, ZEL--
THAT'S NOT WHAT I'M LOOKING FOR.
I'M HERE BECAUSE I REALIZED I WAS DOING THE SAME THING TO YOU. I WALKED OFF.
I NEVER GAVE US... I NEVER GAVE YOU A CHANCE TO TALK.
I KNOW HOW THAT FEELS, TO HAVE THINGS LEFT UNSAID. AND IT FEELS TERRIBLE.

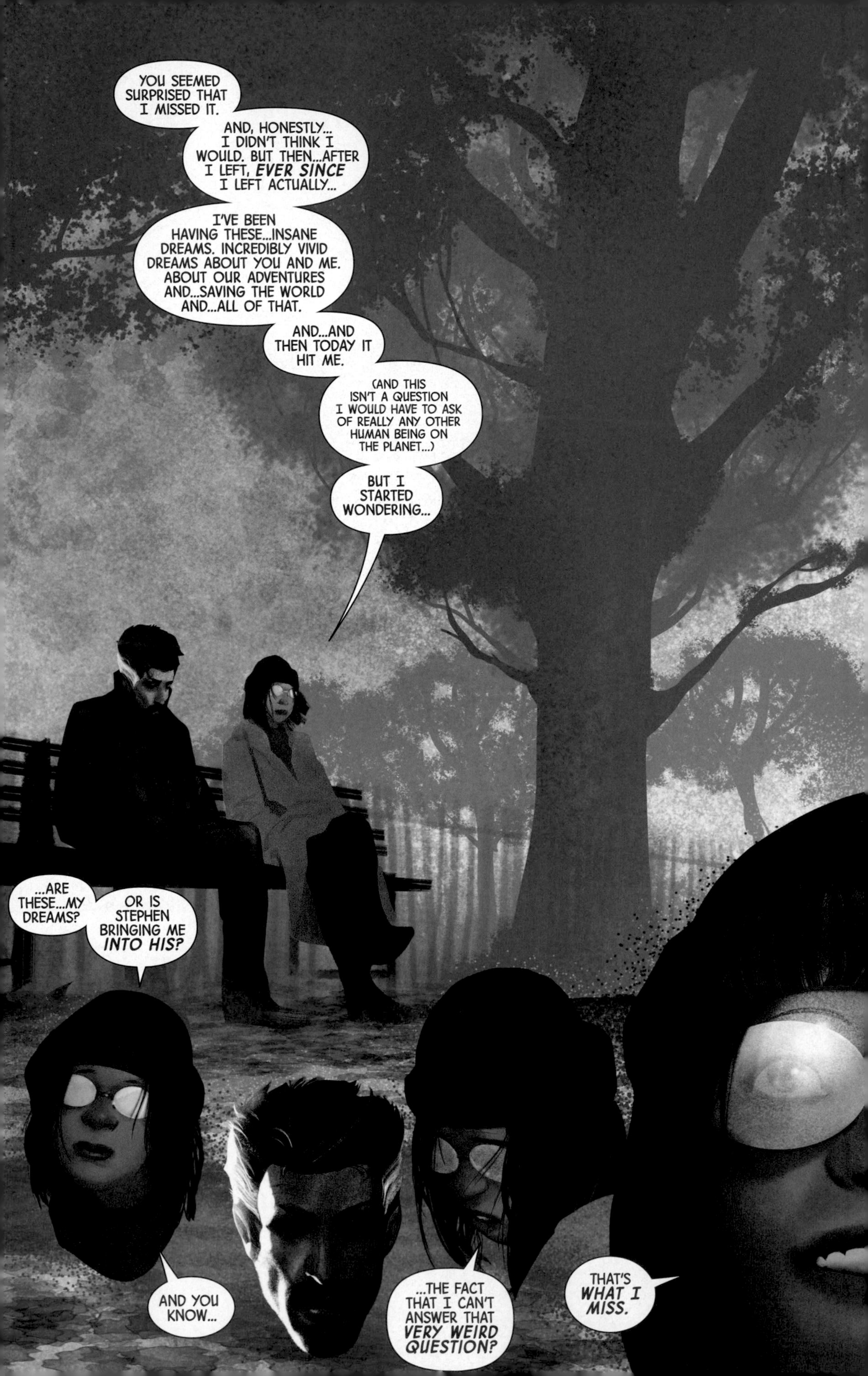
YOU SEEMED SURPRISED THAT I MISSED IT.
AND, HONESTLY... I DIDN'T THINK I WOULD. BUT THEN...AFTER I LEFT, EVER SINCE I LEFT ACTUALLY...
I'VE BEEN HAVING THESE...INSANE DREAMS. INCREDIBLY VIVID DREAMS ABOUT YOU AND ME. ABOUT OUR ADVENTURES AND...SAVING THE WORLD AND...ALL OF THAT.
AND...AND THEN TODAY IT HIT ME.
(AND THIS ISN'T A QUESTION I WOULD HAVE TO ASK OF REALLY ANY OTHER HUMAN BEING ON THE PLANET...)
BUT I STARTED WONDERING...
...ARE THESE...MY DREAMS?
OR IS STEPHEN BRINGING ME INTO HIS?
AND YOU KNOW...
...THE FACT THAT I CAN'T ANSWER THAT VERY WEIRD QUESTION?
THAT'S WHAT I MISS.

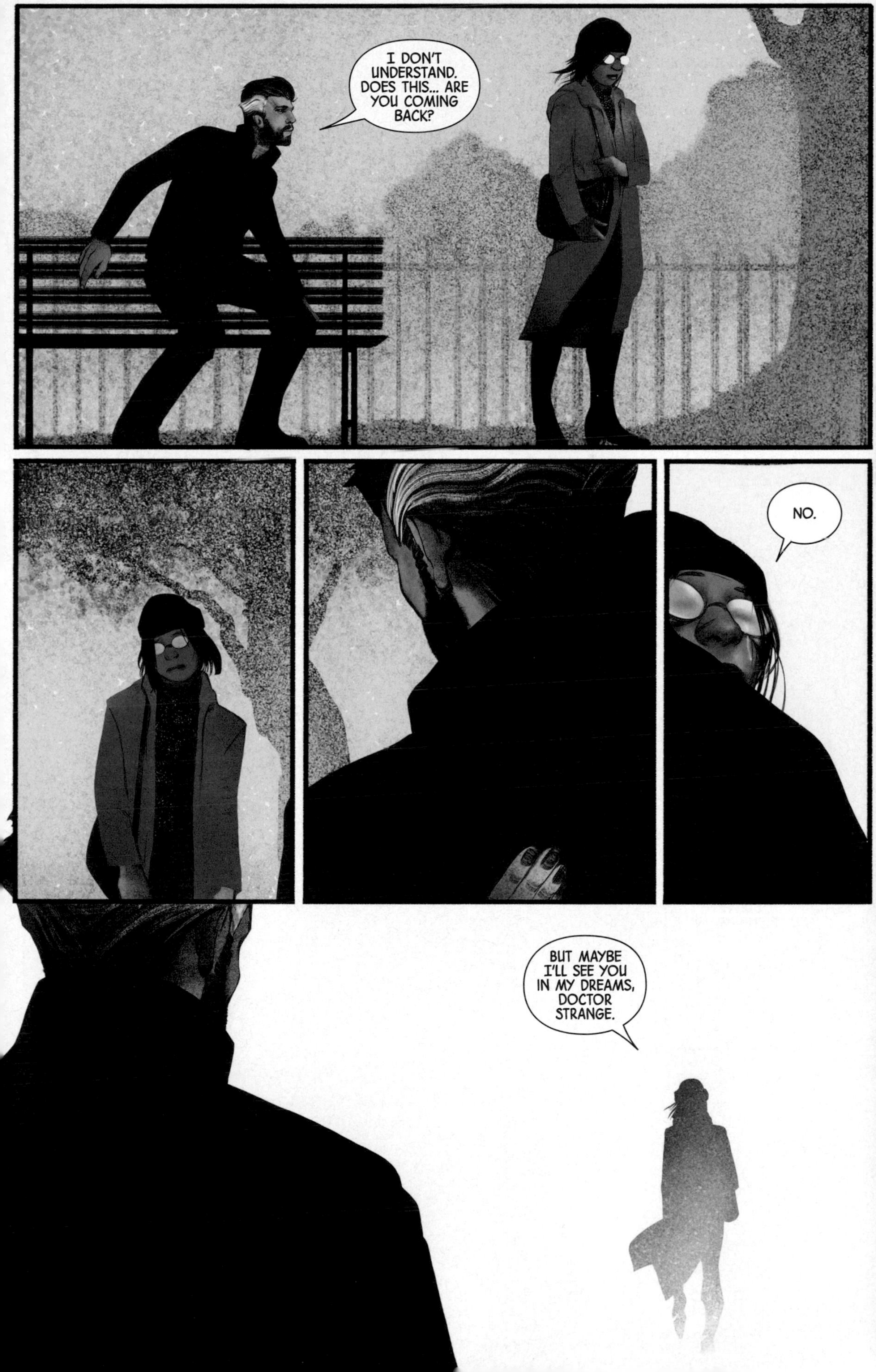
I DON'T UNDERSTAND. DOES THIS... ARE YOU COMING BACK?
NO.
BUT MAYBE I'LL SEE YOU IN MY DREAMS, DOCTOR STRANGE.

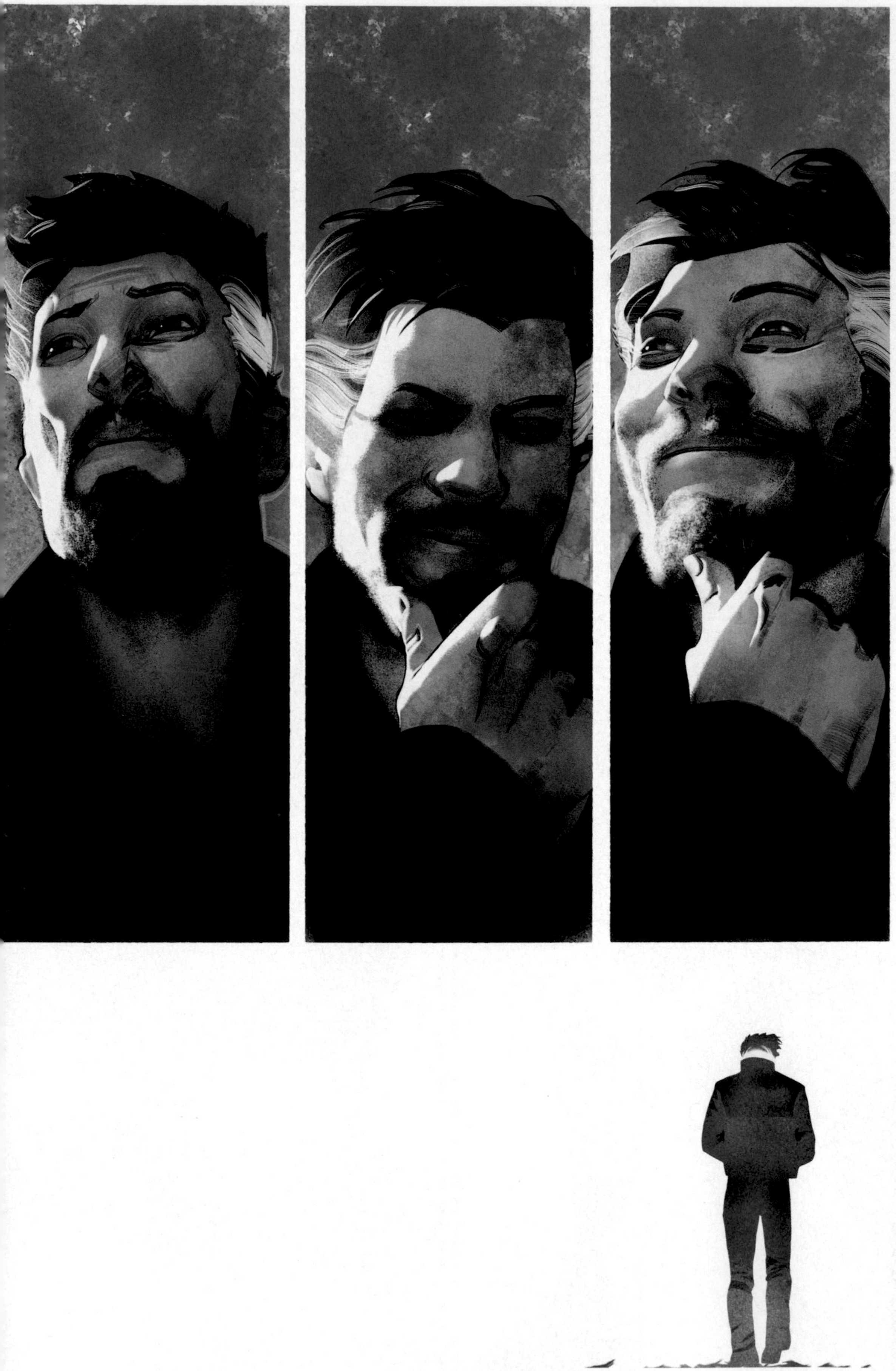

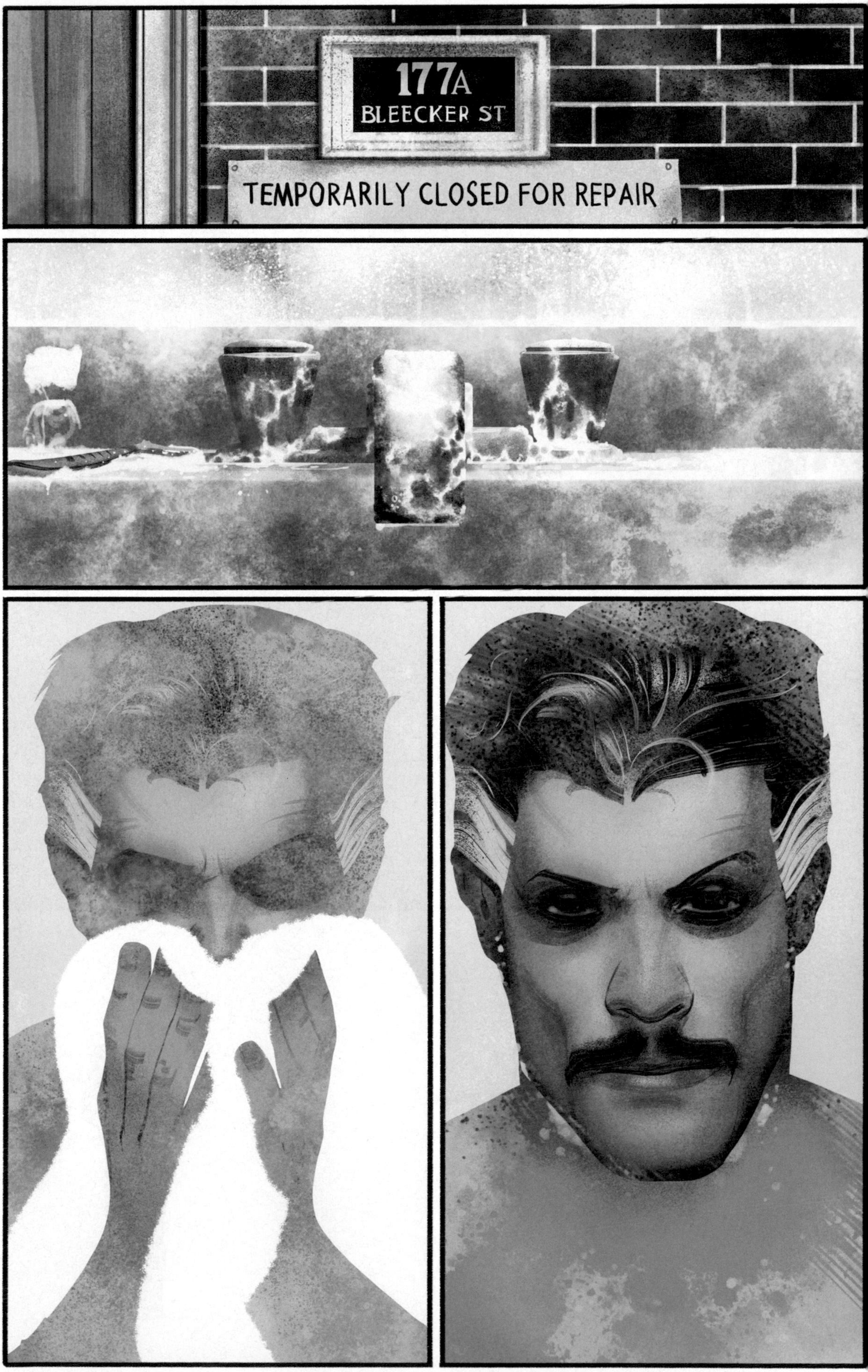
177A
BLEECKER ST
TEMPORARILY CLOSED FOR REPAIR

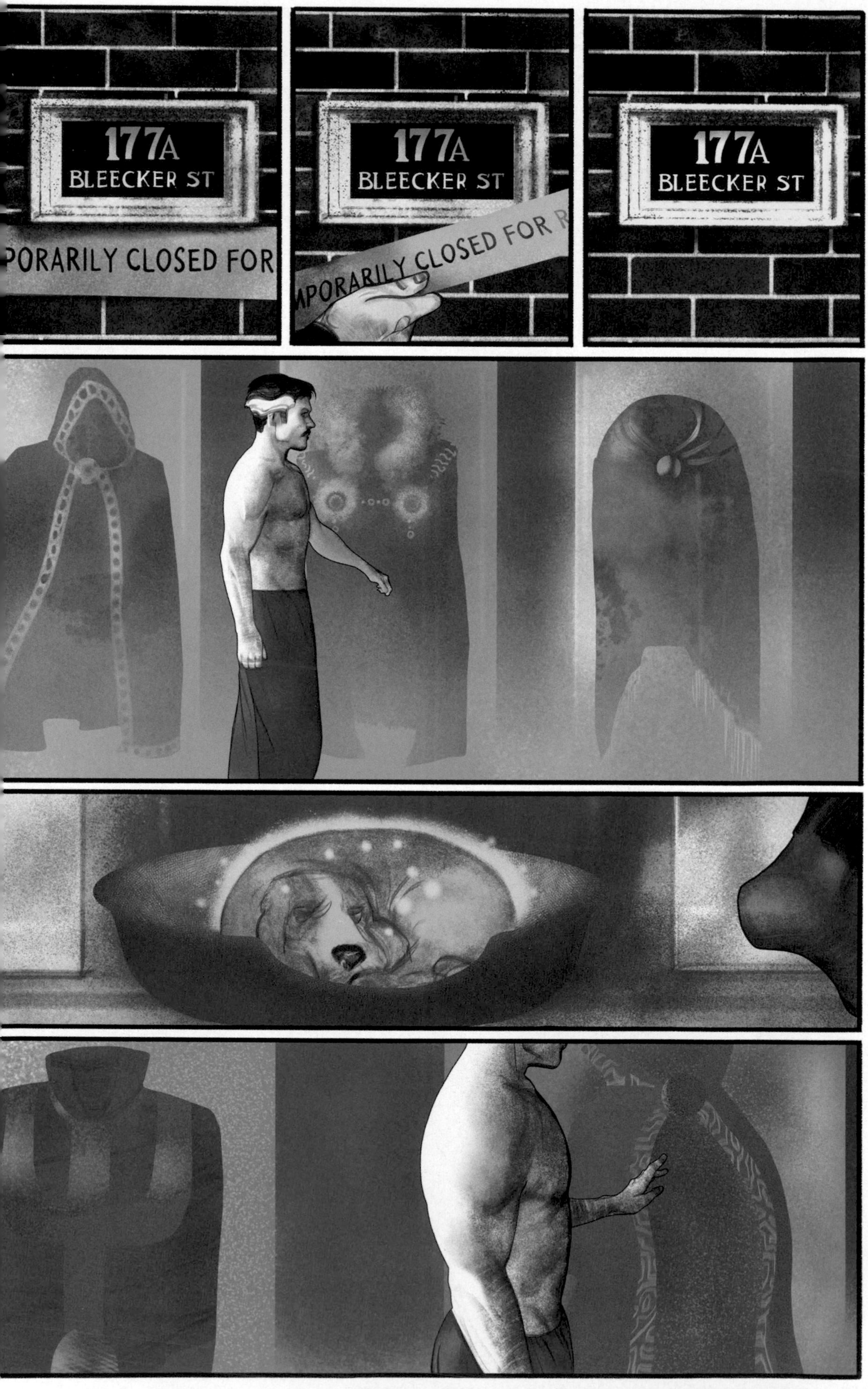
177A
BLEECKER ST
PORARILY CLOSED FOR
177A
BLEECKER ST
MPORARILY CLOSED FOR
177A
BLEECKER ST

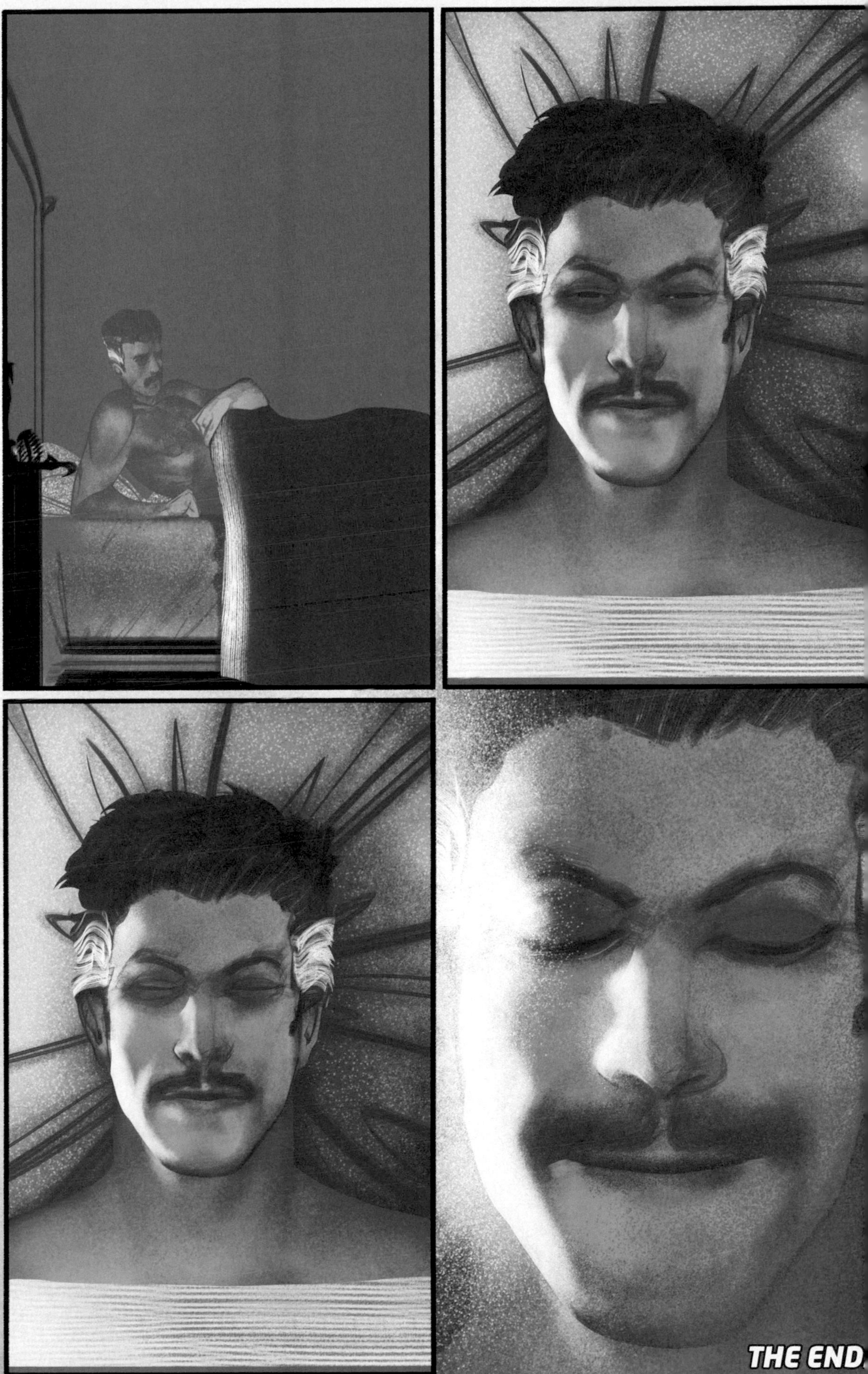
THE END.

I STILL REMEMBER HOW UTTERLY TERRIFIED I WAS TO WRITE THE FIRST ISSUE OF THIS RUN A YEAR AND CHANGE AGO.

I WAS AT HEROESCON IN NORTH CAROLINA, A CON I HAD SCHEDULED BEFORE I GOT THE CALL FROM MARVEL TO DO THIS BOOK. AS A RESULT, I WAS SWEATING BULLETS ALL WEEKEND BECAUSE, WHILE I WAS SITTING ON PANELS AND SIGNING FOR YOU GUYS, IN MY HEAD I WAS A MILLION MILES AWAY TRYING TO MOVE MY FURNITURE INTO THE SANCTUM AND TRYING MY BEST TO FIGURE OUT HOW TO ORGANIZE IT ALL WITHOUT SCUFFING THE HARDWOOD FLOORS.

I KNEW THE BASICS OF MY FIRST ISSUE, THE BIG BROAD STEPS. THE LOKI STUFF, THE THOR SCENE, THE ENDING. THE DOG. BUT I COULDN'T FIGURE OUT FOR THE LIFE OF ME HOW TO OPEN MY FIRST ISSUE.

THAT'S A RECURRING STRUGGLE FOR ME. IF I CAN ONLY FIGURE OUT THAT FIRST PANEL, I CAN GENERALLY GET THE REST MOVING. BUT ON **STRANGE**, I COULDN'T GET THERE. I COULDN'T BREAK IT. AND IT WAS DRIVING ME INSANE.

"BUT WAIT! JASON AARON IS AT THIS SHOW", I THOUGHT, "I'LL ASK HIM!" AFTER ALL, HIS ARE THE (ENORMOUSLY SCARY) SHOES I'M ATTEMPTING TO FILL HERE.

I DID EVENTUALLY GET AROUND TO ASKING JASON ABOUT HIS TAKE ON THE SORCERER SUPREME. IT WAS, OF COURSE, INSIGHTFUL AND AMAZING AND I'M NOT GOING TO TELL YOU A WORD OF IT. THOSE SECRETS ARE FOR ME. AND FOR WHOEVER ELSE WRITES THIS BOOK AFTER ME AND WANTS TO KNOW.

I WILL TELL YOU ONE THING, THOUGH. THE THING THAT UNLOCKED THE FIRST PAGE FOR ME. AT THE END OF OUR CONVERSATION, JASON LOOKED ME IN THE EYE AND HE GAVE ME THE BEST ADVICE HE'S EVER GIVEN ME.

"IT'S ALL YOURS NOW. DON'T @#$% IT UP."

I KNOW THAT SOUNDS FUNNY, BUT IT WAS A GENUINE BREAKTHROUGH FOR ME.

I SPENT SO MUCH TIME WORRYING ABOUT WHAT CAME BEFORE ME THAT I HADN'T OWNED THE BOOK YET. I HADN'T FLIPPED THAT MENTAL SWITCH IN MY HEAD THAT SAID, "THIS IS YOURS NOW. MAKE IT A BOOK YOU WOULD WANT TO READ."

AND SO THAT'S WHAT I TRIED TO DO. AND TO THAT END, I HAD MY FIRST PANEL. IT WAS SOMETHING I HAD TO SAY TO MAKE IT ALL SEEM REAL. I HAD TO OWN IT. SO, I BEGAN MY FIRST ISSUE WITH A DECLARATION OF SORTS.

TO MYSELF AS MUCH AS TO YOU, THE FANS:

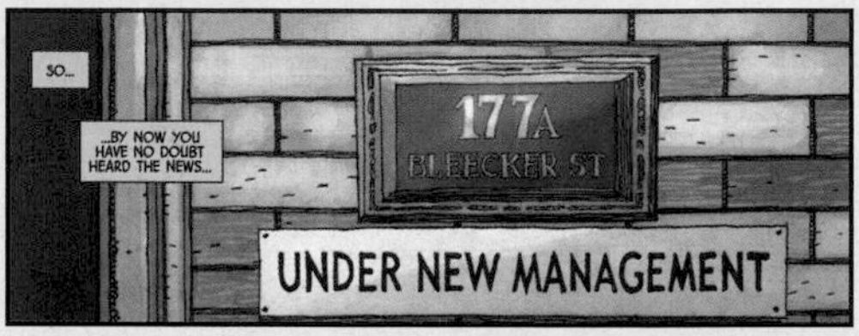
SO...
...BY NOW YOU HAVE NO DOUBT HEARD THE NEWS...
177A
BLEECKER ST
UNDER NEW MANAGEMENT

I HOPE YOU'VE ALL ENJOYED WHAT WE'VE DONE ON THE BOOK DURING MY TIME AS MANAGER HERE AT THE SANCTUM SANCTORUM. I'VE TRIED TO GIVE IT MY LEVEL BEST, AND MOSTLY, I THINK IT'S WORKED PRETTY WELL.

A HUGE THANK YOU TO GABRIEL HERNANDEZ WALTA, JORDIE BELLAIRE, NIKO HENRICHON, MIKE DEL MUNDO, ROD REIS, SZYMON KUDRANSKI, FRAZER IRVING, KATHLEEN WISNESKI, AND PERHAPS MOST OF ALL, NICK LOWE FOR MAKING THIS THE BEST GIG OF MY CAREER TO DATE.

I HOPE YOU ALL KNOW HOW MUCH I APPRECIATE AND RESPECT YOU AND YOUR INCREDIBLE WORK.

SO, YEAH... THAT'S MY TIME, FOLKS. I LEAVE YOU IN THE CONFIDENT HANDS OF AN UP-AND-COMING WRITER WITH A GREAT DEAL OF PROMISE NAMED (SQUINTS AT SOLICITATION COPY) MARK WAID. I THINK HE'S GOT A BRIGHT FUTURE AHEAD OF HIM, THAT ONE.

IT'S ALL YOURS NOW, MARK.

TAKE CARE OF MY DOG FOR ME.

AND DON'T @#$% IT UP.

THANK YOU ALL SO MUCH FOR LETTING ME PLAY IN THIS MAGICAL WORLD.

IT'S BEEN AN HONOR AND A PRIVILEGE.

EXCELSIOR.

-DONNY CATES
AUSTIN, TEXAS
2/20/2018

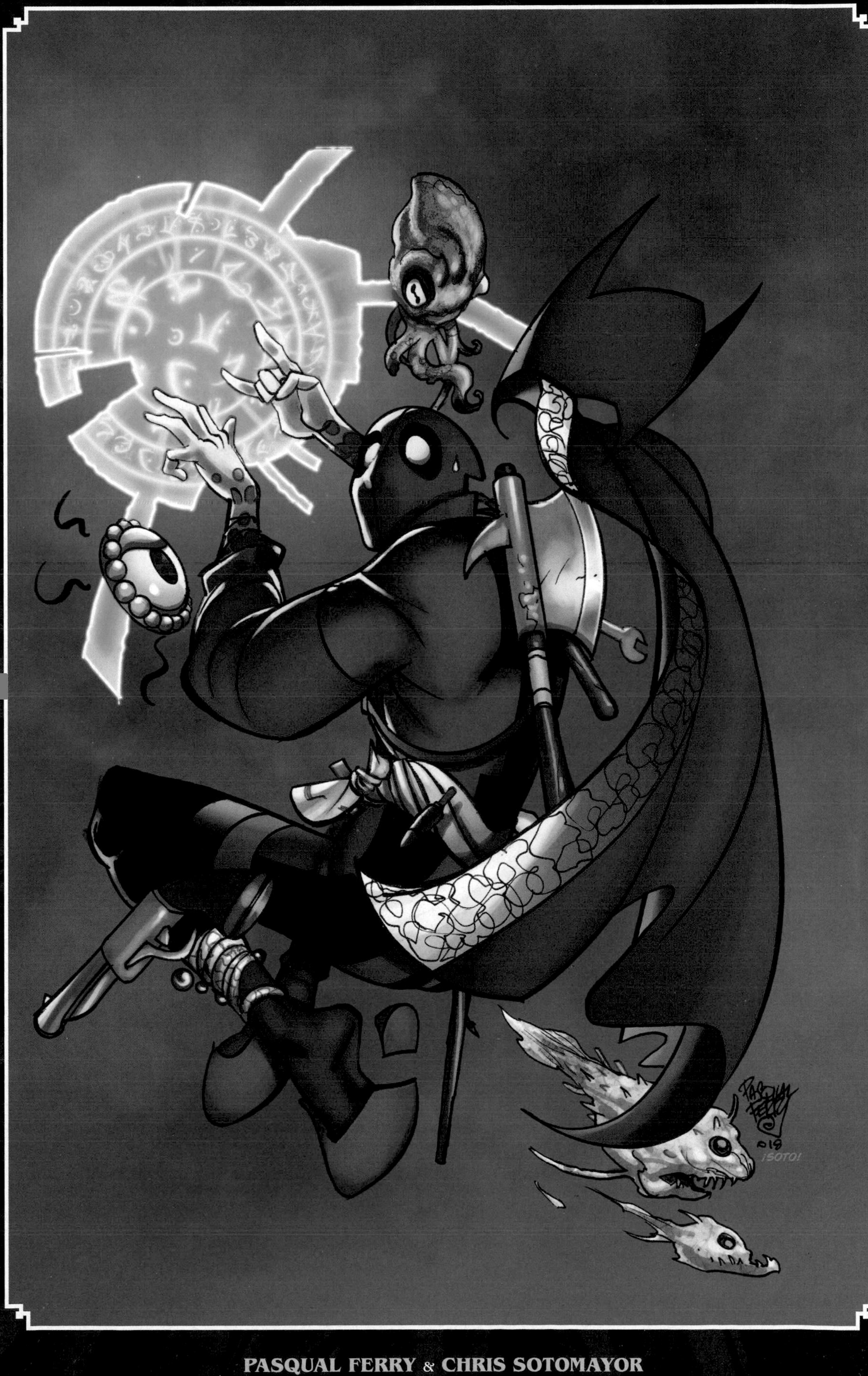
PASQUAL FERRY
'18
¡SOTO!

PASQUAL FERRY & CHRIS SOTOMAYOR
390 DEADPOOL VARIANT